D0398895

THE DEATH OF SPIN

George Pitcher

RETIRÉ DE LA COLLECTION UNIVERSELLE
Bibliothèque et Archives nationales du Québec

JOHN WILEY & SONS LTD

Published in 2003 by John Wiley & Sons Ltd, The Atrium, Southern Gate, Chichester, West Sussex PO19 8SQ, England

Telephone (+44) 1243 779777

Email (for orders and customer service enquiries): cs-books@wiley.co.uk
Visit our Home Page on www.wileyeurope.com or www.wiley.com

Copyright © 2003 George Pitcher

All Rights Reserved. No part of this publication may be reproduced, stored in a retrieval system or transmitted in any form or by any means, electronic, mechanical, photocopying, recording, scanning or otherwise, except under the terms of the Copyright, Designs and Patents Act 1988 or under the terms of a licence issued by the Copyright Licensing Agency Ltd, 90 Tottenham Court Road, London W1T 4LP, UK, without the permission in writing of the Publisher. Requests to the Publisher should be addressed to the Permissions Department, John Wiley & Sons Ltd, The Atrium, Southern Gate, Chichester, West Sussex PO19 8SQ, England, or emailed to permreq@wiley.co.uk, or faxed to (+44) 1243 770571.

This publication is designed to provide accurate and authoritative information in regard to the subject matter covered. It is sold on the understanding that the Publisher is not engaged in rendering professional services. If professional advice or other expert assistance is required, the services of a competent professional should be sought.

George Pitcher has asserted his right under the Copyright, Designs and Patents Act 1988, to be identified as the author of this work.

Other Wiley Editorial Offices

John Wiley & Sons Inc., 111 River Street, Hoboken, NJ 07030, USA

Jossey-Bass, 989 Market Street, San Francisco, CA 94103-1741, USA

Wiley-VCH Verlag GmbH, Boschstr. 12, D-69469 Weinheim, Germany

John Wiley & Sons Australia Ltd, 33 Park Road, Milton, Queensland 4064, Australia

John Wiley & Sons (Asia) Pte Ltd, 2 Clementi Loop #02-01, Jin Xing Distripark, Singapore 129809

John Wiley & Sons Canada Ltd, 22 Worcester Road, Etobicoke, Ontario, Canada M9W 1L1

British Library Cataloguing in Publication Data

A catalogue record for this book is available from the British Library

ISBN 0-470-85048-5

Typeset in 9.5/13pt Melior by Mathematical Composition Setters Ltd, Salisbury, Wiltshire
Printed and bound in Great Britain by Biddles Ltd, Guildford and King's Lynn.
This book is printed on acid-free paper responsibly manufactured from sustainable forestry in which at least two trees are planted for each one used for paper production.

To Mobbs,
who still wants to live with a writer

CONTENTS

PREFACE

O n a City desk as a young journalist on a mass-circulation newspaper, I was once told that I was writing a story for just six people in the financial markets who mattered. More frequently, I realised that we were writing for our colleagues and rivals in Fleet Street rather than for the readers. Like Planet Westminster, the world of journalism and communications can be both metropolitan and parochial and we in it need to be alert to the dangers of re-telling stories to each other. I have tried not to adopt that mentality in writing this book, partly because this is a book for the lay reader, who nevertheless may be an interested observer of the culture we call 'spin', and partly because my editor wouldn't let me. So I trust that the obvious in-jokes and point-scoring have been excised. But the difference between an illuminating anecdote and being a media-luvvy is a fine one, so I hope readers will appreciate that it's the world I know and forgive me for the inward-looking nature that is its characteristic. A further implication of an insider writing a book like this is that it is necessarily subjective. It is neither a 'how-to-spin' handbook, nor pretends to be an exhaustive contemporary history of spin-culture. So you won't be told how to do it and there are some popular figures missing that I think are either not relevant to the subject of the book or boring. That said, most books on this subject have either been dry and worthy management or political manuals or scary exposés of high-profile figures. I hope that what follows is neither – but rather a guided tour through the rat-runs below and beside the corridors of media, industrial and political power as the spin-culture of our times rose and fell. If nothing else, it might explain to a number of bewildered relatives where we've all been these past 20 years or so.

George Pitcher

Acknowledgements

Anyone who has ever been in journalism knows that research amounts to a visit to the clippings library – true, the source may be on-line now, but it amounts to the same thing. The equivalent for communications professionals is the ability to plunder the intellectual property of one's colleagues. In this regard, I am blessed indeed. I co-founded our consultancy a decade ago with Charles Stewart-Smith and since have been privileged to plagiarise one of the finest communications minds of his generation. I am also in debt to my partners for their variety of political, industrial and commercial insights – they are Amy Kroviak, Ben Rich, Andrew Sharkey, Chris Springham, Douglas Trainer, Simon Whale and David Wheeldon. Further insights have come from my governing board, chaired by John Booth, and I thank John Preston and Nick Taylor for wisdom. Further thanks: All the colleagues who have covered my back at the office while I wrote this book, especially Jon Bennett, Jo Bird, Daniel Guthrie, Emma Leeds and their account teams. Despo Ptohopoulos was endlessly tolerant and supportive of me in the field, Bonnie Dixon researched and helped me to remember what I was doing in the Eighties and Christina Lau kept me wired with the patience of angels. My colleagues at Financial Issues, Jonathan Dewe, Clive Horwood and Adrian Thomas, educated me in the fixed-income markets, while Richard Bridges made sense of equities. Importantly, if anonymously, many figures in Westminster and Whitehall spoke to me and trusted me with what they said – you know who you are. Infonic's brain-boxes taught me all I need to know about corporate exposure to the internet – Mark Bunting, Roy Lipski and Orlando Plunket Greene.

Tom Bentley, James Wilsdon and Eddie Gibb at Demos for encouragement, a platform, a pamphlet and a whole lot more. Peter Wilson of Delta Pearl and Strategos thought of questions about corporate communications that nobody else had and one day, albeit briefly, made me a visiting lecturer at INSEAD. Then, substantially, there's the team at Wiley that made it happen – my editor Sally Smith, Julia Lampam, Tracy Clayton, Amie Tibble, Sandra Heath and Benjamin Earl; plus Martin Key for the copy edit. And, finally, if you've just bought this book, or perhaps just borrowed it, thankyou.

INTRODUCTION

Things could only get better in 1997, or so the triumphant supporters of the UK Labour Party believed as they celebrated their first election victory for nearly 18 years. Western stock-markets were gripped by what the chairman of the Federal Reserve called an 'irrational exuberance' that was going to push the longest bull market in history into the new millennium. Bill Clinton's Democrats had been, surprisingly, returned despite his peccadilloes. There were only distant rumblings of a Millennium Bug that might wreak havoc on the world's computers. There was no global war on terror. In the UK the Tories had been marginalised, the Queen Mother was still looking forward to the celebrations of her 100th birthday, Peter Mandelson was Minister Without Portfolio at the Cabinet Office and David Beckham had not yet been sent off against Argentina. Enron was a highly successful energy-trading company and business was booming. It is my contention that the West was also gripped by a spin-culture that in the UK had developed in the early days of Margaret Thatcher's premiership and in which the appearance of things enjoyed precedence over their content. The new imperialists and colonisers were the global brands, whether the background fabric of society engineered by Coca-Cola or Microsoft, or the fabric itself in the shape of Nike, Benetton or Lacoste – what they wore defined the masses and was a mark of success. Failure – for British generations the honourable mark of the heroic underdog – became a mark of, well, failure and 'loser' moved into the international English lexicon as an expression of casual contempt, rather than of respect and pity. Winning at all costs, whether in business or in politics, became the new credo. It defined New Labour, the new white-hats, and pushed the equity markets. It was a culture that venerated appearance and promoted position over priority. This book is about the rise and fall of that spin-culture.

Contemporary culture is most easily defined by personal experience. For me, two events that will have passed entirely unnoticed by national news networks and the world of politics marked the rise and fall of spin. The first was my unremarkable departure from newspaper journalism in the early Nineties to join the emerging spin-culture. The second was an equally unremarkable after-dinner speech I gave nearly a decade later to mark the demise of that culture.

When I left *The Observer* at Christmas 1991, my leaving do was in the cellar bar of the Red Lion in Whitehall. The venue was to gain some notoriety in spinning circles some years later, when, in 1998, it became the stage on which Charlie Whelan performed his swan song, a brief too far on Chancellor Gordon Brown's intentions for the euro.

My colleagues had ritually prepared the mock-up of an *Observer* front-page with a 'good riddance' theme and only some of the not-so-tearful tributes referred to my intended future career as a spin-doctor. This was a relatively new job-title at the time. Those who followed American socio-cultural trends were aware of it, but the role, the job, the 'people who live in the dark' as Labour's Clare Short was to call us, were yet to become a villainous part of popular culture. I went to a *Private Eye* lunch in 1992 where the term came as news to editor Ian Hislop, who suggested that in my case 'spin-proctologist' might be more appropriate, with apparent reference to what I spoke through. This may not have been entirely unrelated to me telling him that he should quit the newly-created *Have I Got News For You* because Paul Merton was frying him. (More than a decade's worth of highly successful Hislop performances in HIGNFY later, this probably ranks among the worst piece of image advice I have ever proffered. Anyway, I was never invited again.)

By the mid-Nineties, 'spin-doctor' was part of common parlance in metropolitan and some provincial circles. I remember it was a term of abuse at the Tory Party conference in Bournemouth in 1996. In his etymological column in the *Independent on Sunday* that year, Nicholas Bagnall made an attempt at identifying its provenance:

Sailors were spinning yarns to each other in Nelson's time and could hardly be blamed for trying to shorten a tedious sea voyage by stretching the story. It must have been the landlubbers who borrowed the phrase to suggest that yarn-spinners were liars ... The spin, as practised at Westminster, has nothing to do with yarns of wool, nor with the webs spun by spiders. It comes from baseball – spin-doctor was first used in the States in the 1980s – though here we think of it more in terms of cricket. In either case, deception is the name of the game. The bowler (or pitcher) hopes the batsman (or batter) will forget that balls he is delivering are not always the balls he seems to be delivering.

Perhaps consciously, this echoed Michael Heseltine's *tour de force* at that year's conference, when he sent up the studious Shadow Chancellor Gordon Brown's 'neoclassical endogenous growth theory and a symbiotic relationship between investment in people and infrastructure' as something he had learned at the knee of his even more academic economic adviser Ed Balls – 'It's not Brown's at all, it's Balls.' Spin-doctors had grown up quickly in the UK, now operating at the level of presentation of economic theory, not just sorting the media at street level. Ed Balls is a Fellow of the Royal College of Spin Surgeons, rather than a sawbones media-mountebank.

They were said to have American parents, legitimate or otherwise. This derivation would have it that we were always pitchers, rather than spin-bowlers. (Your author's name, incidentally, is genuine.) Whether or not spin-doctoring was an import from the States, there is something of a chicken-and-egg conundrum as to whether it came from New Labour's communications' bunker, supposedly under the command of Peter Mandelson, or whether it surfaced first in the British media and was subsequently ascribed to New Labour.

The Guardian, probably the strongest media-trend monitoring service on the street, is a suspect in any investigation into the naming of spin. Political Editor Michael White and former City Editor and Washington correspondent Alex Brummer appear to have first claim on the term 'spin-doctor' in a *Guardian* article as far back as January 1988. A decade later, *The Scotsman* was writing about how everyone had a spin-doctor and that even the Queen had given the role some sort of royal warrant with the appointment of Simon Lewis, the public relations cheese to his brother William's journalistic chalk-stripe at the *Financial Times*, as communications secretary. James Kirkup recorded that the job-title was first whispered during the Republicans' presidential campaign, coined to help 'clarify' George Bush's statements to journalists. And, boy, did they need clarifying. For the Democrats, the diminutive and phenomenally sharp-witted George Stephanopoulos provided the counter-spin, later becoming a key adviser to President Clinton. During the 1994 presidential campaign, the Democrats' chief media strategist, James Carville, was married to one of Republican candidate Bob Dole's advisers, Mary Matalin, who stepped down when Dole eventually decided that there could be a conflict of interest between the day job and the conjugal bed.

Kirkup went on to record the trick of distracting the public from potentially embarrassing facts as a key talent of the new breed of spin-doctors. The satirical movie *Wag the Dog* was just out in 1998 and portrayed Robert De Niro as a spin-doctor hired to distract attention from the president's sexual peccadillo. His strategy is to start a war with Albania and the president is swept back to power. Whether life has imitated art or vice versa, Margaret Thatcher's re-election poll ratings on the back of the Falklands War, George Bush's popularity when he drove Saddam Hussein out of Kuwait (history will judge his son's scrap with Iraq) and Bill Clinton's successful sabre-rattling at Iraq during the Monica Lewinsky affair show how powerful the technique has proved to be.

The use of alternative 'news' to knock negatives off the front-pages is nothing new in politics, however much outrage might be generated by the supposedly original spin-sin of suggesting that the day of a terrorist attack in the States might be a good one on which to bury bad news. But there was a sense that something new had developed in British politics and, more broadly, in all the establishment institutions, from the Church and the Royal Family to the arts. It no longer mattered in the Nineties what something was, it was how it appeared. You no longer argued about an issue, you argued a position.

Presentation had become all – from business, where perceived value had become actual value in the fixing of share-prices, to the theatre and movies, where it no longer mattered so much what it was, but what your opinion of it was. Across society there was a new vacuity; style was not just more important than substance, it overcame it. We no longer seemed to discuss what something was, but what we thought of it. Over the past 20 years, the media, industry, politics, the establishment and the arts have conspired to bring us not their constituent parts, but a presentation of what they would like us to think they are. There should be a term for this, for the zeitgeist that we have come to live in: It is a spin-culture – and that is what I shall call it in this book.

Maybe it originated with the lurid manipulations surrounding Clinton's Zippergate or maybe with Derek Draper in the UK boasting about the names on his pager and the '17 people in New Labour that matter', of which, of course, he was one. Maybe it came from the efficiency with which New Labour ran its media management because if there's one thing that the British electorate mistrusts, it's efficient politics. But, whatever the cause, a decade after the term had been introduced to British society, it had become a solid pejorative. It is not just that the opposite of substance in politics or commerce has become spin, it is that anything of which one disapproves has become spin. Thus by mid-term in the first New Labour parliament, the Prime Minister was only rarely referred to in his own right on communicational matters and more usually as 'Tony Blair and his spin-doctors' or some variant. Political, economic and, indeed, commercial debate is blighted by a dearth of dialectic, for the easiest and most damning knock-out critical conclusion of the new antithesists is 'it's all spin'.

What does that mean? At one level it means a lack of substance, interpretation parading as fact, image creation at the expense of tangible evidence. But the intuitive, tongue-jerk response of 'it's all spin' is symptomatic of a deeper malaise in our collective consciousness. It implies that there is little of value in our institutions. The rare exception of something of true worth proves the rule that the majority is vacuous and superficial. From its genesis in business and politics, spin-culture has infected our arts, our secular institutions and our faiths. For all that is not gospel truth or true art is part of the spin-culture that we have developed for ourselves.

There is evidence that the primacy of this spin-culture is about two decades old, though its roots are buried in the liberalism and social revolutions of the second half of the twentieth century. And there are signs that it has run its course – most visibly in politics, where spin-culture is a most apparent irritant, but also throughout commercial life, where shareholders and corporate activists are no longer tolerating shallow justifications of greed and gluttony. François Rabelais held that nature abhors a vacuum and it may be that the entire socio-economic structure that spin-culture supports will implode on itself. From the black hole that spin-culture's collapsing star will have created may emerge new forms of political, commercial, institutional and artistic life – and this book heralds them. But spin-culture has to die first – which brings me to the other unremarkable event; the one that made me hear spin's death-rattle.

I was invited, in early July 2000, to give an after-dinner speech at the Athenaeum Club in London's Pall Mall. My hosts were a dining club called the City & Westminster, which sounded like an interesting axis of power, and I was provisionally billed as 'A Spin-Doctor Confesses'. The guest list of the C&W did not suggest that I would be addressing a broad spectrum of politics, or indeed anyone from the left or even centre-left of that spectrum. As one Tory friend disarmingly emailed me before the event: 'I expect the form to be cocktails at 7 and holocaust denial by 9.'

In the event, they were very kind, listening attentively and even laughing in some of the right places. My audience was a mixture of Thatcher's Tories and some blue-chip industrialists, with a sprinkling of intelligence services and journalism and I was pleased, given that these were constituencies that are likely to be hostile to the spin-doctor's craft, to be reasonably well received.

But, then again, that may have had something to do with having changed the title of my address to 'The Death of Spin'. Any predominantly right-wing audience could be forgiven in the summer of 2000 for indulging in a little *schadenfreude*. The BBC had just led on the news that thriller-writer Ken Follett had laid into Prime Minister Tony Blair for being, among other things, 'unmanly'. Ken and his wife, New Labour MP Barbara, had been, if not image-makers, then image-subsidisers of The Project, so this bit of literati froth stained Number 10's crisp linen a little. The Project had originally been focused on forming an axis of power with the Liberal Democrats that would keep the Tories out of power for a generation and possibly forever; later, however (and after the size of Labour's 1997 majority precluded any such deal with the Lib Dems), The Project had spread its remit to the implementation of the 'Third Way' programme of market-friendly social democratic policies. The fact that the media took seriously what the PM's press spokesman called Follett's 'self-indulgent ranting' marked an early battle in the trivia-versus-spin war that would develop between the Prime Minister's office and some quarters of the Press.

On its own, this chattering-class spat might have been treated as a seasonal bit of fluff, like the first cuckoo story of the silly season. But the PM had just called for drunken young yobs to be frog-marched to cashpoints for on-the-spot fines, only to be smartly contradicted by police chiefs. That was nothing compared with the humiliation that was to follow, when his 16-year-old son, Euan, was found face down in his own vomit in Leicester Square, in his West End première as a young hooray. (In fairness, the performance ran for one night only.)

Memos had started to leak from Number 10 in what looked like an orchestrated campaign further to discredit New Labour's image machine. Blair himself was seen to have declared concerns that the Government was perceived as weak on the family and on crime and called for a high-profile initiative 'that I can be personally associated with' (hence, presumably, the great cashpoint sanction). This was followed by the revelation that Blair's focus-group guru, Philip Gould, had written a panicky memo to the effect that The Project was in deep trouble with the electorate.

The Blair family retreated to their royal villa in Tuscany for the millennium summer holidays, but the image crisis wasn't quite over. Blair *père* had appeared on the front of Sunday newspapers clutching his newborn son Leo at his christening in the Sedgefield constituency. This had angered the PM, as it had been contrary to agreements with the Press with regard to limiting intrusion into the family's privacy. (The angry reaction also demonstrated that, contrary to opinions expressed in some newspapers, the Blairs have never actually sought to exploit the birth of Leo for PR purposes.)

In what looked like a fit of pique, the Blairs cancelled their Tuscan photo-call, a quasi-royal exercise in which early photos are exchanged for privacy during a holiday that coincides with a period of yawning space to fill in newspapers. With the Blairs reported to be chippy about the Press – perhaps for the first time – an ill-humoured photo-call was reinstated.

But the Blairs could reflect, as the Tory Press had been quick to point out, that the sure touch with the media had appeared to desert them. This should not matter much – all prime ministers, indeed all in the public eye, have their ups and downs with the media. But it mattered all the more to Blair, as the icon of New Labour, because of the alleged presidential style of the new regime. New Labour had galloped to power in 1997 on media stallions, trampling John Major's dead-beat PR into the turf – the spin-culture mattered to Number 10. It followed that its demise would matter too.

With hindsight, the spin-culture was in rude health for the first three years after the great victory of 1997. The PM's personal ratings were astronomically higher than any of the opposition, parliamentary or from within his own party. Meanwhile, former tabloid political journalist Alastair Campbell, as new Press Secretary, protected him from the media wet-work of politics through the application of classic newspaper personnel management – a combination of fear and favour, in this case applied to lobby briefings with parliamentary correspondents. An early review of the civil service's information system, combined with an alleged and uncharacteristic laddish edge that made the last memorable PM's Press Secretary, Bernard Ingham, look and sound staid by comparison, helped establish Number 10's communications machine as a paradigm of the new spin-culture.

Sure, there were communications hiccups along the way. Not just with policy – the failure of the repeal of Clause 28 and the control-freakery of devolved assemblies in Wales, Scotland and London, to name just two. Governments should expect problems with the communication of policy implementation. But there were also crises in the communications machine itself. Peter Mandelson had to resign from government twice. The first was as Trade and Industry Secretary, after it emerged that he had an absurd mortgage arrangement with Paymaster-General Geoffrey Robinson, whose own offshore financial arrangements were producing some negative PR for the Government. The second, over what turned out to be misplaced sensitivities, attached to the granting of passports to the Hinduja brothers. Less significantly, the likely lad of Number 11, Charlie Whelan, had to quit Chancellor Gordon Brown's side, as a spin-doctor who failed to realise there was more to this business than promoting your own man's interests over others. (Campbell took this point on board early on.)

But these peccadilloes could – and were – cast in the light of New Labour growing up. It had been a long time in opposition – nearly 18 years – and there were bound to be growing pains in New Labour's adolescence. Occasionally, even New Labour could be expected to be found lying face-down in its own puke. Overall, the spin-culture was in robust good health and the spin-doctor had arrived in Britain. Special advisers in Government blossomed. In the corporate, commercial world, spin-doctors were in demand as never before. The telecoms and information-technology revolutions were driving corporate globalisation by the late Nineties. Nation was speaking unto nation like never before. And they needed to know what to say. Communication was sexy. Communication was the new rock 'n' roll. It followed that good communications advice was a hot commodity. By this time, more undergraduates wanted to enter PR than journalism. The hubristic claimed that PR was not only at the boardroom table but in the Cabinet Room too. Note that the Chancellor married a PR professional, Sarah Macaulay of 'Integrity PR' firm Hobsbawm Macaulay.

But somewhere, at the start of the twenty-first century, it all started to go wrong. Spin became the new sleaze. It became healthy to talk of its demise. Maybe it was the Dome. Maybe it was a more general disenchantment with New Labour policies, or the lack of them. Quite suddenly, the spin-doctor became a pariah, a sell-stock, someone with whom not to be seen in polite society. Some would claim that this is nothing new. And it is true that there has always been a somewhat paranoid disregard for PR among journalists – and to some degree, it is a reciprocated contempt. When Matthew Parris, then *The Times*' parliamentary sketchwriter, wrote in the mid-Nineties that he hated PR, I replied in the same paper that, since journalists and MPs regularly appeared at the bottom of league tables of respectability and trustworthiness, then if Matthew hated PR it was definitely a trade I wanted to be in.

Historically, journalists have resented PR people because they hold the power-supply of information – and they have found it fun to bite the hand that feeds them, like rebellious teenagers turning on their parents. PR people have disliked journalists because they have their own minds and don't do as they're told. But there is a new mood in the air that goes beyond normal professional hostilities. Spin-culture is the new decadence and its extermination appears actively to be sought by what used to be called 'all right-thinking people'. It was fleetingly fashionable – now almost any effort at advocacy in communications can be met with the charge that it is spin, which means that it is a lie, or at least obfuscation. There is an argument that we should perhaps not take all this too seriously – politics and its practitioners have long been dubious in the public mind and traditional public relations have traditionally been treated with Anglo-Saxon scepticism. 'You would say that, wouldn't you' is an attitude prevalent in the UK and relatively rare in the US. But my point is that the opposite of substance is not spin. Good corporate or political communication is about dialectics. And to be dialectical, you have to hold a position. That means the skills of advocacy. And you can't advocate the absence of something. It follows that good communication requires (or demands) substance; it doesn't seek to replace or usurp it.

The problem arises where communicators usurp their subjects. The danger signs are apparent when spin becomes the story itself. An early symptom of this may have been the BBC2 documentary by Michael Cockerell broadcast in July 2000, which, over 80 minutes, purported to be a fly-on-the-wall examination of how Campbell managed the media court at Number 10. In the Spring of 2002 spin was bizarrely made the top story by the embarrassments of Stephen Byers as Transport Secretary and rather soppy allegations and counter-allegations about the PM's vanity at public occasions. Much of this is silly – all of it is less important than peace in a prosperous economy, which is the pious priority of government (the maintenance of power being the less pious one). But a star burns brightest before its implosion.

It may be, then, that the early years of the twenty-first century were, in the biblical sense, spin-culture's last days. If so, its demise will be an event to look back on from the vantage point of a replacement culture. But, in any event, communications functions have become important in the conduct of politics and business and are a formidable industry in their own right. So, if the peculiar phenomenon known as spin is to wither on the grapevine, we should know what to require and to expect when the communications industry emerges chastened on the other side of change.

This book examines where spin came from, where it is going and what happens next – not just in politics and business, but also in the wider environment of communication as a means of advocacy. I have spent two decades in the media – in round terms, the first in journalism and the second in commercial communication. The book covers those decades, partly because I was there and therefore I know about them, but more importantly because it was 20 years ago that Thatcherism found its communicational feet and, I contend, the modern spin-culture emerges from that period, changing the conduct of politics, business and the media.

I have larded the narrative with re-edited excerpts from diaries, notes and articles that I wrote at the time, which I hope are illustrative and relieve the analytical text of unbroken pomposity. I hope, too, that they help the spinning of the yarn.

MEDIA

How the West was spun

Spin wasn't invented during the past 20 years, or even 20 years ago. There really is nothing new in spin. So long as there have been peoples to be influenced, there have been spinners. St John spun the teachings of Christ, in the sense that the synoptic gospels dealt with what He did, while John addressed what He meant. Tacitus spun the Roman Empire (there are rumours he tried to muscle in on Emperor Hadrian's funeral). Cardinal Wolsey spun Henry VIII to the Pope, though the penalties for failure were rather greater in those days. William Pitt the Younger spun George III, superbly counterbalanced by the satirical caricatures of James Gilray. In the modern era, the great press barons – Harmsworth/Northcliffe, Rothermere, Beaverbrook, Kemsley, Camrose, Hartwell and Astor, all in the shadow of America's William Randolph Hearst – created fresh demand for the statesman's interpreters, or spin-doctor as we would call them today. Sigmund Freud's nephew, Edward Bernays, was doing it for major American consumer-product corporations before the Second World War. In our own day, Prime Minister John Major had journalists Sheila Gunn and Sarah Hogg, wife of junior minister Douglas Hogg, and the awesomely clever Jonathan Hill – though Back to Basics, Wait and See and the Cones Hotline would suggest that the art was enjoying only a primitive revival. Harold Wilson had Joe Haines and, further back, Winston Churchill had Brendan Bracken and Queen Victoria had Benjamin Disraeli (or, possibly, vice versa). But 20 years ago there was a turning point, the start of a new communications age, whose components, from the financial markets to industry and politics, would conspire to bring us the spin industries that underpinned our spin-culture.

Twenty years ago Margaret Thatcher found her prime ministerial feet at Number 10. Depending where you stood in the political spectrum of the time, this was either the dawning of a new age of enlightenment (Boris Johnson, Conservative) or a time when mothers' milk curdled in the breast and crops began to fail (John O'Farrell, Socialist). Too many portents have been ascribed to the rise of Margaret Thatcher. It's true that if you were unfortunate enough to be a miner, or a nurse, or a print-worker in Fleet Street, nothing would ever be the same again, but she was led by her times as much as she was a leader of them – at least, initially. The grocer's daughter from Grantham, a hard-working meritocrat who nevertheless at first embraced a grand old Toryism (with affirming appointments such as that of Francis Pym and Peter Carrington), while bringing into the front-line the new mercantile class (such as Cecil Parkinson and Michael Heseltine), was truly classless. Not in the sense of her anointed successor, John Major, who managed spectacularly to be completely devoid of class, but in the sense of being beyond class, even – perversely enough – above class.

She did not, however, personally impose this classlessness, or anything else, on the Press. She barely knew or cared that the Press was there. Again, depending on where you stand on Mrs Thatcher – whether, by preference, on her reputation or on her throat – she was either uncompromisingly single-minded or dangerously ignorant in her apathy and/or contempt for the Press. Bernard Ingham, who started as her Press Secretary (following the brief tenure of Henry James) and finished as her apologist and faithful Boswell, dictated the Prime Minister's press policy in a manner that was potentially far more dangerously autocratic than any move that Alastair Campbell could later make in the same role for Tony Blair.

Blair has been known to read a newspaper and, more significantly in this comparison, to worry about what it said. Thatcher ignored the Press. Not that she made a conscious decision to avoid it – the truth is that she barely noticed it. Ingham pressed upon her his own carefully edited highlights and lowlights of the morning's papers. As like as not, this would include the consistently supportive tabloid The *Sun*, which was vital for the almost sexual stimulation of the new C2D2 aspirant middle-classes that were to keep her in power for more than a decade, and the Tories that she spawned for the best part of two decades.

Ingham was able to provide the Prime Minister with an altogether narrower and more biased view of the British Press than Blair has ever received. This one operational characteristic makes Ingham a far greater spin-doctor of Thatcher (though not, please note, *for* Thatcher) than Campbell could ever be of Blair. It also made Ingham, at a time when the British Press was getting into its commercial stride, one of the most powerful people in the country. It is worth reminding ourselves of this after his re-invention as the bluff, cartoon-Yorkshireman media pundit. Under his communications command in the Eighties, the Lobby was prone to every bit as much spin and counter-spin as any modern equivalent. I have theivil-service Lobby briefing papers from 9th February 1984 as an example. Leader of the Commons John Biffen briefed the Lobby shortly after 4 pm on the Cabinet's deliberations ahead of the Budget. The confidential civil servant's papers record Biffen's comments as follows: 'Cabinet this morning had been one of the most bland, miserably disappointing and boring meetings he had ever been at. It was absolutely awful; there was no lively debate, just unctuous self-satisfaction.' The 'unctuous' was directed at Chancellor Nigel Lawson. By the following morning, having seen the Lobby briefing and, more importantly, having briefed Margaret Thatcher, Ingham was calling Biffen a 'semi-detached' member of Cabinet at the Lobby briefing. Biffen left Cabinet after the 1987 election. Ingham cannot afford to ride too high a horse when it comes to criticism of today's in-fighting between spin-doctors.

Like Alastair Campbell after him, Ingham was rocketed to the role of *eminence grise* from journalism more by luck than ambition. Ingham worked his way from local and regional Yorkshire papers to *The Guardian* in the Sixties; Campbell through a Mirror Group Newspapers training scheme to political commentary at the flagship title and on the long-defunct *Today*. Ingham was a head of information at the Department of Employment in the early Seventies when Willie Whitelaw turned up from Northern Ireland as Secretary of State with his loyal press lieutenant, Keith McDowall (Mr Brenda Dean, trades unionist and later thorn in Thatcherism's side). Ingham and McDowall were old journalistic rivals; McDowall on the *Daily Mail*'s industrial beat versus Ingham's soft social democracy as a reporter on *The Guardian*. Ingham felt McDowall's appointment at Employment keenly and touchingly called staff in one by one to ask 'where their loyalties lay'. He was soon off to the Department of Energy under Tony Benn and in the late Seventies was an under-secretary at the Energy Conservation Trust. In Churchillian terms, these must have been his wilderness years – though it is only subsequently greater achievements that make them so; otherwise they're just a career. It was from the arcane challenges of energy conservation that Ingham was plucked by Thatcher to be her Press Secretary on her accession in 1979. He was the first head of profession – the government-information top job – to come from outside the Central Office of Information. There were cries of politicisation and, interestingly in the context of subsequent history, Ingham resisted the title. But Thatcher insisted – a phrase that could stand as the story of Ingham's life.

He was to bring professionalism to the Government Information Service (GIS), later to become the Government Information and Communication Service (GICS). He took his leadership seriously and placed his personally tutored information operators – 'Bernard's Babes' – in the key departments of government. He still commands loyalty and respect among the remnants of his White-hall legion. To outsiders, his media oppression and repression was of the folksy 'bunkum and balderdash' variety and, with his bushy eyebrows and grandpa jawline, he looks altogether more like the harmless saloon-bar patriot than the hook-nosed and sneering school-bully that is Alistair Campbell's caricature. Neither of these caricatures is true to life – caricatures are no more true to life today than they were in Gilray's time – though in retirement Ingham grows to resemble his more. Campbell may have the insecurities of the bully, but he has the sensitivities that the bully lacks. Like Ingham, he has had to conceal them to avoid his old press milieu smelling blood. For Ingham it was the bluster; for Campbell the bully. But these are images from the press gallery and the lobby briefing. They carry weight because they are the images with which the media are presented and which they consequently purvey. This is what business people call the demand end of the commercial equation. The real power – as retail superpowers such as Tesco, Sainsbury, Safeway and Asda know – lies at the supply end. Control your supplier – in the case of a Number 10 Press Secretary, that's the Prime Minister – and you're really in your Government's driving seat.

But, tempting as it is to make Thatcher responsible for everything that occurred on the cusp of the early Eighties, it was not her ascent, nor Ingham's media control of her, that developed the spin industry. She was a political child of her times – come the hour, come the woman. The factors that made it possible for Britain to elect a woman as Prime Minister for the first time and to take such a belligerent, stubborn and radical right-wing reformer to its collective heart for two further general elections were many of the same socio-economic factors that produced a media that could be manipulated.

The first of these factors is sociological. Post-war journalism in the second half of the twentieth century developed from a straight news-driven agenda (supported by classified advertising and executed by tradesmen who did apprenticeships as school-leavers and were from the literate working or lower-middle classes) to a polemical profession in the ownership of middle-class graduates. This process was spurred by improved education and a consequent increase in mass literacy and a developing prosperity that further drove a growing industry in display advertising. The influence of changing fashion should also not be underestimated. There had always been a romance to journalism – the hard-bitten, gumshoe reporter or the nobby foreign-correspondent (*vide* the young Winston Churchill) who reported from the imperial front line before going on to do something better.

But sometime after the Second World War, when rationing and austerity had gone, the educated middle-classes started to consider it a real career choice. It may not have acquired the standing of the law or accountancy, but after *Citizen Kane* (1941) and the Sunday-newspaper absorbed angry young man of *Look Back in Anger* (1956), and sometime during the photo-reportage from the Vietnam war in the Sixties and *The Washington Post*'s destruction of Richard Nixon's administration in the Watergate scandal in the Seventies, there grew a kind of inverted middle-class snobbery about journalism. In a terminology that has oddly spanned much of the era, journalism was cool. The apparent liberation from the old order of the Sixties provided extra momentum. Deference to authority was binned, encouraging the well-to-do to air opinions that could be – in the new journalism, should be – iconoclastic and clever. Journalism, some 80 years after Karl Marx had tried to get things moving in politics, had become dialectic. According to media-watcher Stephen Glover: 'Successful journalists tend to be better paid and better educated than they used to be. Leading politicians are less well educated than their predecessors, and many of them are not as rich. The new media class has vaulted over the political class.'[1]

Coffee-bar politics had been joined by café-society journalists. These were people schooled in debate, used to diversity of opinion and, indeed, greedy for opinions. Newspapers suddenly needed opinions and journalists could not meet the demand from their own back-catalogue of education. They needed to buy in opinions and arguments. The bars of Fleet Street began to ring less to the talk of scoops and more to the reasonably learned arguments of who was right and wrong in politics or trade. And as soon as journalism started to have opinions of its own – rather than exclusively the opinions of its proprietors, with all other space given to dispassionate news reporting – there was a market created in commentary, the currency of which was opinions, which could be traded. To this trade came the professional advocate. Journalism had effectively become part of a nascent spin-culture.

If an early factor in making the media spinnable was bourgeois and sociological, it was followed by another that was brutally commercial. The desire to own newspapers was changing from the rich man's indulgence in something unprofitable, which never-theless provided political influence, to something that could be made very profitable, which consequently forced political influ-ence. The old British Press aristocracy had owned newspapers to enhance political and social standing at a financial cost to them – it was almost a social cachet to demonstrate how much they were able to lose. The new press barons, led by Rupert Murdoch as a paradigm, but variously including Conrad Black, David O'Reilly,

---

[1] *The Spectator*, 29th June 2002.

Lord Hollick, Richard Desmond and shareholders of such publicly-listed corporations as Pearson, endeavoured to make money from the media, which coincidentally brought them political and some ambient social standing.

This had two important effects. The first was to expand their newspapers' formats in a quest for new and richer seams of advertising revenue. The old news agenda was subsumed in a mania for lifestyle content – supplements for cookery, fashion, gardening, motoring, the arts, travel and health proliferated. Gender and sexuality has never been far from advertising people's minds. Women's journalism, honourably pioneered on *The Guardian* by Polly Toynbee and Jill Tweedie, was developed elsewhere as a further journalistic ghetto that could be ascribed its own advertising budgets. But whether it was toys for the boys or tungsten-lined pattie-pans to accompany autumn recipes, there was a growing and insatiable appetite for content as newspaper staffers failed to fill from their own reservoirs of knowledge and experience. At the heart of the newspaper, in politics and in business news, there was a demand to expand to accommodate both new readers and further advertising space to reach them.

Particularly in business coverage, which had hitherto been technical stock-market reports, there grew new, separate sections, with vast space devoted to the burgeoning neo-economy in retail financial services – even vaster spaces were created in aeroplanes to jet financial reporters to sunny places that were suitable for announcing the launch of a new unit trust or pet-insurance plan. Reporters were never going to find enough from their own resources to fill the newspaper space available. Again, journalism became spinnable as it sought material.

The Fleet Street diaspora in the Eighties made its own contribution to the PR supply industry that was growing around the new journalistic prosperity. The emergence of Thatcherism had created the political environment in which the new commercial class of newspaper owner could take on the Fleet Street print unions. These unions had exploited the financial indolence of the old press barons, for whom newspaper profitability was a low priority. Murdoch was the first to seize the opportunity in 1983, moving his Times Newspapers almost overnight to a plant in

Wapping that offered an altogether more emollient cost-base. The subsequent lock-out of trades unionists and suspension of publication was a symbol of the early Thatcher years – rioting workers, pickets and violent police on horseback were eerily prescient of what was coming down the line for the miners. As a corollary, a newspaper industry that had been broken in at Murdoch's rodeo, made obedient and supine, would be less well equipped independently and robustly to cover the grotesque human tragedies of the break-up of mining communities. It could not have been a deliberate strategy substantially to break the printed media's will ahead of the war with the miners, but it happened nonetheless.

Paul Routledge was *The Times*' industrial correspondent, who effortlessly breached protocol by reporting the Queen's observation on her visit to the paper's old offices in Gray's Inn Road that the miners' dispute was 'all about one man' to a BBC crew (she was presumed to mean Arthur Scargill, not energy secretary Peter Walker). Routledge never crossed the picket line at Wapping, lost close friends, severely restricted the options for his career progression and, until recently, drank on Tuesdays with his fellow Times Newspapers' 'refuseniks'. I've sat at dinner with Routledge at the stratospherically-establishment Brook's Club on a Tuesday night and listened to him in class-war with a captain of industry. He gave and gives no quarter still. But after *The Times*' dispute, Routledge's journalistic prosperity was the exception that proved the rule. It was never just about the print unions. The new, cool, post-war journalism was broken too; particularly it marked the final demise of the labour and industrial group within journalism. With the likes of Routledge dispersed, it would be easier for outsiders to lead the journalistic agenda to their advantage. Again, journalism had become spinnable.

Newspaper managements have not attracted the greatest talent over the years. That was very significantly why the unions had been able to develop such a restrictive-practice stranglehold on the industry. So, the rest of the newspaper groups followed Murdoch's lead from Fleet Street. The diaspora consequently had one further consequence for the intellectual independence of the Press. There used to be a collective, geographical pride to Fleet Street. It's why some of us went there. I was quoted in one of those 'Quotes of the

Week' columns as saying 'You spend years getting to Fleet Street and then all the bloody papers move'. The comment echoes a regret that journalism lost its homogeneity when it quit the Street. It became the subject of literary nostalgia in the style of Alan Watkins' serially re-published short walks down Fleet Street.

By the late Eighties, there was no major newspaper group left in Fleet Street. There is no room for sentiment among old hacks for its passing, but it was a market for information, like the Rialto bridge in Venice. It was an employment market for journalism – either side of the last war, you could be fired and cross the Street and be in alternative remunerative employment within the hour – a remarkable labour model during economic depressions. Stories that couldn't be used for proprietorial reasons were traded with rival papers in the bars. There was strength in numbers. All that went in the march for efficiency in the Eighties. Liver-disease figures in EC4 may have improved (one theory as to why nearby Bart's Hospital lost it's A&E facility), but British journalism lost some of its identity when it left Fleet Street. For all its faults, it was an identity in which it took some pride. The old rubric for those who want to be in charge is that you 'divide and rule'. Outside influence has had an easier time of it since Fleet Street divided. Again, journalism became spinnable.

How newspapers were
divided and ruled

16th March 1988 – Princess Alexandra comes 'to open' The Observer's new offices. We've been 'open' some time – open-plan, open-minded, open-to-offers, except when they're open. The industrial-strength sniffer dogs come in the morning – one over-enthusiastically sniffs David's office seat and leaves with a yelp. Melvyn stands out at the end of the Business section, by the lavs, somewhat self-consciously, like a colour-sergeant being ribbed by the NCOs behind him. He seems to be the only one who isn't anxious to ingratiate himself and, possibly as a consequence, gets a full seven seconds with the Great One, attended by Tiny and the odd flunky, who I take to be Edward du Cann. There's a photo-call and health correspondent Annabel Ferriman's little girl makes the mistake of standing in front of Tiny, whose great hams of hands not-quite-gently move her out of the way. It's truly marvellous to see a largely republican newspaper fawn like this – there's nothing like leftie journalists for soiling themselves when the nobs turn out. 'And how do you enjoy your new building?' she graciously enquires. 'Oh, it's very light and airy, ma'am,' says a cringing twerp. For which the properly prepared answer should have been 'We feel like a bunch of airline check-in clerks, Your Royal Highness.'

When *The Observer* moved from St Andrew's Hill, just off Ludgate Hill, in the spring of 1988, the management gave us little folders, describing the exciting facilities, such as the wine-bars and restaurants of Queenstown Road in Battersea, that would greet us when we arrived in the new white-and-grey mausoleum just south of Chelsea Bridge, Marco Polo House, designed by an architect with a pony-tail and a period mansion somewhere like Oxfordshire. Excited young Lonrho executives strode about the editorial floor with mobile phones the size of Vienetta ice-creams on their belts. Lighting was of the upward, ceiling-reflective kind from giant Grecian goblets with floor switches that got hammered during their warm-up periods. There was full-length smoked Perspex. And it was suddenly VERY hot.

One of the subs had brought a revolving fan from the old office, which worked for a while until the temperature plummeted and the production department was working in fingerless gloves and balaclavas. One of the belted mobile phones – called Dave, I think – pitched up and told us solemnly that we now worked in a 'perfectly controlled atmosphere'. A computer adjusted the air-conditioning in response to the temperature outside – in Battersea Park, presumably. 'Then why are we f******freezing?' The fan, an heirloom from the old homestead, was confiscated. One or two of us lived in fear of a more personal visit from the clip-board apparatchiks: 'Your management has gone to a great deal of expense to make this a perfectly controlled atmosphere – I'm sorry, but you're just too ugly to work here.'

The paper's editor, Donald Trelford, had described the move from Blackfriars at his first address to staff in Battersea as 'a bridge too far'. Rather more presciently, the *Telegraph*'s wise-owl of the industrial circuit, Roly Gribben, who had moved with his paper to Docklands, remarked that, by contrast, *The Observer* had 'gone west'. The heart was no longer in the place. There were too many indolent and overpaid grey-heads who had lost the plot. There were still to be moments of gut-wrenching high emotion and drama. Farzad Bazoft was summarily hanged on a spontaneous investigative mission to Iraq. Canon John Oates, rector of St Bride's, the journalists' church in Fleet Street, led prayers around his desk, which became a shrine to him and his journalistic cause.

I collected a lot of stick from properly cynical colleagues for applauding Melvyn Marckus when he arrived at the office on the morning of the publication of *The Observer*'s eccentric mid-week edition carrying the Department of Trade & Industry's Inspectors' Report on Mohammed Fayed's acquisition of Harrods from under the nose of Tiny Rowland, our proprietor. Whatever the charges from rival papers – some sincere, others plain jealous, others yet fearful for their own exposure at the hospitality trough of Fayed at the Paris Ritz and elsewhere – the DTI Inspectors had vindicated *The Observer's* relentless pursuit of Fayed by publishing a viciously critical report on him.

John Merritt further developed his extraordinary talent for investigative scoops, in failing health, by gaining access to a remote island to which Greece had secretly consigned its severely mentally handicapped and, even as he began to die of leukaemia, exposing the shortcomings of the National Health Service in London from his hospital bed.

But these were already echoes of a passing glory. The wreck of Battersea Power Station was meant to be reclaimed as the hub of a vibrant new South Bank to Chelsea, but it stood like an eyeless metaphor for the exhausted power of *The Observer*. We used to say that whatever economies management had managed to exploit by the move to Battersea must have been more than expunged by the taxi bills for actually getting anywhere where anything was happening that readers might want to hear about.

Editorial conferences would consist of a quorum of the grey-owls at the top of the table, like the praetorian guard of the groves of Academe, parading knowledge of middle-east politics during the Gulf War. Below the salt, riff-raff such as Routledge and I flicked paper-balls and gags and occasionally interjected questions like 'What are we actually going to put in the paper?' After some flirting with the *Independent, The Observer* was sold to The Guardian Trust in 1993, precipitating the grotesque spectacle of *Observer* journalists grabbing champagne bottles from catering staff who were about to lose their jobs to pop in front of the television cameras. An honourable and exciting world was ending, not with a whimper, but a pop.

Such worlds were ending elsewhere, as Fleet Street émigrés became part of a new commodity industry. Putting a brave face on it, journos spoke of the River Thames as the new River Fleet, connecting *The Observer* in the west with Express Newspapers and the *Financial Times* at the southern bridgeheads of Blackfriars and Southwark respectively, before continuing downstream to Times

Newspapers at Wapping and the *Telegraph* titles on the estuary at
the Isle of Dogs. This took no account of tributaries that might
connect with Associated Newspapers on Kensington High Street
(owners of the *Mail* titles) or *The Guardian*, unmoved up Farringdon
Road. But it's true that we tried to maintain a collective soul and a
convenient, equidistant meeting-place for all of us for leaving parties,
catch-up drinks and trysts was Fleet Street. There, we watched in
some bewilderment as Goldman Sachs built its Tardis in the old
Telegraph building – strangely bigger on the inside than it looked on
the outside – and threatened to absorb the Black Lubianka of the
Express (it now has) and looked in some sadness at the dark, satanic
mills of *The Observer* (now demolished) and the Daily Mail & General
Trust, which decayed at the foot of Whitefriars Street, the owners
having neglected to sell before the collapse of property prices at the
end of the Eighties.

In the spirit of the New River Journalism, I took one of the new
(and now largely extinct) Thames cabs to the *Sunday Telegraph* in
the Isle of Dogs to visit Richard Addis, then the paper's Deputy
Editor, latterly Editor of the *Daily Express* and resuscitator of the
Toronto Globe & Mail, before returning to revive design at the
Financial Times. As someone occupying a parallel dimension – I
first met him when we were rival diarists in the trade press, when
he had pinned the label of his jacket to his arm 'because there's no
point in wearing an expensive one unless people know' – Fleet
Street had been like sheltered housing. He was safe there. Now,
taking his expenses chitty to draw cash from a bank in Docklands
for lunch on a barge, he was like a saintly padre in a gold rush
shantytown. In the New World, but not part of it.

He made the transition, of course, as did most of us. Even those
who claimed a preference for ancient mechanical Remingtons,
hammering out copy on 'threes' and subbed in blue pencil, were,
within a month, revelling in the joys of being able to move
paragraphs about on screen, spell-checks and word-counts – not to
mention naughty messages to colleagues. But for the communications industry – what was to become almost universally known
within a decade as spin – this period represented an opportunity.
Removed geographically from where the action was and demoralised by mismanagement and rationalisation, the newspaper

industry was like a scattered herd of wildebeest – and the lions, lionesses, jackals and jackalesses of the public relations industry recognised that.

If nature abhors a vacuum, then the communications industry – if it's any good – should love it. It should suck matter in and the PR industry should be the provider of such matter. In their new technological palaces, the newly remote journalists were grateful for visits from outsiders with information. For the political desks – where spin has become the fashionable *bête noire du fin de siècle* – there has always been the lobby system, firmly anchored in Westminster. That is where spin developed its most visible presence, though, in truth, it had been there forever, more of which later. On City and Business desks, the geographical departure of the printed media from Fleet Street – mid-town between the City and Westminster with a psychological strength in numbers – made us more vulnerable to vested interests.

It may have cost their clients a small fortune in taxi fares, but the City desks of national newspapers – many of which returned to separate offices within striking distance of the Square Mile – grew accustomed to visits from financial PR magnates, such as the urbane and charming Anthony Cardew, the urbane-and-charming Nick Miles, then of Tim Bell's financial wing Lowe Bell Financial, and the U&C Alan Parker, whose financial PR hot-shop Brunswick was sweeping all before it. But the departure from Fleet Street, geographical and psychological, was only part of it. The arrival of the technology also took its toll. As I say, the screen-based wizardry was exciting initially. We became carried away by silly little novelties, such as the ability to receive Reuters and PA at our desks and to send messages to each other in the office (this was before e-mail proper).

But the technology brought something altogether more sinister too. It had been the intention of newspaper managements, led by Murdoch's Times Newspapers, to introduce efficiencies that required the breaking of the print unions, with their restrictive practices that had inflated the cost-base of newspaper production for generations (they alleged). This meant that the printers and compositors – those gentlemen and a few ladies whose skilled trade was to make up pages with scalpels from acetates, for the making of plates of each page in the bowels of the newspaper factories around Fleet Street – were to be replaced by screen-based technicians.

This also meant more than the loss of romance of receiving a warm first edition from the 'comps' (compositors) downstairs and taking it across the Street to swap with one's journalistic 'oppo' for comparison. It meant, crucially, that not only was page make-up – the job of the comps – being replaced by the new technicians, but the role of the sub-editor was eroded too. The sub-editor, in old Fleet Street, was a whole lot more than a technician. He, or (occasionally) she, had already been through the reporting mill, knew about how to construct a story, could 'copy-taste' and had an intuitive eye for the cock-up of a reporter under pressure and was, consequently, a safety measure that could save a newspaper hundreds of thousands in potential libel damages. They would form part of the 'back-bench', where the senior editorial talent of any shift resided. The *Mirror* would have wished that these traditions had been so assiduously maintained when a feature it ran on the prosecution of Leeds United footballers was ordered for re-trial in 2001 after an interview it published proved prejudicial.

The highly experienced editorial individuals of the production desks were being progressively replaced by technocrats who could make the story fit. As modular page designs increasingly pandered to the abilities and demands of the technocrat, the unsung heroes of the subs' desks were despatched. I'm not saying that the technocrats were cynical collaborators with newspaper managements in the qualitative demise of the sub-editors – not all of them anyway – nor that talented subs didn't make the transfer suucessfully to the new technocracy. Furthermore, I'm not saying that there aren't technocrats doing screen-based make-up with great editorial talents. Headline writing in Britain is still the best in the world. But the technological revolution removed a layer of editorial management that it neither strategically intended to, nor has been to the benefit of the British quality of journalism. Quite the reverse – that quality has suffered.

Where there was a back-bench with the inherent qualities that the old sub-editorial system engendered, the reporting (not to mention the commentating) functions of a newspaper were exposed to a level of objective quality control that no longer exists in the same strength. It follows that journalists – and it is most dangerous at the level of the young and inexperienced – can get more into their newspaper unchecked, qualitatively or quantitively, than they could before the Fleet Street diaspora. The effect is exacerbated by competitive rationalisation – there are fewer reporters producing more for their newspapers. However diligent they are, more of a lower quality is reaching the reader.

The opportunity for vested interests is a significant one. The advocates and spinners in industry and politics have a greater opportunity than ever before successfully to argue their case into the British Press. This is not, in itself, a pejorative factor – one of the factors underestimated in the public obsession with spin is that there is livelier and more open debate on a wider range of important subjects than there has been to date. More vested interests are able to participate.

But there are also clear dangers. The technological revolution has made the Press far more susceptible to the spin-culture of such vested interests. The price of the British Press's freedom, in this regard as in so many others, is constant vigilance. I have confined my analysis of the media revolution in this regard to the Press. Broadcast media have not been exempt from similar pressures, though their own technological revolution – the dawning of the digital age – has not had the same potentially catastrophic effect on quality as is the case in newspapers. Allegations of dumbing-down aimed at the BBC are often levelled by those who complain that policemen are looking younger – it's a rite of passage for the middle-aged. Nevertheless, the quality of television journalism has suffered, not least through the franchise break-up of ITV regions by the Thatcher government – an element of policy that the Baroness appeared even herself to regret. Competitive pressures invariably and often justifiably strike at the cost-base of operations.

ITN, the independent television news service that served the regions, has been heavily rationalised over a decade and a half. When my colleague, Charles Stewart-Smith, was a producer at ITN in the Eighties, he had enough mobile crews in London at his disposal to cover outside-broadcast stories. By the time he left in 1991, he and his colleagues enjoyed no such luxury. ITN was simply forced to decide which events to provide pictures from and which to do as studio-based exercises. The opportunity for independent commercial provision of pictures, from principals in the story, has been an obvious one. It's an opportunity that has been woefully ignored by the PR industry, but historically that has been because its practitioners don't understand and are afraid of broadcast media. But this broadcast issue is one that has arrived and does require commercial communications management.

The BBC, meanwhile, has been too obsessed with public-service broadcasting to play its part in the development of the debate over vested-interest content. It has often appeared that the BBC's attitude, whether on radio or television, is that if it hasn't been in the papers, then it isn't news. Given the way that newspapers are going, as previously described, this attitude leverages the influence of a spin-culture. Under the politically-aware Greg Dyke, who took up the director-generalship in 2000, the BBC has addressed its fading reputation. Significant was the appointment of Jeff Randall as Business Editor in 2001. The BBC's business coverage had hitherto been earnest talking-heads, gushing hagiographies of money-makers, or the impenetrable economic analyses of intellectuals such as Peter Jay. The appointment of Randall, who had re-launched *Sunday Business* after the Business editorship of *The Sunday Times*, signified an intention to popularise the BBC's business coverage and – a shock to the BBC system – to break stories. It also signified that the BBC wanted to play business to the public it served on an equal footing to politics. Meanwhile, another former newspaperman, Andrew Marr, a former editor of the *Independent*, was being encouraged to do rather more than stand on College Green, speculating on what was in the minds of government ministers. Oddly, there have been charges of dumbing-down at the BBC from old-guard commentators. In fact, what Randall and Marr have been doing at the BBC is dumbing-up – bringing the non-specialist and general viewer into the worlds of business and politics. The same principle applies with Evan Davies as Economics Editor. The challenge for all of them has been how increasingly to make their subject matter broadly accessible, without condescending to the viewer or patronising those on whom they report. It should also be noted that, with the broadening of appeal of the BBC's coverage in politics, economics and business comes a wider sphere of influences and vested interests. The BBC has grown under Dyke's stewardship to be a greater contributor to and participant in the spin-culture in which it operates. How could it be otherwise, when its business coverage is no longer simply aimed at industrialists and City financiers, but at anyone with an interest in money, and its political commentary appeals to the electorate, rather than a small clutch of drones around College Green?

Popularisation – what the snobs call dumbing-down – and rationalisation have changed the British media. The latter makes them more vulnerable to a spin-culture, while the former makes them a more valuable tool of it. These are threats. But business, as well as politics, teaches us that where there are threats there are opportunities. Competitive rationalisation in newspapers and broad-casting – and the broader commercial appeal of both – may have produced some qualitative threats that are alarming in some quarters. The digital age, meanwhile, brings untold communicative opportunities. It is now time to turn our attention to those opportunities.

It's sometime in 1993 and I'm in the bath at Beach House beside the Exe estuary, which we rent from time to time for Welly Weeks, the children's half-term breaks. I'm on a mobile phone to Richard, whom I'm trying to persuade to become the finance director of our burgeoning communications consultancy enter-prise. Richard is an old friend from financial-journalism days. He rose through the Investor's Chronicle to the Telegraph City desk to writing its Questor Column, seducing the odd tabloid reporter along the way. He also took a First from Oxford and is one of the brightest young men of his generation – he would exclaim on planes, at lunches or in the office 'But I don't want to be a journalist'. So he quit, lived in a garret and rode a bicycle, took an MBA and made his way in equity fund management, or global asset management as we must now call it. And no, he gently explains, he won't be our FD: 'I just like to wander up to a Reuters screen, find out all I need to know about a company and decide whether it's worth investing in or not.'

One of the modern equivalents of policemen looking younger and having to make our own entertainment, as subjects for the middle-aged with which to bore their children, is the speed of the information-technology revolution. Vocabulary changes not just between generations, but within generations – my six-year-old recited funny website addresses in the summer of 2002. Some years previously, a screen in a newsroom told me 'It's now safe to turn off your Macintosh.' Had our teachers told us, as we arrived at school in the rain, that this would be a perfectly plausible professional instruction in our adult life, they would have been sectioned. As our friends email through their BlackBerries, we might remind them that in the mid-Eighties estate agents had mobiles the size of house-bricks, attached to re-chargers like a Jeep's spare petrol can. Or we might say, which is also true, that there were no international fax facilities at the time of the Falklands War in 1982.

You can always throw in that the early Amstrad personal computers in the Eighties were the size of Seventies' colour-television sets and rather more clunky in their operation. The laptop that this was written on is rather slimmer than some of my daughter's GCSE exercise books. As I once heard Frances Edmonds remark in respect of mobile phones, this is the only time that you'll find a room full of men arguing about who's got the smallest. The propagandists of the info-tech revolution can become over-excited. Even Nicholas Negroponte, the founding editor of *Wired* magazine, in his otherwise seminal book *Being Digital*, at one point appears to suggest that Jumbo-jet simulators are now so advanced that they offer a more realistic experience than flying a real one. At another, he predicts the demise of the novel. While we should all accept that the technology will continually bring with it new delivery formats – whether we down-load music from the internet or read Jane Austen on a palm-pilot – one doesn't have to be a complete old fogey to observe that there is no evidence for the demise of the linear narrative, either in literature or in movies. But then I never thought it was safe to switch off my Macintosh.

It is now held to be axiomatic that the info-tech revolution has the economic equivalence of the Industrial Revolution. It doesn't. The commercial development of the internet has more in common with the invention of the telephone. But this is not to suggest that there are not changes in the lives of anyone who has to communicate on a daily basis and profound changes in the lives of those of us who earn our livings in the processes of communication. It's not just those of us who had to run warm first-editions across Fleet Street and the PR people we used to bump into on the way who have been affected by these changes. It's the stockbrokers in the City who used to have young runners to take their closing positions round to the Stock Exchange. It's the multinational that can abandon the milk-run around the universities in favour of reaching graduates through their lap-tops, whether they're in the JCR or Jakarta. It's the ability to order your groceries from a global retailer like Wal-Mart's web-site and collect them from a depot by the station.

This is the stuff that entire industries grow very excited about. And rightly so. One of the buzz-words of the revolution has been disintermediation. This means the cutting out of traditional distributive dog-legs in industries. In financial services, for example, the markets were democratised by this process – the implication was that the decision-making clout was transferring from financial institutions to investors. Whatever the implications for brokers and independent financial advisers – who may or may not be disintermediated, depending on where they fit into the distributive process – the relevance to those of us in the media and its professional supply industries is that this represents empower-ment at the receiver's end and direct communication at the point of transmission.

The issues for us are twofold: Firstly, to what degree are traditional media themselves being disintermediated and, secondly, as a consequence, what does that mean for the professional suppliers of information, the PRs and spinners? The first point to make is that the pluralism that further channels of information supply bring to the market enhance competition between those channels and increase demand for information as well as the opportunity to see it published in one or more formats. So that's good news then.

The less-good news (spin-doctors try not to say bad news) is that much of the Press is being remorselessly disintermediated. The financial markets primarily take their information on-line from Bloombergs (the relatively new kids on the block), Reuters and Dow Jones. At the end of the last century not a month passed without a brave band of newspaper journalists quitting the Press for a dot-com equivalence – Hugo Dixon's departure from the chair at the

Lex column at the *FT* to found breakingviews.com being paradig-matic of the trend. Benjamin Wegg-Prosser, a former lieutenant of Peter Mandelson and latterly head of politics at *Guardian Unlimited*, the on-line business of the newspaper group, told me in early 2002 that 38 per cent of its site visitors didn't read *The Guardian* – the implication is that there is a generation emerging that won't read newspapers at all: 'Ten years ago, people were saying that the internet will kill newspapers – that hasn't happened, but the next five will make a difference.' This is tremendously frightening for the PR old guard, for whom the prospect of dealing information in real-time, rather than for a fixed edition every 24 hours, is tantamount to being told that there's no time for lunch.

But the really bad news for traditional PR is that on-line information services empower not only the consumers of informa-tion, but also the sources of it. Companies can reach their target audiences themselves – not just through their own web-sites but also through other internet constituencies – and they can do so globally, quickly and very often outside the bounds of regulation. Researching a company a decade ago, we had an Extel card index or a physical cuttings library; now we use a search engine and distinguish (or try to) between objective information and the company's own material.

This has serious implications, the first of which is that PR agency functions are dead and dying. There cannot be a continuing justification, in an era of global on-line corporate communication, for middle-men to distribute press releases, compile performance tables, post interim and preliminary financial results and field queries. If client companies don't recognise the efficiencies of taking these functions technologically in-house, their shareholders should.

There is one agency function that will temporarily outlive the others, like a widow left in the big old house. Copywriting is enjoying an extended lease of life through the pluralism of the new media. The proliferation of on-line delivery channels is woefully under-serviced with qualitative content – most of what we still see is 'garbage at the speed of light', as management guru Tom Peters dubbed it in *Fortune* magazine in 1994. Otherwise, communications agency functions that have not already expired will do so. It is consequently incumbent on communications advisers to raise their game or get out of it. To remain in the game means managing the change from the old methods of communication to the new.

More importantly, it means the management of communications content, rather than its distribution. That means ever more leadership of issues at the higher echelons of corporate manage-ment. Initially that was a boost for spin-culture, but quickly it moves the communications process beyond the management of message to the business of policy-making. And that, in turn, means hammering a seven-inch nail into the coffin of spin – for we will no longer be interpreting the message, but forging the policies from which the messages arise.

It's often said that all professional service providers – lawyers, accountants and auditors, bankers, corporate financiers, venture capitalists *et al.* – are management consultants now. And it's true that globalisation has driven the expansion of the likes of McKinsey & Co, Accenture and accountancy-firm conglomerations such as PricewaterhouseCoopers and KPMG International. The collapse of Andersen for its auditing of the fraudulent accounts of energy-trading colossus Enron has been purgative of a profession that had grown too consultative and less professional. But, within a decade, it is these straitened management consultancy groups that will be pushing forward the communications agenda. And it is these groups that could progressively challenge, in corporate commu-nications, the advertising-led global marketing services groups, such as WPP, Omnicom and Interpublic. This is the opportunity that arises from the threat to traditional PR services, which can be characterised within the rise and fall of spin-culture. Whether the opportunity can be seized depends on whether there is sufficient substance behind the spin-doctors, whether they are to be found in corporations, PR agencies or management consultancies. To establish that we need to look at where they came from.

April 1987 – We gather, a press corps of about 10 plus around 60 breweries equity research analysts, in a hotel foyer at Heathrow and shoot the breeze as though this was the most natural thing in the world to be doing. But, looking back, it is odd. The food and drinks group Allied-Lyons, under siege from Australian corporate raider Alan Bond, has acquired spirits group Hiram Walker – some say as a 'poison-pill' defence against Bond. Allied has chartered a British Airways Concorde for a week to fly we giants of financial and business commentary around their plants in North America and Europe. First stop, glamorously, is Prestwick to tour a whisky distiller. The pilot tells us as he opens the throttles that Concorde has never flown out of Prestwick before and he's 'not sure the runway is long enough – but here goes'. We make Toronto in a little over three hours. Her Majesty's Press Corps open a book at the rear of the plane on how much this is costing Allied. A deputation of analysts complains that the press contingent isn't being respectful enough. The PR man tells us airily that if this trip puts a penny on the share price it will all have been more than worth it. As it turns out, market-makers cautiously mark-down stock in the absence of any research in London (it's all on the plane) and Allied loses 5p. From Toronto, we cross Lake Ontario – low fuel pay-load, so it's a 'sporty take-off' – to Windsorville, a tiny airport, and the local populace has turned out to watch the great white bird land. The pilot tells us he has permission to do some 'recreational flying to show off this beautiful aeroplane'. A City man opposite me crosses himself. We feign an aborted landing, cut in the after-burners to make it sound dramatic and bank away, pulling our first little G, at an angle 'steeper than we would usually use with passengers aboard – but we hope you're enjoying it'. We do a low fly-past, breaking some glass in suburban greenhouses and land like rock stars – 'The Beastie Boys' says Pat Donovan of the Independent, which, because of its newly-published piety, insists on 'paying' for its correspondent's trip. We have police outriders on Harley-Davidsons to get us through the crowd, who want us to wave at them. In the Hyatt in New York, which is like Superman's grotto, the Evening Standard's man becomes over-emotional and files home a piece that starts 'Buy. Buy. Buy.' Tessa Curtis of the Telegraph has dug a real scoop out of the City crowd and the rest of the daily papers are filing furiously to catch up. I tell the PR man in the coach that it doesn't look like there'll be much left for the weekend papers. He looks around conspiratorially: 'What no one has written yet, George ... is how great this company is.' That's it, is it? Dr Julie Feaver of Mackenzie's is sitting in the back, palely murmuring 'stop it' at the tourist commentary. We disembark at dinner-time and Concorde takes away the night –

three hours from New York at 9 pm we arrive in Cognac at dawn and our hosts at Courvoisier hand us balons. The day passes in a haze and then there's a final dinner. Allied's chairman Sir Derrick Holden-Brown has arrived with his wife. I separate him at pre-prandials and walk into the vineyard, eyed suspiciously by my colleagues, to stand up a little unrelated story about Martell. I give the vote of thanks after dinner, suitably disrespectfully in a poor imitation of Ben Elton. We stay up drinking and playing pool all night, our second-running without sleep. We transfer to Heathrow and limos take us home with samples of the product we've visited in the back – drinks like Kahlua and Maker's Mark bourbon. My wife tells me she's pregnant again and we celebrate until I fall asleep in the conservatory, like a roadie. Next morning I fly Jumbo from Gatwick to Boston with fund manager Fidelity – at least there's time to sleep on the plane. My watch can no longer stand up to the time zones and I buy a girl's Swatch off her in the street for $20. Ersatz Aussie John Jones of the Mail on Sunday *and I fly down to New York to cover how the British election is greeted on Wall Street (it isn't). In the journalists' bar Costello's on 44th East, we laugh that we have been sent by Magellan, Fidelity's hugely successful equities fund. I don't know what all this is meant to be achieving, but it beats working.*

Financial PR isn't the heartland of today's spin-culture. That has been occupied, reluctantly of late, by the communications machine surrounding New Labour – in particular the fast-breeding reactor that has produced 70-odd special advisers in Government (policy-writers very often, but spin-doctors in the media minds – and perception is all), compared with 11 when Tony Blair entered Number 10. But, from the end of the Seventies and particularly in the Eighties, financial PR was where the money was made. It was where the power of spin – as it then wasn't called – was discovered and developed and from which, ultimately, the commercial disciplines were to be learned that informed the development of a political spin-culture.

The financial markets in EC3 were spinning like tops more than a decade before the word spin was heard in SW1. This was partly down to the strength of the old GIS, the arm of the civil service that ran departmental information in a bureaucratic fashion under

Heads of Information, down through Senior Information Officers to Press Officers. Bernard Ingham was head of the GIS during the Eighties. New Labour presided over its partial dismemberment during the late Nineties. But it wasn't only the strength of the GIS that resisted the development of spin-culture in the Eighties, it was the commercial weakness of spin-doctors in the political field that delayed its development in Westminster.

While spin developed among the financially canny in the City, Westminster still had bow-tied parliamentary lobbyists who thought that effective communications amounted to introducing their clients to sympathetic backbenchers over a good lunch and running parliamentary monitoring services. Given parliamentarians' capacity for freeloading, they may have been right. But it held back the development of slick, commercial communications in Westminster until New Labour's nascent PR operation, directed by Peter Mandelson, shook up the Government's communications processes, cut the dead wood out of the civil service's communications functions and promoted the role of special advisers.

On the other side of the political wire in commercial land, Tim Bell had also spotted the opportunity. Recognising the margins and growth potential of PR over advertising, he had abandoned his Saatchi & Saatchi roots, bought out the PR sections of Lowe Howard-Spink Bell and formed Lowe Bell Communications (later Bell Pottinger, under the publicly floated holding group Chime Communciations). Whatever Bell's eccentricities, all too well documented elsewhere, he was one of the first operators to recognise the opportunity of leveraging corporate and financial PR into the political arena during the Eighties. He was assisted in this endeavour by his proximity to the Prime Minister, Margaret Thatcher, and her intuitive obsession with business, fostered by husband Denis.

With his company's engine in financial PR firing on all cylinders, under the chalk-stripe-and-cheese and highly successful partnership of Piers Pottinger and Nick Miles, Bell could subsidise early inroads into the political arena. On occasion this involved lying on the PM's carpet at Number 10 in order to think more clearly during the 1987 election campaign, so informal was Thatcher's relationship with her principal spin-doctor.

Through the financial service, Bell had access to British industry at the highest levels. In turn, he could provide British industry with access to the PM, who played her part perfectly in flattering industrialists with her attention (briefed by Bell). Bell was also demonstrating to the PR world how you could take the fee twice – once in the City and once in Westminster. The fee could be, and was, propagated elsewhere by other firms, which successfully made a specialist distinction between communications in Parliament, the City, media, the regions, between businesses and any other sub-set that could be imagined and distinguished for budgetary purposes.

Less theatrical, but every bit as commercial in bridging the mid-town between the City and Westminster, was Dewe Rogerson. The company was born of a partnership between Roddy Dewe and Nico Rogerson, the latter clearing off to New York relatively early, leaving Dewe, who had grown up in commerce with the likes of James Hanson, a PR master of all he surveyed in the City. Before Thatcher's minor industrial revolution got underway, Dewe Rogerson harboured the urbane Tony Carlisle and an earnest but talented number-cruncher called Cary Martin, who had arrived from market researcher MORI where he had conducted an annual survey of PR companies' effectiveness among British industries. Interestingly, Dewe Rogerson had headed the poll.

Carlisle had developed a considerable talent for talking down difficult journalists from the side of his mouth and had become the firm's deputy chairman. Dewe told me years later: 'I gave him the title to shut him up and the bugger made a job out of it.' That job turned out to be, with his faithful baldrick Martin, to sell the Government's privatisation of the public utilities, such as British Gas and BT, to the electorate – both in the sense of selling the principle and selling the shares. Carlisle came up with the strategy of 'perception of scarcity' to persuade British investors they needed to compete to buy shares in industrial assets that they had previously owned as taxpayers. The programme was formidable, made the firm and its shareholders rich and drove sections of the GIS, such as those who worked for Mike Granatt, as Head of Information at the Department of Energy during the electricity privatisation, up the wall. But, like Bell's efforts in Downing Street, the process was the transfer of the new communications in the financial arena into the parliamentary and political arena.

They didn't know it at the time, but during the Eighties Bell and Dewe Rogerson, by imbuing Parliament with the new commercial communications disciplines of the City, set the stage for the spin-doctor of the Nineties. Bell (now Lord Bell), in a particularly spectacular piece of anachronistic revisionism, is today often described as 'Mrs Thatcher's favourite spin-doctor', a term that had yet to be coined in Clinton's campaign camp across the Atlantic when Bell was operating as such. Given the fairly sorry state of British parliamentary lobbying in the Seventies and Eighties – a dark heritage that found its nadir in the exposure of Ian Greer Associates' commercial access to Government ministers by Granada and *The Guardian* – it can be said with some justification that professional spin-doctors would not have found a footing in British politics so easily had it not been for the professional development of City PR.

The paternity of City PR is widely attributed to the late Stanley Gale, an ex-Deputy City Editor of the *Daily Express* and the *Evening Standard*. Gale was consistently approached in his journalistic capacity by companies concerned about the presentation of their results and he consequently founded Shareholder Relations in 1958, when Angel Court Consultants (founded in 1960) was a glint in the eye of Dewe and Rogerson. I have a note of a conversation I had with Gale in the financial PR hey-day of the mid-Eighties. It tells us much of what we need to know about the subsequent development of financial PR and how both good and bad practice developed in the modern political spin-doctor. He told me: 'A scoop is something that one of the parties does not want published. When it is published because the parties concerned do want it published, it is not a scoop – it is a leak. The purpose of that system is twofold. First, it is an attempt to swap news for views – the PR hopes that in exchange for exclusives a City Editor will support his clients when needed. Second, predators want the shares of their targets in the hands of speculators and a well-placed tip in the financial pages of the Press can aid that purpose. I have heard some PRs tell their clients that they can find out what a Sunday newspaper is going to print –

and they have. I have even heard them say that they can go onto
the stone and have copy changed.'

Gale had never heard the term spin-doctor then, but with a little
judicial manipulation of the words (a spin-doctor's skill, after all), one
can see its relevance to the spin-culture of more recent times. Replace
PR with spin-doctor, the City editorial references with their political-
desk equivalents and clients with politicians and it could (perhaps
should) be pinned to the wall of the Number 10 press office and in
other government departments besides. It is Gale's rubric by which the
modern, leaking spin-doctor lives and dies – as Chancellor Gordon
Brown's former representative, Charlie Whelan, might confirm.

City PR has much to answer for in the shaping of the modern
spin-doctor. The kindest way of putting it is that the growth of
financial operatives, mobile phones pressed to heads, has always
been multi-faceted. It had the colourful individualist, such as John
Addey, acknowledged as the most prominent City PR of the early
Seventies – said to have been the first to have sat at a merchant
bank's boardroom table – a position that many have since claimed.
He had a butler, a flat in Albany off Piccadilly and was chauffeured
by Bentley to meetings. He also had a loose-tongued lunch with
Private Eye, a run-in with Sir James Goldsmith and an ill-fated court
action that nearly ruined him.

There were Brian Basham and John Coyle at Broad Street
Associates, whose aggressive knocking-copy display advertise-
ments eventually invited a ban from the Takeover panel. The
global businessman, in the form of the genuinely funny Peter
Gummer (now Lord Chadlington), who despite, or possibly because
of, his brother John being a Tory minister, never appeared to make
the bridge with Westminster, except informally. The donnish
intellectual, Tony Good, whose publicly-listed Good Relations
was outrageously sold from under him as he struggled to find his
bearings (and his lost clothes, as it happens) in a hurricane in
Florida. And showman Alan Parker, from an immensely talented
family that includes his late father Sir Peter, former chairman of
British Rail, and ubiquitous screen-actor brother Nathaniel. With
congenital energy and indefatigable bonhomie, Parker Junior built
Brunswick, pre-eminent in second-generation financial PR. Angus
Maitland, who pioneered investor relations for publicly-quoted

companies and who honoured the interests of his own shareholders at Valin Pollen International, as it collapsed on a deal too far. But, whatever the achievements of its doyens, the City crowd of communicators has contained within it both the creativity capable of the development of an entire new consultancy industry, as represented by the cast-list above, and the seeds of its own destruction. Were it gender-specific, one might refer to gentlemen and players, but a more appropriate description of the two sides of this PR psyche is the operator and the spiv, not least because they were to be replicated as such in British politics in the late Nineties.

The operators were (and mostly are) first-class advocates, persuasive in their dialectic, who recognise that, as in politics, there are at least two sides to any position and that clients should have access, as in law, to the best professional representation. In other quarters, the spivs ramp shares, rather as some spin-doctors have ramped one minister against another in the New Labour Government. I have always been dubious about the notorious Friday Night Drop, which has enjoyed various attempts at exposure by friends such as Damien McCrystal (in a television documentary) and Patrick Weever (supporting ill-fated litigation against former employer the *Sunday Telegraph*). This is allegedly the system whereby PRs inform Sunday paper City editors of forthcoming price-sensitive company information, for parties they represent to sell shares off the back of a rising price on Monday as a result of the printed tip.

Sure, it goes on. I recall, in an echo of Gale's experience with regard to PR claims of being able to change a newspaper at the stone, bumping into a well-known City PR man leaving the *Sunday Telegraph*'s office on Fleet Street as I went to swap our first editions one Saturday evening. He seemed flustered to be caught there, as the commissionaire explained to me that he had no copies as yet. 'Here, have mine George,' he said. 'On one condition – you promise not to tell your editor you have seen me here.' Sadly, I'm obliged to honour that promise, even though the editor now works for the PR man.

Another friend – now a Baptist minister, though the career change is only partly related – told me that he watched astonished on a Friday evening as his City PR colleagues had two City editors on the line and simply 'broked' the share-tips between them. This is simply the trading of information as a commodity – rather as Max Clifford has formalised celebrity information into a commodities market. Far more dangerous, to my mind, was the largesse that was extended by City PRs to financial journalists during the economic boom of the Eighties. The proximity and mutual interest that this generated began to make some company desks look not unlike fashion writers in their lickspittle relationships with sources of information and their access to them. This was particularly true of some quarters of personal finance journalism – the upstart younger sister of City journalism.

Some of the flavour of it is reflected in the compilation of notes that starts this chapter. I remember vividly the day the music died. It was 19th October 1987, Black Monday, the biggest crash in world equity indices since 1929, the FTSE index of leading stocks falling by 26.04 per cent in two days. They claimed to have weathered the storm, but City PR would never be the same again. As budgets and entire companies disappeared, the spivs had to defer to the operators. The new commercial communications disciplines that were transferring successfully to the world of politics came out chastened. A new discipline had to be forged.

In 1988, Anthony Cardew, a PR elder statesman of surprisingly tender years who was then chairman of Saatchi-subsidiary Grandfield Rork Collins Financial, told me: 'What has changed principally since the early Seventies is that we have increasingly moved towards full management consultancy.' The full management consultancy to which he referred had now to embrace the world of politics on behalf of clients if it was to find a way forward in the recessionary aftermath of a stalled economy. It was that, or a return to issuing press releases of company results. It was this prospect, rather than any alleged emulation of Clinton's Democrat team's communications techniques in the States, that spurred the spin-culture in politics in the UK during the Nineties. Little did we know how the political climate was looking for such a service and that, when the desires of the City and Westminster met, their union would give birth to the new breed – the spin-doctors.

12th October 1991 – Mid-morning on the Saturday shift of The Observer. *Business Editor Melvyn Marckus calls Nick Goodway, Deputy City Editor, and me into his office for an impromptu editorial conference. As usual, Melvyn hasn't been to bed since*

*Thursday, his eyes are swollen with fatigue and he has a cigar lit.
'Here, I've got this,' he says, floating a sheet of paper across his
desk. 'What do we do with it?' Nick reads it first, inscrutably
stroking his moustache, then hands it to me. It's a letter from
Lord Hanson, chairman of the eponymous conglomerate that has
amassed a predatory 2.8 per cent stake in ICI, to his leading PR
man, Tim Bell, dated Monday 26th August 1991. Hanson is
evidently exercised by a leader in the* Mail on Sunday *by City
editor Lawrence Lever, headlined 'Is Hanson such a good
gamble?' The letter is worth quoting in full.*

'Dear Tim,
Since we reduced the direct approach (from us) to editors *et al.*,
we have had lots of advice from you, most of which seems to
address how best we should keep the institutional investors
correctly informed on Hanson. I think you're missing the point.

At that time we left you to spread the Hanson gospel to the
media and politics, without involving us directly. What you had
to offer us was based on 'who you know' and that you would be
serving us best by influencing them indirectly but constantly.
We've left that to you while we've been working, as agreed,
directly on the institutions.

We're disappointed with the press recently, exemplified by
this article. Libellous, in our opinion, but a clear puff from Alan
Parker who shows himself to be running circles around us. Alan
Parker to advise ICI on financial matters? He can't even advise his
own father on how to submit a national radio bid ... What kind of
clown is he? How about exposing *his* expertise for a change.
Come on, chaps, let's do *something*. He spends his client's money
trying to discredit *us*. Can't you dispel all this garbage in advance?
Who is Lawrence Lever[2] anyway? I've never heard of him, but by
now all the media should have the *true* story and realise that they
shouldn't be able to get away with blatant puffs like this? And
your own loving relationships? Apart from Jeff Randall[3] and Ivan
Fallon[4] and John Jay[5] – who contact us direct – everyone else

[2] Financial journalist, *Mail on Sunday.*

[3] Business editor, *Sunday Times.*

[4] Columnist, *Sunday Times.*

[5] City Editor, *Sunday Telegraph.*

seems to have drifted against Hanson and comment is deteriorating. This letter is intended to show our unhappiness.

It's not for us to tell you how to do your job, but it is up to me to judge the results. Let's just take one thing. Parker and Co have managed to imprint in the media's mind the 'Lord White Lifestyle'[6] lie, to the degree that even you partly believe it, judging from what I hear from you about our dispelling it. Shouldn't you be addressing this – and the minor bloodstock deal – day, night and holidays too? After all this time, Parker's still making plenty out of it.

I think we're entitled to better results. Weekly strategy meetings are a waste of time. We've put our faith in your ability to *sell* Hanson to your contacts. You know what a great story there is out there, but it's not getting through. You *know* what we need but I begin to have my doubts. Each time I raise them, back comes a message: 'May we get together to discuss ... ' You know your story sufficiently well by now to sell it for us.

You're in the communications business so I hope you won't mind this frank communication from me. I know you'll understand that we're entitled to look for some positive results and to let you know when we don't see them.

Sincerely, James.'

'So what do we do with it?' repeats Melvyn. Nick and I make some grown-up noises about this just being a memo between a client and his PR adviser and, as such, it's not on the main highway of business interest. There's a pause. Then we both say, practically in unison, 'So let's run it big on the front.'

In the event, that proved to be the correct journalistic decision. This may have been just correspondence between a client and his PR man, but Lord Hanson was no ordinary industrialist and Bell, confidante of Margaret Thatcher, was no ordinary spin-doctor. The letter's contents were said to have been around elsewhere, but newspapers more reverential of the correspondents had declined to refer to them. They came to regret that as the story ran as a follow-up in the dailies throughout the following week. The *Financial Times* of 15th October reported that: 'Institutional investors said

[6] Lord White's lifestyle, particularly his fondness for horseflesh, had attracted considerable press attention.

yesterday that Hanson must change its own managerial style and take account of criticisms over its corporate governance instead of simply blaming its public relations advisers for not getting its message across.'

For Bell, who passed off the incident breezily in public, the dressing down had made him look less sure-footed as the doyen of British PR. Thatcher had fallen from power the year before and Bell's era of networking appeared to be coming to a close, his finger no longer on the industrial, as well as the political, pulse. Nick Miles, at that time running the financial practice of Lowe Bell, phoned to tell me at the time that Bell had rung him to say 'Listen, Nick, I know ...' – he repeated for emphasis – 'I *know* that George Pitcher got that letter.' Wrong again. I just knew where we might find him that weekend for reaction, so the phone call came from me. Bell's magic touch was deserting him. Lord King, chairman of British Airways, was said to have mused over his copy of the *FT* that we might look back on this episode as a turning point in the fortunes of both Hanson and Bell.

We all thought that might be the case. It was wide of the mark. Bell went on successfully to float Chime Communications, the holding group for Lowe Bell, later Bell Pottinger. Hanson de-merged the Hanson empire in the mid-Nineties into four separate public companies, focused on chemicals, tobacco, energy and building materials. Though Hanson himself had lost the wizardry of Lord (Gordon) White to the great racehorse trainer in the sky, no one could claim that the heady days of takeover were followed by a period of failure. But Hanson's splenetic memo did mark a change in the communications atmosphere. The day of the energetic and well-connected message deliverer was drawing to a close, as the recession set in. In a sense, the PR sport had gone. The Eighties were finally over.

FINANCE

MONEY ON A SPINNING PLATE

Politicians are fond of talking of industrial revolutions as a good thing. This is no time for a history lesson, but the original one of steam, iron and textiles began the process of wholesale migration from the rural economy that, two centuries later, is being played out in the final demise of British farming. It might be added that it also institutionalised urban poverty, which gave birth to the urban underclass that remains a problematic British social anachronism today. The industrial revolution of the past 20 years is widely accepted as a social advance. This view is considerably assisted by the economic high ground of metropolitan prosperity driven by advances in information technology and telecoms. Politicians of any major party are less keen to consider that in the last fifth of a century we have closed the coal industry for political reasons, run down our steel industry, sold our utilities substantially into foreign ownership and our motor industry entirely so.

Looking back, it is almost impossible to believe that the Tories could have got away with the privatisation programme of the Eighties. Not that it wasn't logical, or even necessary after North Sea revenues had been frittered away. What I mean is that the level and standard of the Government's handling and communication of the process was at best arrogant and at worst cack-handedly incompetent.

December 1988 – We shuffle into a Government briefing room on Millbank for the publication of the Water Bill, the first legislative step towards the privatisation of our tap-water, drains and sewers. Environment Secretary Nicholas Ridley is at his chain-smoking chippiest and, hiding behind his horn-rims, condescends for his country. There's the rather hippy 'it's-like-privatising-air' contingent on the floor, but Ridley waves them away. Everything is going to work much better because there's going to be competition. The man from the BBC, with genuine curiosity, asks how you can introduce choice in the water industry, making the point respectfully that consumers have no alternative but to drink the water from their taps. 'Yes they do,' snaps Ridley, losing the script, 'they can drink Perrier.' The press seats hum to the murmur of 'Let them drink Perrier' – he may not have said it, but we know what he meant and it'll make my column. The Cabinet minister in charge of water privatisation is paraphrasing Marie Antoinette and, really, it sums up the other-worldliness of this Government. The shame is that Ridley can't lose his head like the Mistress of Versailles.

The privatisation charabanc was probably kept on the road by the GIS. They were frustrated and infuriated, as often as not, at the intervention of private-sector PR operators. But there can be little doubt that the slick sales techniques of the privatisation shop Dewe Rogerson and the patch-up ministrations of Tim Bell kept the exchequer receipts coming, to subsidise the income-tax cuts on which much of Thatcher's tenure depended.

It was no mean feat. The sale of the second tranche of BP shares in 1987 straddled the world-wide collapse in share prices, but they got it away anyway, assisted by Chancellor Nigel Lawson discreetly underwriting the offer for the public punters. Three years later, Lord Marshall, chairman of the National Power, the pre-privatisation electricity-generation colossus, tried his best to disguise the true cost of decommissioning nuclear power stations which were nearing the end of their useful lives. He also wanted the energy-generation industry privatised as an integrated whole, partly to protect his beloved nuclear, with the National Grid, which would have protected his obligation to supply. Mrs Thatcher was fond of Marshall and he thought he could get away with it. He had kept the lights on during the miners' strike, at one time legendarily managing to get the National Grid to work backwards. But Energy Secretary Cecil Parkinson had a way with the PM and out-manoeuvred the old public-sector panjandrum.

When the true, hidden costs of the nuclear industry emerged in the due diligence process, Parkinson was in an arithmetical mess and was moved aside to Transport to make way for former chief-whip and leader of the House of Commons John Wakeham. Best known latterly for his resignation from the chairmanship of the Press Complaints Commission because of his proximity as a consultant to and non-executive director of collapsed US energy trader Enron, Wakeham had been a fiercely effective and popular Chief Whip. A tough operator behind a schoolboyish exterior, he lost his first wife to the IRA Brighton bomb at the Conservative Party Conference of 1984 and suffered terrible leg injuries himself. We used to meet in offices overlooking Buckingham Palace's gardens and Wakeham would lie in a winged leather chair, puffing on a large cigar with his leg across a large pouffe. He was a picture of the relaxed statesman, in control and with time on his hands – it was only his civil-servant assistants who let on that he had to sit like this to relieve the agony of the metal in his leg.

Wakeham pushed through re-pricing of electricity as a commodity with the 12 distributive area chairmen (also facing privatisation) and told me at the time: 'Nobody resigned – or at least nobody resigned long enough for it to get in the newspapers.' With his patrician and sometimes mischievous permanent secretary John Guinness (later chairman of British Nuclear Fuels), Wakeham manfully pulled the nuclear industry from privatisation, leaving a duopoly of National Power and PowerGen for flotation. To accept levels of debt on its balance sheet that were arduous but necessary, PowerGen had to be threatened with a trade sale to Lord Hanson. But this curiously constructed industry, with its dismembered nuclear parts, was successfully transferred to the private sector, despite its Machiavellian politics.

The significance for the development of a spin-culture is that, looking back from the distance of more than a decade, the privatisation of the electricity industry was a mess. The Government collected its £9 billion or so, but it muddled through. And it wasn't just electricity and water that adopted Heath Robinson flotation techniques. It was widely claimed that Sir Denis Rooke, as chairman, had 'bullied' erstwhile Energy Secretary Peter Walker into privatising British Gas in 1986 as a single supply and distribution business. The monopoly would have to be tortuously broken up by regulators in the Nineties. Rooke as the bullying monopolist is an attractive image – but it is wrong in this instance.

Walker succeeded his mortal enemy Nigel Lawson at Energy as part of Thatcher's plan to bring Walker 'into the tent'. Walker had been identified as a dangerous potential dissenter from Thatcherism. Consequently, he had been given Agriculture and had made a success of it. He was despatched to Energy with instruction to make as much as possible from the sale of British Gas. Walker told Thatcher that he would do it his way and that meant no interference from Lawson, now at the Treasury; this was a deal that Thatcher accepted. Walker was effectively privatising Gas in a bi-lateral agreement with the Prime Minister, cutting out the Chancellor. Walker saw Rooke months before the flotation and told him that he could keep Gas intact if he did as he was told – in short, that he could keep his monopoly on Walker's terms. Thus Walker steered through the flotation of Gas as a monopoly with no interference from the industry or Cabinet colleagues. His relationship with the PM was one of extreme lese-majesty, compared with his colleagues – on one occasion he cut her off three times while asking her to hold on an old key-and-lamp phone. Walker was a fearsome political operator, if not phone operator, but his autocratic deal-making was symptomatic of the shambolic way in which privatisation was being conducted under the sheen of expensive PR and advertising. 'Tell Sid' was the catchline of a populist television campaign that persuaded the public that it must oversubscribe the Gas issue or miss a wealth-creation bonanza – the vaunted 'perception of scarcity' strategy. But, behind the scenes, public assets were being peddled as if by gangsters in a black-market stitch-up. Sid wasn't told that. And the stitch-up was not always competent – British Telecom had been privatised two years before Gas so that it might compete effectively in the private sector, but the regulatory restrictions placed on its monopoly interests in the UK meant that it couldn't effectively compete at all.

Other than Dewe Rogerson and Bell, all this was done without the serried ranks of spin-doctors that the New Labour Government was to employ more than a decade later. Politicians, such as Wakeham, largely spun themselves, with some assistance from the civil-service machine. But, to a significant degree, privatisation drove the spin-culture as vast state-owned corporations found that they had to justify their existence in the private sector. It also exemplified an object lesson for spin-doctors that were to follow – all need not be as it seems, or it may not seem to be what it is. The art of privatisation was to sell the public what it already owned as taxpayers and subjects. The mountebank school of communications had arrived and spin-culture was to take it into politically new territory. It is only one short step from selling the public what it already owns to telling the public that things can only get better under socialists with Tory policies.

But there was another great contribution that privatisation made to the development of a spin-culture. When Mrs Thatcher came to power in 1979, there were fewer than two million private share-holders; estimates vary, but by the end of the programme of utilities privatisation in 1990, there were between nine and 12 million. The new share-owning democracy brought with it new accountabilities for companies and for Government. Companies had to communicate with their shareholders as never before and not just sophisticated, City institutional shareholders. They had to communicate, horror of horrors, with members of the public. The new PR discipline of investor relations was about to undergo radical revision. The trend caught on throughout the FTSE index. 'Open' and 'accessible' became watchwords. And it didn't stop there. Nationalised industry staff now found themselves exposed to private-sector prosperity – the 'fat cats' at the top might attract the media attention, but staff and employees had to be retained, 'incentivised' and, at its simplest, shown that life was better in the private sector. The mission statement ('Our aim ... etc.') was adopted and adapted from the States and nailed up in shiny new receptions. Furthermore, environmentalists had to be appeased, for fear that regulators might impose new sanctions or restrictions of trade. That generated a whole new industry in the communication of green credentials, the antecedents of non-governmental organisation (NGO) communications techniques. Similarly, customer satisfaction had to be delivered by utilities as well as retailers, partly because it said so in the mission statement. Not only that, but customers needed to be told they were satisfied. More communications.

By 1995, Will Hutton, sometime editor of *The Observer*, had re-coined the term 'stakeholders' in his seminal book, *The State We're In*, which became cast as a guidebook to the New Labour creed.

Industrial audiences, like political ones, were diversified and complex and the demarcation lines between them blurred. Politics, the financial markets, the environment, staff and customers all needed messages delivered and the old communicational disciplines were falling down. Spinning a line in Westminster in isolation no longer sufficed – you had to know how it would play in the City, with Greenpeace and among employees. Privatisation had been a catalyst to this revolution in political and industrial communications. Companies and their communications demands are consequently entirely different to their equivalents of the late Seventies and early Eighties. The Tories had not only de-regulated the City to allow foreign professional financiers in, they had brought the speculative investments of the masses in with privatisation too. This was an intriguing variation on the old principle that the purpose of the Stock Exchange was to transfer the savings of the poor into the pockets of the rich once in every generation. But live by the stock markets and you die by them – as the modern crisis in equity-linked pension provision demonstrates. The old City had known the risks of the gambling tables it played. Open to all-comers, the games had to be played a different way – and that presented a challenge to the way the City communicated, as much as to the way it traded.

> *January 1991 – It's dawn and I'm somewhere in the City, at one of the great stockbroking houses, which sadly has to remain nameless because of the story that follows and the security of the people in it. But the story is about securities, not security. The Gulf War is starting and I'm watching screens – television and dealing – for signs of action in the air and in the oil price. A little before 8 am, the Prime Minister, John Major, appears in Downing Street, looking tired. The dealers gather round the screen, looking more tired. The PM burbles what PMs burble and the dealers return to their desks to deal. I find myself standing by the great knighted chairman. 'Are you long in oil?' I ask. 'Not too bad,' he replies. 'Number 10 tipped me off about this last night, so I could adjust our position.' As our conversation develops, it dawns on him that I may not be a member of his staff. He pales and stalks off. Later, the PR staff tell me he didn't say that – I can't run it anyway without independent witnesses. But it would have been one hell of a story.*

The relationship between the City and politicians has always been an on-and-off love affair. The Tories have always conducted proceedings rather like the oil industry; the Government is upstream, providing unrefined and crude capitalist policy, while downstream the City refines and markets it to make money. In this way, the Tories have traditionally used the City to make it look like the party of economic prosperity. Labour, by contrast, has never really understood it. Old Labour just thought it was evil and never really tried. It has been astonishing to witness how ill-briefed are Labour MPs when they quiz an industrialist or banker at a select committee – there remains little real understanding of the relationship between profits and investment (and that's true, it has to be said, of many Conservatives too). New Labour has tried, bless it. And it took some ribbing for doing so – *vide* Michael Heseltine's withering send-up in the House of Tony Blair's 'prawn cocktail offensive', the supposedly reassuring dining tour of the City ahead of the 1997 election. But New Labour meant free markets and there were visible signs of enlightenment. Chancellor Gordon Brown's first initiative after the 1997 election victory was to establish the Bank of England Monetary Policy Committee, so that interest rates could be fixed for the first time free of political interference. He may also have been considering that if Britain were to be an early entrant to the euro-zone, at that time still a real possibility, then it would not be unhelpful for a New Labour Government to be free of the responsibility for fixing interest rates.

The City has been drawn over the past two decades into being an integrated part of political spin-culture. That process started in the early Eighties. I remember sitting high above Victoria Street in the old offices of the Department of Trade, with Cecil Parkinson lounging on a sofa in his monogrammed shirt, beside him a lady from the GIS who was rather oppressively taking down everything he said in fearsome shorthand. He was striking a deal with Sir Nicholas Goodison, then chairman of the Stock Exchange, to abolish single capacity in 1984 (to replace the old restrictive practice of jobbers and brokers on the Stock Exchange floor with dual-capacity market-makers). It was this initiative that led directly to the City's Big Bang of de-regulation in 1986. By allowing foreign interests to own British financial institutions for the first time, the

Big Bang had two direct effects on the City's role in politics. Firstly, it broke the cosy cabals of the Square Mile. Insider-dealing had become illegal in the Companies Act of 1980, but the City had still operated until 1986 substantially on the principle of 'I'd have some of those'. A mutual interest in the *status quo* had prevailed between the City and Westminster, in which it was generally in the interests of both to leave each other alone. Now it was to be populated by Americans, Germans, Swiss and Japanese who cared little for the British political scene, other than for being allowed to trade in London unrestricted. And politicians had a vested interest in keeping these foreign institutions in the City, to maintain London as the pre-eminent European financial centre. A new dynamic between SW1 and EC3 had to emerge. Secondly, it was precisely this internationalisation of the City that made it attractive to politicians. From being the engine of a British economy within Europe, the City was now part of a global stage and, as such, a more visible component of foreign policy and relations with other Governments than it had been previously.

After the Big Bang in 1986 came the Big Crash in 1987. I was – with that intuitive feel for the big story – on holiday in Italy at the time, and thought the headlines on the British papers referring to 'storm' and 'crash' were late stories about the hurricane that had blown through Britain during the previous Thursday night. In many respects, with the cushion of more than a decade between, the worldwide meltdown of equities was the perfect storm, bringing together a number of negative aspects in world economies to shake out the dross within them. In communications terms, it got rid of some of the drearier of share-tipsters in City PR. A new breed of communicator, steeped in the heady wine of the wider share-ownership experiment of the privatisation years, was to emerge – one who not only knew the importance of addressing markets, but also of addressing shareholders, institutional and retail. It was this slicker, more knowledgeable operator who was to drive financial PR to the hegemony in communications functions that it enjoyed by the early Nineties. Shareholders were the most important target audience for the most senior executives in industry; their communicators had to reach them and the constituency was now a global one.

In the States, Bill Clinton emerged as the steward of an unnervingly prolonged period of growth in the American economy. By 1996, the Chairman of the Federal Reserve, Alan Greenspan, was saying the US equities market was suffering from 'irrational exuberance'. In Britain, global asset management firm Phillips & Drew was claiming that as much as 40 per cent of value was set to come out of the American market, which was bound to have a domino effect on the British equities market. It was to have to wait a while to be fully vindicated. Clinton was spinning plates to keep voters – very many more of whom were active equities investors than in Britain – content that the economy was as safe in Democrat as in Republican hands. It was vital that American investors' fingers were not burnt, particularly during the difficult years of the Monica Lewinsky affair. Many US voters hoped that the return of a Republican President, albeit on a dodgy vote, would see a more prudent approach to the American economy, but George W. Bush's early promise that his administration would allow personal-pension money to be gambled on Wall Street didn't suggest it. Nor did his adoption in 2002 of the language that he had used for prosecuting the war on terror in his pledges to pursue the fraudsters of corporate America, who had brought about a collapse in American confidence after Enron and WorldCom, demonstrate much intuitive grasp of the financial markets. What he does know is that 9/11 further politicised the markets – the collapse of equity markets is a sign of weakness in the face of what Bush sees as the enemies of democracy. America continues to spin its markets on sticks – and so long as that situation prevails, it will need spinners to do so.

While there isn't as yet the same ineluctable relationship in Britain between the equities and currency markets, voting intentions and the politics of the free world, New Labour's spin-culture owes much in this specific regard to the Clinton communications manual of the Nineties. It may be that New Labour can embrace financial markets as the Tories have in Britain in the past and as the Democrats have in the States. But the development of the role of markets on both sides of the Atlantic has joined financiers and politicians at the hip. It follows that to separate a multinational corporation's political communications from its financial communications is to misunderstand late twentieth-century capital markets. The two arenas are today mutually dependent. The age of the politico-financier has dawned – and he needs advice.

> *April 1995 – I'm watching Sir Rick Greenbury before the Employment Select Committee in the House of Commons. The chairman and chief executive of Marks & Spencer clearly does not want to be there, but unlike members of his peer group who have sat before this Star Chamber for fat cats, he is not being given a hard time. This is because he has just chaired the Greenbury Committee on executive pay and is consequently seen as part of the inquisitors' camp, rather than one of those wicked plutocrats who siphon shareholder value into their personal bank accounts. But word has it that Sir Rick has not enjoyed his tenure in the chair of what is more formally known as The Study Group on Directors' Remuneration. Perhaps he doesn't enjoy being accountable to a bunch of pettifogging bureaucrats at the Confederation of British Industry and these self-important committee politicians who don't understand business. His performance is tetchy and impatient. At the end, he is thanked and dismissed. But Sir Rick isn't finished. He reaches into a bag by his side. If this were America, men in dark glasses would speak into their sleeves and semi-automatics would cock. But Sir Rick pulls out a plastic M&S apron emblazoned with the words 'If you can't stand the heat, get out of the kitchen'. It elicits a polite chuckle from the committee members, but it's actually quite a sad moment. This is the moment when we realise that Sir Rick should be wearing that apron, perhaps baking muffins for local scout groups to enjoy on the lawns of his country estate, on sunny afternoons when less wise men are fighting boardroom battles with their non-execs in sweaty City towers.*

Sir Rick Greenbury's career at M&S lasted for nearly five decades, but his last years at the helm cannot have been happy ones. By the end of the Nineties, he had divided his dual roles of chairman and chief executive – a little belatedly, perhaps, for someone who had adopted a public role in corporate governance – and pretenders at M&S were squabbling and infighting over his succession. M&S, for so long not only the bellwether of the British retail market but also of Middle Britain's taste and decorum, plummeted in value in the estimation of customers and shareholders alike. As the man at the top, occupying both great positions of the corporate state, this must have been, at least in substantial part, Greenbury's fault. He had failed to institute a corporate structure that anticipated and met the pluralistic challenge that emerged from new generational clothes retailers such as Next and The Gap. M&S's detractors too often fail to credit Greenbury with the High Street colossus that he built in the second half of the twentieth century. Nevertheless, the Greenbury who developed M&S into the force that it was also became its agent of regression. He was, in the Nineties, both an old-fashioned retailer and an old-fashioned businessman.

Old-fashioned, in business management terms, means command-and-control, in the style of GEC's late Lord Weinstock. It means commanding shareholders' earnings, as well as respect. It means controlling the company's strategy and its cost base. These responsibilities at M&S were, as at GEC, for years vested in one person. It was not a form of corporate governance to which Greenbury confessed – far less endorsed as a regulator – but it was widely regarded as autocratic as a management style. This is not control-freakery in the modern, political and particularly New Labour sense. That is more a symptom of insecurity. Command-and-control structures in the corporate world are invariably the result of over-confidence, rather than the lack of it. Greenbury would be the arbiter of the coming season's fashion collections at M&S. What post-punks, Goths or former new romantics were going to wear when they grew up and bought semis in the provinces was being decided by a middle-aged man who thought novelty aprons were funny.

It comes as little surprise that M&S's command-and-control management structure embraced communications. Greenbury wrote his own press releases. He decided summarily which journalists to speak to and what to tell them. Being on-message was agreeing with what Greenbury had to say. The M&S press office, for a protracted period of its history, felt like a resource for obstructing journalists from reaching management and answers. M&S was a not untypical, if extreme, manifestation of command-and-control. British – indeed western – corporations of all kinds are constructed on the pyramidic model, at whose apex is an individual commanding a board of directors with ever wider strata of management and peons below them. Value is contributed upwards; remuneration and information is cascaded, in return, downwards.

The Darwinian corporate game is, through a process of natural selection, to mutate your genetic management skills so that your species reaches the top of the pyramid. More straightforwardly, what you do is apply your management specialism to a battle of survival of the fittest. Accountants used to have the correct genome map to reach the chief executive's chair. Then marketers were found to be most suitable to prosper in the corporate environment. More recently, information technologists and statisticians have done well. Needless to say, public relations executives and communicators have been driven by a primal instinct, over the three decades or so that they can be identified as a specific genetic variant in the corporate species, to rise from the swamp and drag themselves ashore on the sustaining feeding grounds of executive predators. Gather any collection of corporate communications executives together and before long – perhaps as a means of primitive genetic recognition – they will start talking about PR being taken seriously as a management function. Professional journals and associations, such as the Institute of Public Relations (IPR) and the Public Relations Consultants Association (PRCA), have aspirational default positions. In the absence of anything else to discuss, correspondence columns and seminar platforms will vibrate to claims that the PR professional is to be taken as seriously as any other management discipline.

It is now widely-held that communications is sufficiently highly regarded as a management function to warrant representation at the board table, or at least on the management executive. There are still perceived hereditary impurities to be bred out before PR can be truly cross-bred with the predominant management species of accountancy and marketing – but so long as PR breeds as a subset of marketing, it will get there, runs the practitioners' argument. But there is a problem with this. Centralisation of management functions that require anything other than mechanical execution suffer as a consequence of their loss of contact with the talent, creativity and intelligence of remoter, non-centralised parts of the organisation.

You can centralise cost-accounting, buying (in markets without product diversification), distribution and group strategy. You cannot and should not centralise functions of personnel such as recruitment, regional marketing and sales. Such experiments, particularly as a result of rationalisation as a consequence of merger or acquisition activity, are invariably a disaster.

To centralise communications functions is similarly misguided. New Labour's endeavours to centralise communications operations in the corporate centre of Number 10 have been ill-conceived. In the same way, companies that centralise communications functions are courting disaster. This is particularly so where communications operations in the field are separated from the corporate centre by something as large as the Atlantic Ocean. You may as well operate communications responsibility from another planet, as a number of American corporations with interests in Europe have discovered to their cost. The problem will be exacerbated by the communications fiefdom that is created at the corporate centre. Those who aspire to a centralised communications executive are likely to be the least suitable to run it. In the rush to be taken seriously, as the kind of suits who attend executive committees and the boardroom, centralised communications executives are mutations of self-importance and status addiction. They are unlikely to be communicating effectively with anyone other than their CEO – and then only on their own behalf. There are exceptions to prove this rule among the western world's corporate affairs directors and vice-presidents (communications). There are those with a strategic wisdom and a talent for street-level implementation (though the latter is more a characteristic of a head of media than a director of communications) who can and do operate effectively out of a corporate centre. But they are rare and becoming more so as a consequence of the regional fragmentation that, bizarrely, globalisation brings along as a side-effect of trying to fulfil the same strategy everywhere.

A further weakness of centralising communications functions is that another, smaller, self-contained managerial pyramid is created within the group structure. A director of corporate affairs (UK) or a vice-president for communications (US) may have three communications departments reporting to him or her in the shape of public and/or parliamentary affairs, a press office or head of media relations and very possibly internal communications. Additionally, there may be environmental, regulatory, consumer/customer relations, investor relations or a variety of other communications resources reporting in to the executive through the communications chief. This is assuming that there is a single individual with overall responsibility for communications. Far more likely, on the British model, is that there will be a head of government relations (or public affairs), investor relations (as in financial communications) and corporate communications. Government relations may report directly to the chief executive officer (CEO) or sometimes through the company secretary; investor relations will report to the CEO through the finance director and a head of corporate communications will invariably have a direct report to the CEO as chief hand-holder. This model is subject to infinite reorganisation and re-naming of parts. But what it means is that the CEO's office divides and rules discrete communications functions – so ultimate authority and quality-control of communications are controlled from the CEO's desk, with a variety of mini-empires vying for preferment; the CEO could preside over a number of specialist and pyramidic communications functions. This is probably inefficient, but as a fact of business life means that responsibility for communications is represented at the board by the CEO.

Communications departments have always had empire-building as their driver, ever since they inveigled themselves into the management lexicon. But a cumbersome, centralised communications department looks particularly inappropriate in the modern commercial environment, now that a stakeholder society aspires to fragmentation of communications messages into bespoke, personalised formats, supported by personal communications technology, rather than the one-size-fits-all messaging of the mass media age. This does not represent an argument for maintaining fragmented communications management functions for the CEO's divide-and-rule purposes. Rather it means that communications functions are so diverse and serve such a variety of management purposes that communication needs to be a healthy virus, infecting all areas of corporate activity, not a single department with its title on the door.

The centralising question is further complicated by the relationship between these fragmented critical constituencies for communication. I remember Richard Handover, the chief executive of WH Smith, telling me of the City analyst who was swayed less by the briefing from the new management than by his young daughter, who had confided that a visit to Smiths on Saturday morning was a treat for her. For every such intuitive analyst, there will be a dozen dry fundamentalists poring over earnings before interest, tax, depreciation and amortisation (the sometime trendy ebitda) and the historic yield curve. But modern organisations know that they cannot ring-fence and protect discrete communications functions and constituencies anymore. It's not an industrial development; it's a social development.

The customer influences the spouse who works in the City, who is a member of Amnesty and surfs the internet to join in activist chat-rooms with correspondents, some of whom may work for the company from which he is about to make an on-line purchase. Except, he decides not to, because a friend, who works for an NGO, has just texted to say that their political supporters have called for a boycott in the European Parliament.

Just as communications constituencies fragment, so it becomes vital for the corporation to address them holistically. This is the argument deployed by internal empire-builders to suggest there is a case for centralisation of communications management. But it's not so. Communications functions have to be released from the silos, or they develop a bunker mentality – they cannot be in touch with the complexities of fragmented markets. And, in any event, without light there can be no growth. Those with a responsibility for communications have to be released to do their work away from the corporate centre. There is risk in this – but, again, if they love you they'll be back. This is the case not for communications being taken seriously at the boardroom table – as expounded at a thousand PR seminars – but for the boardroom table being taken seriously in the communications function. By all means allow the power-dressed director of corporate affairs (or whatever they are called) to sit on the executive, but take away their corporate-centre power-pyramid and create a budget that goes to work where it matters – in the critical constituencies of your organisation's communications effort. Don't, whatever you do, allow them to justify structure or action with the module they did on communications for their MBA.

Only in part does this make a case for contracting out communications resource. While it is true that a budget of £250,000 will buy considerably greater external communications resource than it will create value in an internal department, with its overhead, employment law, pensions, national insurance and private medical insurance, that is not really the point. What companies have to start to understand is that there is another reason why communications should not be at the boardroom table, where its guardians have spent entire careers labouring to place it. Whisper it softly, but that's because communication is not a management function. It's a human function. In a way that marketing, or balance-sheet management, or corporate strategy, or earnings growth, or even human resources (personnel) is emphatically not a human function.

To claim its place at the boardroom table is tantamount to claiming a place, with a job title (and a PA and a water-cooler), for intelligence, or aptitude, or foresight, or sensitivity, or vision, or energy, or ambition. Communication is a human talent, rather than a human resource. In the wildly fragmented, though integrated, markets that companies need to address to enhance their prosperity – using media that are no less fragmented – the implications of this are radical. Companies do not so much need to hire communications professionals as to learn how to communicate. It's a responsibility for individuals to take on, rather than for departments. For many in corporate life, this will be a daunting challenge. But it represents the only really practical way forward. When companies sub-contract their business acumen, by hiring management consultants, the result invariably is – or should be – the identification of solutions that the company cannot deliver. Similarly, a message that, for whatever reason, the principals of an organisation cannot deliver themselves is likely to be untrue, inappropriate, wrong or unbelieved – by sender and/or recipient. It follows that the job of good communicators must be to develop an organisation's ability to communicate, not to do its communication for it, other than in the specific functions of company spokespeople.

It further follows that executives should not hire professionals to have their education or their charisma for them. Communication needs not to be a part of the board, but to be invested in the board and those who argue otherwise – who push for the dedicated communications function at board level – are seduced by their own spin-culture. (And that brings us nearly to the dot coms)

February 2000 – The West Country. I'm staying for the weekend with the group chief executive of a global drinks company. He is leaning over the bannister, railing against the misvaluation of internet stocks. This is not simple jealousy that a new stock-market sector should be so much more prosperous than a company such as his in the allegedly 'old' economy. Nor is it principally about the intellectually unsound premise on which the dot-coms are valued – though nebulous multiples of hypothetical future revenues for companies that have yet to make a profit fuel his ire. No, what has really got his goat is that the dot-coms have created a false bear market in stocks such as his own. 'Our brokers are being phoned by shareholders who tell them to sell our shares and buy a dot-com – any dot-com,' he rages from the landing. Companies such as his are now prevented from buying back their own shares to create liquidity in the market, because that liquidity is simply going to be re-invested in the dot-coms, which have the equity markets under some sort of voodoo trance. And for what? So that a bunch of pony-tailed entrepreneurs can go 'post-economic' by their thirtieth birthday and sharp, young 'incubator' fund managers can make a fast turn. I'm reminded of Jeff Nuttall's comment on the vapid new arts movement of the Sixties: 'You don't have to be a drunken navvy to throw up in the face of that lot.'

If privatisation, by the very early Nineties, had brought the equities of huge state-owned corporations to the people, requiring those companies to address new audiences from the City to politics and the environmental lobby, by 2000 the internet was taking the rise out of our shareholding democracy. This was essentially because the internet was and is neither State-owned nor owned in the private sector. It is un-owned. The concept of ownership cannot be applied to it, without which industries are unlikely to be able to imbue investors with any long-term desire to own the shares. It could only be a matter of time before it was disowned by the equities markets in which it had been valued so absurdly. This came as very bad news for those endeavouring to build real businesses through internet distribution (such as Amazon, the book retailer), or for established industries embracing the new distributive conduit – the so-called 'clicks and mortar' businesses. But it was also bad news for the communications industry. The mega-privatisations of the Eighties had demanded of major companies that they communicate with diverse constituencies of stakeholders. This made a major contribution to spin-culture, developed throughout the caring and sharing Nineties in the more austere aftermath of the conspicuous-consumption years of the Eighties. It was to be dot-commery that was to turn spin into a demon in the financial markets, undoing much of the advance in communications skills of the previous decade.

Martha Lane Fox, co-founder of Lastminute.com, an on-line late-reservations service for anything from skiing holidays to basketball matches, said as much when asked for the reason for her company's phenomenal value at flotation: 'It's all hype.' Companies don't live for long on hype alone. But inside the internet bubble, company valuations were subject to a virtual reality – you had to don a sort of virtual-reality helmet to see the value and many in the City duly did so. Among corporate finance boutiques and venture capitalists, the attitude by early 2000 was that they were making money, so there was money to be made. Simple as that. This phoney market was further fuelled by the new breed of American-style incubator funds, many of which were venture capitalists on speed, raping nascent dot-com businesses of equity in return for seed capital and demanding a return on that capital, by way of premature flotation on to one of the new-wave equity markets such as Nasdaq, as an early exit.

Lastminute.com had a turnover of £6 million and was making no profits, but was nevertheless valued at some £400 million at flotation. At one stage, such enterprises were 'worth' more than the entire American airline industry. As I say, valuations of multiples of turnover against some hypothetical future earnings are bonkers. But what should really trouble us is the business proposition at its heart. Lastminute – let's drop its dot-com status for a moment and pretend it's just like any other company – is a bucket shop. In the nature of bucket shops, its margins are bound to be wafer-thin. But its shares weren't even close to being priced on that basis, simply because it's a dot-com. We were living in Lilliput.com.

The question arises whether any of this mattered. It did and does, very much. Not just because of the liquidity frustrations expressed by my captain of industry on the stairs of his country home. But also because, while there was a Nasdaq-led raging bull market inside the dot-com bubble, there was a bear market developing outside it, some two years before the bear market proper arrived. During the first quarter of 2000, there was a taciturn stock-market response to the proposed merger of Norwich Union and CGU to form the largest insurance conglomerate in Britain and one of the top five in Europe. Norwich Union's shares fell by 12 per cent and CGU's by nearly as much in the four days following the announcement of their deal. Similarly bizarre was the lukewarm reception for the Glaxo Wellcome/SmithKline Beecham merger. The capital markets had been apparently longing for years for Glaxo to consolidate competitively in the pharmaceuticals industry, yet its shares dropped 30 per cent relative to the market in the first quarter. Anyone would have thought it had failed to find a partner. Meanwhile, the empty promises made on behalf of the dot-com enterprises saw their share-prices soar away from flotation. For the first time in the equities markets, there was no fundamental asset value in valuations. For the first time, it really was all spin. Happily, it couldn't last.

21st May 2000 – The Sunday papers are full of the collapse of on-line sports retailer Boo.com and there is much use of photos of its co-founder, former Swedish model Kajsa Leander, looking sorry for herself. Boringly, nobody observes that Leander is down the Swanee. The heavily male offices of the Business sections have clearly succumbed to her female charms – as, more surprisingly, did investors such as Goldman Sachs and JP Morgan. The giveaways are the 'she draws on a cigarette' or 'she takes a sip of coffee' type of comments. She says she wants 'to chill out', adding that she's 'been working so hard for two years and never taken a holiday'. Perhaps the institutions from which she raised at least £85 million in a series of increasingly desperate financings

explain that starting a business can be quite hard work. This
money has been hosed away on Concorde flights and five-star
living, as well as 'a lot of office furniture'. Her partner, Ernst
Malmsten, adds solemnly: 'Maybe this is the end of people
building a business from scratch themselves.' Er, no, Ernst, but it
may be the end of people building a business based entirely on
hype and then believing that the worst aspect of losing millions of
pounds of other people's money is that you haven't had a holiday
for two years.

Suddenly the Nasdaq market had lost one-fifth of its value and
dot-coms were trading at heavy discounts to their issue prices. By
June, the dot-com emperor was seen to be naked and the collapse
in valuations – as it always does – took good and bad companies
down with it. The FTSE 100 index held relatively firm, as
investors took a flight to quality. 'Old economy' troupers, such as
Scottish & Newcastle, AB Foods and Hanson, ousted from the
index by 'new economy' upstarts such as Psion, Baltimore,
Kingston Communications and Thus in April, were back in the
FTSE by June. But the damage had been done. This damage was
partly to do with the embedding of the notion of a 'new' and an
'old' economy in the national commercial and political psyches.
As in New Labour and the political environment, 'new' is
associated with good, valuable, progressive values; 'old' is the
forces of conservatism – and that attitude has been applied to
industries in the 'old economy' as much as it has been aimed by
New Labour at its political opponents.

There is no new economy. Information technology and the
internet's value-contribution to business is, at best, incremental. A
real step-change, a truly new paradigm, was the one that followed
the industrial revolution of the century before last. So, again, there
is no new economy. The economy is the economy – simple as that.
The likes of Scottish & Newcastle and AB Foods are still with us not
because they are some relics of a past (and discredited) economic
model, but because they are part of the core economy. The trouble
with 'old' and 'new' is that they seem to distinguish qualitatively
between companies simply on the basis of their age and whether
or not they're 'wired'. This is patently absurd, since commercial
longevity must play a part in qualitative valuations, just as we

might take a pejorative view of an internet company that lasts in an index of leading stocks for less than two months in early 2000.

But, in an indictment of the flimsiness to the communications process at this time, 'new' was good and 'old' was bad. The dot-com aberration did much to establish this shibboleth at the turn of the millennium. But that it is consistent with the prevailing view in the Government makes the issue all the more alarming. One doesn't have to be a fusty old force of conservatism to observe that, while anything that is connected to the internet is not intrinsically of value (as the dot-com aberration taught us), nor is everything about New Labour either new or of value. The dynamic between New Labour and the new economy proved to be a dangerously phoney one. Through the dot-com fiasco, we have already learned that the new economy was a chimera – there were fiascos to come that would do the same for New Labour.

If the new economy, as defined by the Klondike rush of investors to the internet craze, discredited its proponents, that was as nothing to the defining effect that dot-com mania had on the emergence of spin-culture. Martha Lane Fox's disarming frankness – 'It's all hype' – was to be echoed by opposition MPs as an easy criticism of Government policy. The dot-com fiasco of the first half of 2000 went a long way towards equating spin-culture with vacuity and hype. Presumably it had not previously been thought of as the weightiest of intellectual disciplines, but New Labour had been thought to have imported slick American spin techniques and Peter Mandelson had been a 'master of spin'. These had been dark arts practised by clever operators with intuitive skills. Spin had, in the public mind, been about power and manipulation. Now the mood was changing, in politics as in business. Spin was about vacuity, lack of value and of substance. It was casually used as a definition of such. You told the truth or you spun. Those who had been seduced by the power of spin began to look less intoxicated than queezy. We should now turn our attention to the changing political scene, where the leaked memos of Tony Blair and Philip Gould from Number 10 showed that New Labour recognised that the electorate was turning nasty on spin. Electors didn't look like they were spun anymore. Nor did they look intoxicated. In fact, they looked threateningly like drunken navvies.

POLITICS

THE CORRIDORS OF PR

14th November 1990 – Committee Room 13, House of Commons. I am here for The Observer *to cover the evidence of Professor Roland Smith, chairman of British Aerospace, and of Lord Young, former cabinet minister and Thatcher's Mr Fixit, latterly with Cable & Wireless, regarding the Government's sale of Rover to BAe. Brussels has suggested that there may have been unlawful 'sweeteners' in the deal, worth some £38m. The Parliamentary Select Committee for Trade & Industry needs no sweetening on this occasion; it is an affable affair, under the chairmanship of Kenneth Warren (Hastings and Rye), flanked by mates such as Keith Hampson, confidant of Michael Heseltine, and Labour's Doug Hoyle. I'm late and, in any event, new to the Committee Corridor. Sheila Gunn of* The Times *is next to me on the press bench and, reminding me of a girl who helped me with my pencils on the first day of school, kindly brings me up to speed with the proceedings. I write a send-up in a column I have at* The Observer, *casting Smith as a bluff northern-inverted snob, confusing the chairman with Frank Warren, the boxing promoter who had recently been shot. The following Wednesday, I receive a letter at the office, on House of Commons paper from the chairman: 'Dear Mr Pitcher, Your article of last Sunday has been drawn to my attention. I am advised that it constitutes a serious contempt of the authority of this Parliamentary Committee and, under the powers invested in me, am instructed to advise you that I may deem it appropriate to bring it to the attention of a full hearing of the committee.' Under his signature, in his own hand, is written: 'PS: I can always be bought with a free lunch.'*

We had that lunch at Lockets in Marsham Street, a restaurant with its own division bell, where Warren had pre-briefed the waiter to serve (and charge for) 1947 Armagnac rather than the house decanter. We bumped into Brian Basham eating crab with a lady companion at the bar and went, as a foursome, to a wine-tasting in Westminster where Sir David Mitchell, MP and proprietor of El Vino, memorably poured some of our wine back in the bottle with the words: 'Do you mind, this is meant to be a *tasting*.' But the abiding memory is that letter. It's sad that a decade later, after the inquisitions into standards in public life, post sleaze, post Nolan and post Wicks on conduct in Parliament, it is almost impossible to imagine a back-bencher, far less the chairman of a select committee, daring to write like that, even in obvious jest. Most importantly, following the new atmosphere of high-church morality that Tony Blair wittingly or otherwise introduced to parliamentary affairs in his first term – though that morality was to start to look fairly tarnished by the second term – there seemed to be no place for play.

Perhaps that is a good thing. While Warren's parliamentary playtime was confined to winding up journalists with send-up letters and telling saucy jokes on the Terrace, the *laissez-faire* nature of politics in the Eighties and early-Nineties had also brought us Jonathan Aitken and Neil Hamilton. The question for us here is whether politics changed fundamentally in its nature over the last 20 years of the twentieth century – from the rise of Thatcher to near the end of the first New Labour parliament – in a similar fashion to the seismic shifts in the media, in technology and in communications. And if the function of politics has undergone such a shift, to what extent has its change matched and contributed to parallel developments in the media and communications? For, if there is such a match, then the likelihood must be that the changes over the two decades in the media, communications and politics are greater than the sum of their parts. And the sum total will have brought us to a spin-culture that can be examined objectively.

Politics is about the serious and the trivial, both of which affect political careers in equal measure. There is probably nothing more serious in politics than wars (real wars, with the deployment of armed forces, not wars on drugs, poverty or miners). And there is probably nothing more trivial than whether David Mellor wore Chelsea strip on the job (he didn't), John Major's Cones Hotline (he really did), Derry Irvine's wallpaper, John Prescott's Jags and Tony Blair's vanity – but they will, with assistance from the media, all have contributed ultimately to the diminishment of political power for the principals involved. To start with the most serious: war. Politicians are fond of referring to a 'period of unprecedented peace in Europe'. Tell that to the Kosovans. But the British prime ministers of the past 20 years have had more war than they should have expected. Thatcher had the Falklands, Major had the Gulf and Blair had Kosovo and Terror before he got to the Iraqi question.

What made these wars entirely different in domestic politics from previous British engagements was television. From the first, faltering coverage of marines yomping and the *Galahad* burning in 1982 – and the bulletins read by the implacable press officer at the Ministry of Defence, Ian McDonald – to the full real-time, living-room experience of the Gulf War nearly a decade later, courtesy of CNN and the BBC's John Simpson breathlessly describing cruise missiles from his hotel window, the conduct of war was brought to the electorate by electronic media, like a ghastly true-life Playstation. Thatcher gamely tried to regain the old political territory – 'rejoice, rejoice' – in which politicians took the gruesome war decisions and told the people to be grateful, but the television medium had become the message. The television genie was out of a jar rubbed by both politicians and their electors and it wasn't to be put back.

The psychological effect of television telling us what's really going on – and it applies to Serbia and the Sudan – is the major communicative contribution to development of politics and its allied spin-culture over the past two decades. Politicians, it has to be said, have been slow to catch on. Towards the end of their last 18 years in power, Tories were fond of mumbling that they 'weren't getting the message across'. This, again, was symptomatic of how fast the media, particularly television, were moving in reaching the essence of what was happening. The Tories may not have been getting the message across, but voters were *getting* the message. It was being delivered by the media, rather than by politicians. And that meant a new form of political manipulation needed to be developed. Spin-culture was deepening. Wars, our own and other people's, provided the most dramatic exemplars of the process through which the electorate started to take direct ownership of momentous events. But television has also played its part in the development of a spin-culture through the politically trivial. Parliament was first televised in the early Eighties. This did have the effect of bringing the spectacle of power to the people. Prime Minister's questions, Geoffrey Howe's withering resignation speech to a frozen Thatcher, the playing to the new public gallery that could seat millions and the squirming background players jostling for position at Budget speeches, were all now in public-broadcast ownership.

The chamber of the House of Commons became wallpaper television, great slabs of it broadcast off-peak, with dramatic soundbites only making the peak-time news. The same, incidentally, applies to the scrutiny of the select committees, which become stages for televised point scoring. Sometimes it's about not being heard too. Tim Bell told at least one client appearing before a committee to place 'a bird with big tits' in the chair behind and to the right of him, since this is the background seat that the fixed camera picks out and 'no one will listen to what's being said'. Whatever the level of sophistication of the media exercise, the parliamentary process is being packaged in tit-bits. This contributed to the attenuation of parliament. Spin-doctors were no longer just writing speeches, they were constantly writing soundbites. Viewers became inured to the sight of politicians strutting their stuff in the mother of all theatres, just as we became horribly inured to the sight of civilians being bombed and ethnically cleansed in Iraq and the Balkans. But access to political policy-making became no less potent because the people were taking it for granted. On the contrary, politicians and nascent spin-doctors saw the opportunity to exploit this new-found popular access. If voters now had access to parliamentary issues, then a new generation of politicians saw the opportunity to play out populist issues to their advantage. One such issue was the stoning of the Fat Cats.

February 1995 – Five years later and I'm back on the Committee Corridor of the House of Commons, but not on the press benches. And it's the Employment Select Committee this time, chaired by an altogether different kind of MP, Greville Janner, who adopts a languid and condescending metropolitan barrister's attitude to the utilities chiefs brought before him, many of whom are straightforward provincial industrialists. Janner's inquiry into executive remuneration in the privatised utilities – the fat-cat report as it becomes known – is a Star Chamber. It's oppressive at the best of times to appear before a select committee and Janner's appetite for humiliating less articulate men makes it the worst of times for many. Cedric Brown, the media-vilified chief executive of British Gas, has to appear twice, on his own and with chairman Dick Giordano. I speak to them in the Corridor – Giordano is perfectly relaxed; Brown seems to have accepted that he's toast. Cedric should be a Labour hero – a self-made man who started out in the gas-pipe trenches and now knows more about the industry than any man in Europe, possibly any man alive. But the fat-cat campaign, undoubtedly politically-driven, smells blood. Janner is enjoying himself. Just before Dick and Cedric go in the dock, Janner is asked in the House about his own highly-remunerative and modestly disclosed interests in training companies and he's altogether more flustered. You make your own luck in this game. As a result, Giordano can play it at his smoothest. At one point, asked to list his non-executive director-ships, he is asked whether he has left out RTZ, one of the world's largest mining concerns. He rolls his spectacles between his fingers dismissively: 'Yeah, I forgot that one. I should have mentioned that.' Next up is Sir Desmond Pitcher (no known relation, though sometimes described by colleagues as my illegitimate uncle), who is chairman of United Utilities. Desmond has had enough – I notice the back of his neck has turned red. The Committee has asked for details of the company's charitable contributions and the suspicion is that they're looking for payments to the Tory Party (there aren't any). Desmond has not supplied these details and Janner's opening question asks why not. Desmond more or less tells him it's none of his bloody business. Janner is enjoying it less now.

There have always been and probably always will be two levels at which New Labour's communications work – the short-term tactical and the longer-term strategic. You can judge the quality of its communications operators on whether their aptitude is for the former or the latter. The fat-cat campaign was a case in point. A pig called Cedric was taken to the British Gas Annual General Meeting in 1995, which must have given Ian McCartney the idea to demonstrate his stature, in so many ways, by appearing at the United Utilities AGM dressed as a pantomime cat. New Labour's opportunists could spot a populist issue to exploit as well as Old Labour at its best – and fat-cattery was one. The strategists took a more measured view. Peter Mandelson, for example, knew that a new Labour Government (as distinct from New Labour, or the new New Labour of his updated book, *The Blair Revolution Revisited*) would, from day one, need to work with the utilities industries – it might even need their co-operation to implement the heralded 'windfall tax' on 'excess profits' to fund the New Deal. The short-termists didn't even know what profits were – it was astonishing during the fat-cat select committee hearings how poorly briefed were some members and how little understood was the difference in company terms, between profits, cash and investment. Mandelson understood – his business understanding is one asset that would have made him an excellent Trade and Industry Secretary had he been allowed to stay.

It follows that, while McCartney dressed up as a pussy cat, Mandelson came to dinner at the Lanesborough Hotel, a converted neo-Georgian hospital on Hyde Park Corner, with Sir Desmond Pitcher, who had become 'King of the Fat Cats' now that Cedric Brown had been driven from the throne. You have to aim off with Mandelson – the charm can make you miss his purpose. But 'Prince of Darkness' and 'Master of Spin' are just risible for those who have known him informally. Towards the end of dinner, he turned to me and asked me to explain what I did. I explained, as best I could, my firm's role with United Utilities. But he didn't mean that – it dawned on me that Peter Mandelson was asking what a communications firm did. He was asking what a spin-doctor was. It may be that he was simply not familiar with the role in a corporate, rather than political, sense. But his innocent line of questioning and his untutored vocabulary led one to suppose that here was a strategist, not a grubby tactician. This view is endorsed by any examination of what was actually filched from Clinton's campaign camp in the States. Philip Gould – King of the Focus Groups – had been seconded to the Democrats for their 1996 campaign and had witnessed the power of 'small-bore' policy initiatives that appealed directly to swing-voters and were pragmatic in their approach to the economy. These were not just adopted by Mandelson in style and in substance, but also in detail – 'Welfare to Work' and 'A hand-up not a hand-out' were slogans lifted verbatim from the Democrats. Mandelson was always a political strategist rather than a press-room spin-doctor.

The same could not always be said of his acolytes. I had a colleague seconded to New Labour's Millbank Tower headquarters during the 1997 general election campaign (as we had people in personal capacities working at all the major parties). Rapid Rebuttal was one of the few media communications techniques learned from the States. It meant prompt and comprehensive response to negative media coverage, which often meant greater coverage of the rebuttal than of the original story. The system was fed by Excalibur, a sophisticated piece of news-scanning, storage and retrieval software, probably of greater importance in its threat to the Tories than in its actual delivery. Perhaps not unlike a microcosm of Mike McCurry's White House, it was a very sexy place to work. You could cut the testosterone and oestrogen with a chainsaw. One colleague reports a well-known figure saying 'I'm so excited I could have sex – oh, that's right, I just have.' Trouble was, this rush of blood carried over into government. If anything, it turned into something scarier – the looting instinct that breaks discipline in a conquering army. It did for Derek Draper and colleagues shortly after the great victory. You simply can't carry on making media hits – and privileged access fed the desire for hits like adrenalin. It wasn't just the Young Turks. The Brave New Labour Government was looking for a new media hit per day.

When the National Lottery operator Camelot's directors were called in by Heritage Secretary Chris Smith for a routine meeting, they were given a dressing down and a week to come up with a scheme for returning their excessive remuneration packages. They reeled from the meeting to find news camera-crews waiting for them on the pavement. It was only later absorbed that Camelot was a private-sector enterprise and the Government quietly compromised. Similarly, McDonalds had a routine meeting planned with Agriculture Secretary Jack Cunningham in 1997 after it had withdrawn from sourcing British beef, driven by consumer concerns over BSE, or mad-cow disease. Intelligence sources revealed that the Government planned to do a Camelot on McDonalds but, in the event, the *Daily Express* led that day with a front-page splash that 'British Beef is Safe Again', reporting that the company had taken a decision to return to British sourcing. The only glory for Government that day was reflected. As I say, you make your own luck.

What was happening was that industry was wising up to the new spin-culture. The fearsome New Labour machine was producing reciprocal responses from those with whom it came into contact. The spin-culture was escalating – and the stakes were rising too. But it wasn't all knee-jerk short-termists. There were and are strategists in the New Labour camp other than Mandelson – and not a few, of course, in the GIS. There was enough talent of the Mandelson variety, for example, to notice as the general election approached that a Monaco-based corporate raider called Andrew Regan planned a break-up bid for the Co-operative Wholesale Society, an icon of Labour heritage. Old Labour could cause untold trouble for New if it was seen in its earliest days of power to preside over the rape of the Co-op. A contingency plan was quietly drawn up in Walworth Road and Millbank. It was never needed, since the youthful Regan shot himself in the foot by purloining confidential Co-op documents. But it was a measure of how subtly Labour could mobilise a pre-emptive media strike in the event of a threat. As with the short-term tacticians, those who had to deal with the Government strategically started to respond in kind. When the spin war escalated, as with all wars, it started to attract public attention. And so the spinners became the story.

It happened to the willing and the less than willing. In April 1995, John Sweeney of *The Observer* wrote one of the more thoughtful pieces about Cedric Brown's persecution. Of the Select Committee Corridor, he wrote: '[Brown and Giordano] are joking with a third party – ah yes, yet another British Gas public relations minion. But this one is different: George Pitcher of Luther Pendragon. George isn't frightened of the Press, least of all *The Observer*, because he used to work for it. George is a professional hitman. What's he doing here? What's his game, eh?' I've often asked myself the same question – as have many of the new breed of spin-doctors who recoil from that job-title. He went on to say that we had lunch later and he asked whether I had arranged the question in the House about Janner's business interests. Apparently, I 'spluttered, said "might have" and ordered another bottle of Chablis'. I suppose spin-doctors have to live with it, but that is a complete fabrication. It was Chardonnay.

31st December 1999/1st January 2000 – It's a little after 9.30 pm on Friday night and I, and a clutch of civil servants, must be the only people trying to leave Parliament Square. We've just handed over to the night shift of the media co-ordination unit at the Government Millennium Centre in the Cabinet Office and, as we're due back on duty at 8.30 am on the first day of the new century, our aim is to get home against a tide of some two million revellers with precisely the opposite intention. We weave and shoulder-barge our way along Millbank until we reach the old British Gas headquarters, now a tower of luxury flats and a metaphor for our new millennial times. We cross Vauxhall Bridge and still the crowds come, as though drawn by a new Messiah. We turn right into Nine Elms and find our taxpayers' taxis by New Covent Garden Market, the closest they can get to Whitehall. After a couple of years of preparation for the possible effects of the Millennium Bug there is a somewhat different keenness to the anticipation of the new dawn among the Government's information team than among the throng with hooters. We feel celebratory and not too apprehensive. But there is an awareness that this midnight, which we have tracked since mid-morning GMT from the Pacific to Europe, would be the first test of whether all that preparation had been worthwhile. Not knowing how easy it will be to make the return journey, I'm back in Whitehall shortly after dawn and wander through the government buildings to the Embankment. From the kind of detritus that used to be left after a royal wedding I'm looking out across the Thames at British Airways' monument to anti-climax, the London Eye, not working and frozen in time from the last millennium. Another metaphor. By contrast, the computers of Britain are working as, in the most part, is the Government. Its charabanc has returned upstream from the rather acrimonious party for New Britain at the Dome and the Millennium Centre, overlooking a trashed Whitehall, offers a reality checkpoint and is visited by Bug minister Margaret Beckett and Home Secretary Jack Straw, who

address an ungrateful nation while we try to look busy in the
background. Tony Blair has already dropped in on his way to the
party and, unushered, has walked in on the pressroom, believing
it to be the monitoring room where the action is. Another
metaphor for the new millennium, perhaps.

As soon as it became apparent that there wasn't to be a techno-
Armageddon on Millennium night, the recriminations started. The
world's computers largely didn't wake up thinking it was 1900 and,
consequently, that they hadn't been invented yet. Much of the
media, however, did wake up thinking it was sometime in the last
century and that if everything had gone right then somebody must
be to blame. This process of thinking follows the age-old media
technique (I've often used it myself) that if there's a disaster in the
public sector, then the Government has not spent enough, and
if everything runs smoothly, then the Government has wasted
taxpayers' money. It was difficult, in the cool light of the
approaching 'real' millennium of 2001, to construct an answer as
to whether the Government's expenditure on the Bug was worth it.
Part of the reason for this is that there were some very strange
figures bandied about in early 2000 as to the extent of this
expenditure. Some wildly speculative figures put the total cost to
Britain at between £25 billion and £35 billion. Those are figures
pulled from the air on which the Government's detractors have
hyperventilated. What private-sector industry spent in total is, and
always will be, quite unquantifiable. Those strange figures were,
incidentally, driven by some fairly strange theories: Cuba's Fidel
Castro, the world's last heavyweight practitioner of communist
spin, claimed the whole Millennium Bug enterprise was a capitalist
plot to make us buy more computer software.

What we do know is that the Government spent some £430
million tackling the Bug issue. It was claimed in the New Year of
2000 (New Labour, New Year) that Italy spent a fraction of this
sum and didn't suffer unduly. Part of the answer to that is that
Italy alone turned red on our screens when midnight arrived in
continental Europe – coastguards were reporting that ship-to-shore
telecoms were down. Perhaps not as critical in the Mediterranean
as it might have been in the English Channel, the world's busiest
shipping lane. Italy was muddling through. A colleague told me

that, for reasons nobody could quite explain, he fielded desperate calls from Italian homes at the Treasury on the Monday morning of the new millennium. Britain was in control in Europe for once.

Uncynical as it may sound to media ears, Britain had the best global Millennium Bug monitoring and tracking research resources in the world. Subsequent stories about the Pentagon losing touch with its satellite defence systems bears out that we led even the US. This expertise proved highly marketable abroad. And it was this intelligence that secured the emergency services, the National Health Service, the utilities and the entire national infrastructure during the millennial rollover. So much for the public sector wasting taxpayers' money. But this was also the resource that enabled Action 2000, the organisation established by the Government to advise and support industry on the Bug issue, to ensure that similar security applied to British business as it returned to work in the new millennium.

The problem with this case for the Government's defence of Bug expenditure is that the principal beneficiary of that investment was invisible, precisely because nothing happened, any potential crisis was averted and we (or, rather, those of us who weren't working) were able to enjoy the party. Invisibility is to be a major challenge for political spin-culture, a point to which I shall return. But, in the case of the Millennium Bug, invisibility of benefit had its apotheosis. It was like arguing that you don't inoculate a school and then complain there's no smallpox. Or, as the Millennium Centre's line for Mrs Beckett had it on New Year's Day, things don't go right by accident (though much went right for New Labour in 1997 as a result of the Tories' accidents).

But Mrs Beckett's line only worked if the threat was a real one. That it was can be proved historically. In the last week of 1999, electronics conglomerate Racal showed symptoms of the Bug when its swipe-card systems went down – a glimpse of the kind of chaos that could have occurred had the Bug got a hold. Could it have done, or was Racal just an isolated glitch? Well, some 12 months ahead of the new millennium, I saw Government research that showed a sea of 'red status' in British industry, the worst category for lack of preparedness. As a result of the Government leading the Millennium Bug issue, British industry is in far better technological shape for the new century than it would have been without this investment. It wasn't just a case of avoiding Bug-related collapse. The knowledge and experience of systems security that the Bug exercise has provided has kept British information-technology expertise at the cutting edge of developments, despite the collapse in confidence and markets early in the new millennium. Furthermore, as a result of the process IT is now taken more seriously in British management than it was before the Bug was addressed. In perception terms, IT has taken off its anorak and put on a pinstripe, which further assists Britain's competitive position with the Americans. In a way, IT has entered the boardroom.

I go into this level of detail on the value of the Bug exercise because it is paradigmatic of one of the main factors in the development of a political spin-culture. Information technology drives the globalisation of markets. If Britain maintains a cutting edge in information technology, it contributes its markets to the world, as well as taking itself to the global market. We might say that Britain is no longer a global power, but it's part of global power. The benefits of this development are largely invisible in old political terms. It's not like a penny off income tax or free milk for schools. Globality and the dawn of the information-technology age are not political initiatives that you can hold in your hand. In domestic political terms, the world leaves the country cold. The issue of the Bug sums up the modern communications challenge for politicians in government – if you can't see it, then it must be all spin.

If there is a central driving force of the Blairite vision, it has to be modernisation. That means – if New Labour is to mean anything – that Britain must be dragged by its ear lobe, grumbling like a recalcitrant Victorian schoolchild, into the twenty-first century. In turn, that means, according to The Project, modernisation of government, of the tax system, of financial markets, of the law (the influence of Cherie Booth QC being a driving force here), of welfare, of industry and, yes, of communications. In the case of the last of these – the one that concerns me and the only one on which I'm qualified to have an opinion – it's no longer simply an issue of 'getting our message across effectively', the plaintive cry of Thatcherites in their twilight years. It no longer works, in an environment in which I can send this book down-line to Seattle or Singapore in a digitised instant, to argue that political messages are something static, domestic and presentational, just so long as one can find a slick presenter. The electorate are being asked to play on a different and immensely larger stage. It's not so much a question in today's politics of getting the message across to the people as of getting the people across to the message.

Talk of new-age political communications, like new-age any-thing, is dangerously close to old-fashioned bullshit. So allow me to apply this pseudo-intellectual thesis to two real political develop-ments of recent years that provide it with some validation. The first is about attenuation and the second is about rationalisation. It was perhaps appropriate that Sir Robin Day should die in 2000 during the political dog days of August, when politicians are at play, and with ill-concealed relief the Press duly filled its newspapers, yawning with silly-season space, about how Day's invention of the aggressive political interview had, ironically enough, killed good political debate. It's argued that lesser interviewers than Day can do the interrupting bit, but not the illumination and, meanwhile, media-trained politicians turn up at studios with pre-prepared soundbites and no talent for political argument.

The BBC's Jeremy Paxman, a scion of the Day technique (and, like Day, a scourge of spin in all its forms), contributed to the debate on political debate in a letter to the *Daily Telegraph*, in which he observed that 'the British Parliament has become less important as the power of government has grown'. He added that 'national governments throughout Europe ... have all become attenuated things as a consequence of membership of the European Union'. He listed some of the reasons for the fundamental change in politics since Day started to practise his trade: 'Globalisation, the EU, the role of the courts, privatisation, the centralisation of what remains of national power, the opaqueness of much of parliamentary procedure, the decay of ideology and, yes, the influence of the mass media.'

Margaret Thatcher, with her 'one of us' bullying abrogation of Tory ideology, her centralisation and emasculation of local government, her re-definition of Cabinet consensus as being the view that accorded with her own and, yes, her presidential style long before Blair was accused of developing one, did much to neutralise Parliament. New Labour, with its condensation of Prime Minister's Questions in the House to one session a week, Blair's relatively modest number of appearances in the Chamber, devolution of local government and propensity to make policy through the media and flag it on the Today programme compounds the attenuation of Parliament. Against this winding down over 20 years of the role of Parliament, is it any wonder that a spin-culture developed outside it, to conduct political debate in the public arena?

It is against the diminishing role of Parliament that the rationalisation of GICS has to be seen. Since New Labour's victory in 1997, alleged control freaks in Number 10 have been the butt of the new spin-culture's critics. This was understandable in light of the new regime's insistence that all ministerial media communications were cleared through the Number 10 press office, headed by Alastair Campbell. The climate of detraction was exacerbated by the communications infrastructure of the pager, to keep potentially errant ministers on-message. This use of by now fairly basic communications equipment was remarkable only in so far as it had not previously penetrated the time-locked world of the Palace of Westminster. Pagers had served New Labour well during the election campaign; it was unremarkable that they should continue to be used in office.

Early in the first week of the new Labour Government in 1997, departmental heads of information were called for a briefing with Alastair Campbell and Peter Mandelson – one of only very few collective meetings that would be held between either of New Labour's panjandrums of communication and the government communication machine. Mandelson and Campbell read from synchronised speeches, the thrusts of which were that the message was everything. There would be no departmental communications fiefdoms and departments would be delivering to a centralised Number 10 agenda – as, indeed, New Labour had delivered to its centralised new leader's agenda in opposition. Civil servants have latterly felt patronised by remarks of Campbell to the effect that they should 'raise their game' in the communications process. But it is widely admitted within the Service that there was a lot of dead wood that had gathered in corners or floated to the top of GICS. The urge to modernise, driven by Campbell but recognised by the talented and intelligent within GICS as necessary and overdue, was supported by civil servants.

Sitting at the vast meeting table of the Old Treasury Room at the Cabinet Office, with its seventeenth-century clock and view over the gardens of Number 10, during the management of the Millennium Bug issue, I was struck by the ability of Mike Granatt, Head of Profession (as the chief of GICS is known), and Mike Ricketts, Head of the Government Millennium Centre (and subsequently head of communications for the London Mayor and Assembly), to develop sophisticated and empirical strategy under extremely challenging circumstances. These were the 'Two Mikes' who were to run the show during the long midnight of the new millennium. There were a variety of public- and private-sector vested interests with diverse political and commercial agendas around that table that had to be coalesced under a demanding Government with very specific performance and budgetary demands. This was 'Yes Minister' re-written as five-act Shakespear-ean history, with the possibility of late adaptation as tragedy.

Bearded and self-deprecating, combined with a capacity for endless diligence and tolerance for selfish factions, the Two Mikes on first sight could be taken for ivory-tower academics. But their political management abilities were painfully underestimated by some who sought to make capital out of the Bug issue. Granatt has in the past taken time out to run the communications of the Metropolitan Police, in addition to departments such as the Home Office and Energy. These are not people who issue press releases about factory losses in the West Midlands. But, if the likes of Granatt are grand strategists for the governments they serve, they remained at the head of a communications machinery that was geared up for a very different era of dissemination of government information. Prior to the centralisation of communications that had its roots in the Thatcher years, government information was like a factory process, supplying detailed information with regard to the activities in Parliament of a range of discrete and highly autonomous government departments. This was labour-intensive, with heads of information at departments running mini-empires of

Never mind that it had grown fat and flabby compared with the austerity that had become the norm elsewhere in the civil service. Campbell was always going to be perceived as the new mill-owner cutting off the income of the workhouse. Had he been a civil servant, the process of rationalisation might have been seen as a necessary piece of self-immolation. As it was, it was to be used as further evidence of centralising communications power on Number 10 and control-freakery.

Campbell's role in relation to the Press is often misinterpreted, particularly by those who have not been a part of the press corps themselves. As a former tabloid political commentator, with the Mirror Group and the now defunct *Today*, he knows intuitively how newsrooms work, both internally and in relation to their sources of information. Those who complain petulantly about bullying tactics, or favours sought from and despatched to favoured journalists, misunderstand the communications process. That is how it works at the newsroom level – it is not something invented by New Labour, far less by Campbell himself. A working journalist will seek to beat his or her competition to the story by any means possible. Mostly these means are legal, though far from invariably so. But in the humdrum process of the working day, the journo will bully, flatter and bribe (not usually with money, but with reciprocal favours) to get ahead. Campbell's talent has been to turn that process around, or at least to meet it on an equal footing, and to institutionalise it.

There are those in the parliamentary press lobby who have whined about the bullying or favouritism – which is a bit like lawyers complaining about the cost of professional advice – and a regular claim was that Campbell had lost it, had forgotten what it was to be a journalist, had grown contemptuous of the media process and simply wanted it controlled. But Campbell's great achievement in the first Blair term was precisely that he didn't go native. Surrounded by politicians with particularly vague ideologies and strong egos, ensconced on Planet Westminster, he resisted losing touch with the world in which the media operate. The question arose after the 2001 election as to whether Campbell could maintain streetwise skills in a more elevated and strategic role. But as Number 10 press secretary he played the media at their own game.

It was these central skills that kept Campbell – and consequently, to a significant degree, New Labour itself – at the top of his game, to the apparent disgruntlement but private admiration of much of the press corps, during Blair's first term and the extended honeymoon, as reflected in the Prime Minister's ratings in the opinion polls.

The real problem was one of centralisation. New Labour was used to being centralised. It had been centralised at Walworth Road; even more so at Millbank Tower. The old habits were not so much dying hard in government as virally infecting the body politic. All conduits of communication were to run to Number 10. But the Government had never run like that. For generations, the machine had run like a medieval royal family. Number 10 was a court; the Cabinet Office was a court; the Treasury was a court. If Number 10 was to become one super-court, with all departments serving the one true king, then local departmental lairds either had to fall into line, leave or be frozen out of the communications action. And there was the court of Millbank Tower, over which Mandelson had presided as Prince Regent during the election campaign of 1997. The power of Millbank had been superseded by the power of Downing Street, as New Labour replaced its siege mentality with the mind of government. New Labour, old psychologies. And old psychologies die hard.

The spin-culture that developed at the heart of government, the political process and Parliament is a direct result of the attenuation of Parliament and the consequent rationalisation of the communications resources that had served it. What is left is a communications superstructure built on Parliament rather than developed from within it, which is sound so long as the Government is delivering. In the absence of policy initiatives – such as the Chancellor's £43 billion public-services spending spree in the Comprehensive Spending Review of 2002 – attention is bound to focus on this superstructure, in a manner that it would never have focused on the comparatively invisible civil-service machine. Blair expressed the same rather differently when he appeared before the select committee chairs for a prime ministerial review in July 2002, the first Prime Minister to do so since 1938. He observed that during Labour's last 18-year spell in opposition 'announcement is the reality' because oppositions are 'not in a position to deliver anything on the ground'. He had come to the not very startling conclusion that things were different when you found yourself in government: 'For Government, the announcement is merely the intention – the reality is that you have to deliver on the ground.' A paraphrase of that might be that, in government you have to do stuff, rather than merely say that you are going to do it. It seemed to have dawned on the PM that something rather more substantial than intent had to be delivered. Well into his second term, content was belatedly going to have to replace style.

A painful lesson for Blair to have learned so late. Meanwhile, announcements of intention, suitable only for opposition, had in government done much to encourage the spin-culture. When there is a dearth of content to be spun, spin becomes the story. What Campbell may have discovered is what experienced politicians have known for generations – when you've run out of tit-bits to feed the jackals, they're likely to turn on you. The painful problem for Campbell is that he is neither an elected politician, nor an invisible and detached civil servant. Caught in the middle, he cannot but help become the story himself. And it's all too easy to call the story 'spin'.

In the political field, spin was known to have tarnished the noble spirit of Blair's Camelot by the time of the general election of 2001 – Gould's panicky memo and Blair's comments about concentrating less on the presentation of policy prove it. But, if nothing else, spin-culture had fallen from fashion by the millennium.

Most fashions fall from favour with some grace. Platform soles and the mullet hairstyle of the Seventies are ridiculed with some affection from the distance of a couple of decades or more. The High Tory manner, combining an effortless condescension with an assumption of natural authority, is a curiosity of half a century ago, inviting nostalgia rather than contempt even in Spartist circles.

Not so with spin. Fashionable among those who practised the new art and feared by those who did or could not during and directly after the New Labour landslide of 1997, spin had not just fallen from fashion by the approach of the millennium, but had become a pariah-occupation and a firmly pejorative descriptor for the smoke-and-mirrors of The Blair Project. At its most contemptuous, it had become a straight synonym for the lies and deceits of the spivs and fixers attached to New Labour.

The London mayoral elections of 2000 brought Labour's embarrassing uncle, Ken Livingstone, to a party being hosted by a political family that had hoped that he had lost touch and with whom they had no intention of sharing The Project. Liberal Democrat candidate Susan Kramer manfully tried to resist the tsunami of popular support on which Livingstone was surfing by repeatedly greeting his campaign with the one-liner 'It's all just spin'. She enjoyed as much success in turning the tide as King Canute. But she did reveal a shift in public perceptions. Spin had ceased to be the dark art, adored and resented but always feared, that Peter Mandelson had allegedly practised like Merlin to Blair's Arthur at the 1997 election. It was just lies, subterfuge and window-dressing.

This was partly the fault of mischievous squires attracting attention to themselves, intentionally or otherwise, in the kitchens of Camelot. Derek Draper, squire to Mandelson, had longed to joust with the knights and had fallen victim to his boasts of access to Court. The Press was happy to play the role of Morgan le Fay, destroying the magic of Draper's trusty pager by holding the mystery of the names it held to the light of day. Similarly, Charlie Whelan, squire to Chancellor Gordon Brown, had underestimated the jealousies of Court and the degree to which the king's own retainers would mercilessly put down any challenge to authority. Whelan was slain by his own sword – that other piece of New Labour armoury, the mobile phone.

It was at about this stage that it dawned on some that spin might be Labour's version of the Tory sleaze that had proved such a vote-shifter in 1997. New Labour's detractors, such as they were in the late Nineties, being a motley and demoralised bunch of war-lords who denied the uniting light of Camelot, seized on such dishonours as evidence of corruption in the new order. Among Tories, this defiant resistance was conducted without any sense of irony, with attempts to move 'cash for access' into the contemporary political lexicon, alongside 'cash for questions'. It says much for the dissolution of the Tories in the late-Nineties that they sought to identify resonance between non-elected Labour apparatchiks seeking to cash in on their election-campaign contacts books on a consultancy basis and the scandal of former Tory minister Neil

Hamilton. The latter had fallen from grace and failed to clear his name in two libel actions over allegations that he took payments from Harrods-owner Mohammed Fayed in exchange for asking questions in the House.

There is no equivalence between the two accusations. Selling access to contacts is a large part of what political consultants do. If there is impropriety on the part of the politicians to whom access is being established, then you have a corruption scandal. That was at the heart of the accusations levelled at Hamilton. But failure to distinguish between an intermediary being paid for access to ministers and those ministers themselves being paid is to abrogate any sense of moral relativity.

In any event, Camelot had greater problems than exercising discipline among its squires. The 'whiter than white' pledge at the time of its 1997 election demanded not only the highest levels of probity, honour and chivalry at the Round Table itself, but the swiftest of corrective action should those standards ever be compromised. Sir Lancelot was Arthur's favourite, but flawed, knight at the original Camelot, whose integrity was violated by his love for Queen Guinevere. Perhaps Peter Mandelson should never have tried to transfer his pre-election role as Merlin to that of a post-election Lancelot. However, falling in love with New Camelot's queen, Cherie Booth QC – an unlikely plot-line – was not Peter Mandelson's flaw. It is alleged that Mandelson was variously in love with money, with celebrity, with parties and famous people. Or with himself, or with New Labour, or that he came to fail to distinguish between the two. Whatever the quality of the amateur psychologists on Mandelson's case, his two resignations from ministerial office in the first Blair parliament presented New Labour's enemies with a proper scalp.

A knight of the Round Table had yielded dishonourably under tournament conditions. This was not a matter of indiscretion among the squires – Whelan caught wielding his master's cudgel at the Red Lion or Draper polishing his sword at the Groucho Club. This was Lancelot banished from the Round Table. This was a knock to the credibility of the New Camelot. As tarnishing as the downfalls of Mandelson were the allegations of corporate sleaze. In the early days of New Labour Government, Formula One supremo

Bernie Ecclestone was revealed to have donated £1m to New Labour's campaign coffers and the coincidence of his sport's exclusion from new regulations concerning tobacco sponsorship proved sufficient cause to require him to take his money back. Later, in 2002, came the Lakshmi Mittal 'cash for favours' imbroglio, in which Blair had evidently lobbied the Romanian premier on behalf of what was claimed to have been a British company for the purchase of a steelworks. It emerged that Mittal had been a significant donor to the Labour Party.

But if these offered evidence of the soiling of Camelot's linen, they were not root causes of the decline of the spin-culture. Actually, they could be interpreted as the kind of thorns that any government has to pick from its side if its opposition is even doing half its job. For the root causes of the decline of the political spin-culture, we have to go further back into New Labour's governmental history. In fact, we have to go back to the first days of power in 1997.

NEW LABOUR: VICTIM OF SUCCESS

3rd/4th May 1997 – In the small hours of the great New Labour victory we're in the Plough in Dulwich, celebrating not just Tessa Jowell's victory with co-workers in that constituency, but witnessing on the televisions throughout the bar the destruction of Toryism. It's like a safe, middle-class, computer-game version of the collapse of the Ceauscescu administration in Romania – sanitised and without real suffering, but with the thrills of seeing a busted and wicked regime brought to justice by democracy. There's no real hate, of course, as there never is in violent computer-games and as there always was when despots fell in eastern Europe. The drinkers cheer as the endless red ticker-tape runs across the screen recording the latest Labour victory. They cheer at the humiliations of the previous regime's icons, such as Michael Portillo. But they also light-headedly cheer the odd blip of blue that appears, recording rare Conservative holds – sporting and generous of spirit, magnanimous in triumph and, anyway, the Tories are no threat anymore. Earlier we had been in the Marquis of Granby, the pub next to Tory Central Office in Smith Square, where they had been selling beer with nicknames like Labour Landslide and Major Hangover. We wander now into the dawn, lighting post-coital cigarettes. It is, of course, sunny. The South Bank resounds to the anthem 'Things can only get better'. The sap's rising and spring is in our step.

Maybe things could only get better. We were starting from a very low base after the Major years – the Cones Hotline, the Citizen's Charter, Back to Basics, Wait and See. If Major had won another election, we might have looked forward to policy initiatives such as Can't Be Too Careful, Everything In Moderation and I'd Better Take My Cardigan Off Or I Won't Feel The Benefit. The regime that had brought us Neil Hamilton, Jonathan Aitken and Jeffrey Archer had been taken out and shot at the polls. The people had stormed the Grey Palace. An entire journalistic commentary tradition had been established on the premise that there was more to John Major than met the eye. How could it have been otherwise? To have admitted the truth would have been to produce a single column and repeat it regularly for the seven years of his garden-gnomic tenure. Now the truth could be told – there was less to Major than met the eye. And the electorate had just taken its revenge on Margaret Thatcher.

There was a childlike and refreshing innocence to the incoming Labour Government. None of them had been in government before, but it was alright because they were nice – nicer than us, in fact – and would never go to jail for telling lies about who paid their hotel bills (Aitken) or who they were having dinner with (Archer). Whitehall chuckled at the naïvety of the Freshers. One story had it that the new Foreign Secretary, Robin Cook, placed a call to his opposite number in the States, Madeleine Albright, and expressed surprise that the call was not recorded in any way, to be told politely by a senior civil servant that he had been in the next room, monitoring every word on another line. Then there was John Prescott, mentioning that his predecessor had left a load of ministerial papers in his office and being told, by another patient civil servant, that this was his departmental briefing file. These stories are not apocryphal – they are reliably sourced – though they may have been embroidered and exaggerated for comic effect. Civil servants need a laugh. There was a gag doing the rounds around this time that Prescott got into a taxi and the driver asked him whether he had 'heard the latest joke about John Prescott'. 'But I am John Prescott,' replied the surprised Deputy Prime Minister. 'Okay,' says the cabbie, 'I'll tell it slowly.' These were largely affectionate gibes, the sort of good-natured joshing that was associated with the camaraderie of the rugby club or stewards' mess. Nobody had told an affectionate joke about a Tory for years. This was like teasing newly-weds.

It wouldn't be long before Blair was denying undue influence from Bernie Ecclestone's £1m gift by saying that he was 'a pretty straight kind of guy' (November 1997), that Cook was being ordered to consolidate his love life by mobile phone in an airport departure lounge and that Prescott was protecting more than his wife's hairstyle in a chauffeured car, culminating in a burly punch-up with a disenchanted voter in the 2001 election campaign. But the newly-weds enjoyed a protracted honeymoon nonetheless, bolstered by the Prime Minister's discovery of his special tear-fighting voice for the death of Diana, Princess of Wales, commitments to things that people cared about such as 'education, education, education', things that people didn't care about but admired such as Britpop and Cool Britannia, a young family and a surprise baby – and a press secretary in Alastair Campbell who understood how the modern press worked.

History will record that this honeymoon lasted, pretty much unmarked by the likes of Ecclestone, Mittal and Mandelson, until Blair's adoption of the role of world envoy for peace in the wake of the terrorist attacks on the United States on 11th September 2001 and the return to tax-and-spend Labour policies in the Budget of 17th April 2002.

The arts and sciences of spin, as exercised by Mandelson before and directly after the electoral triumph of 1997, fared less well along the way. This was only partly down to the telecommunicational affairs of Derek Draper and the personal and professional financial affairs of his sometime mentor Mandelson. The spin culture that had developed during the Nineties, with only some techniques raided from the Clinton camp in the States, had served Labour well after the political demise of Neil Kinnock, the unwitting stalking horse of the 1992 election, and the sudden corporeal demise of his successor John Smith. Rapid rebuttal, the undermining of political opponents, focus groups and the addressing of critical issues at the right times and in the right places were all weapons that had served Labour's renaissance in opposition well. The problem, as the relatively swift deterioration of spin as a fashionable career choice to synonym for lying demonstrated, and as traced in previous pages, was that it was insufficient as a means of government. At least, it was insufficient of itself.

The early years of the regimes of Clinton in the US and of Blair in the UK were distinguished by some similarity. They both prospered politically, for example, from runaway economies that had little or nothing to do with their own initiatives – Clinton's Federal Reserve chairman, Alan Greenspan, confirmed as much when he ascribed ridiculously over-valued equity markets to 'irrational exuberance'. But the Clinton of government, though distracted and undermined by peccadilloes of immeasurably greater damage than anything Blair has had to endure, also created issues of Democratic government that needed active management. In reforming American health services he took on powerful vested business interests, because he deemed it right and had a mandate to do so. His foreign policy aspired to focus and effectiveness, rather than some apparently vague mission for world peace. Blair's ill-conceived tour of the Middle East, in particular his humiliation at a press conference in Syria at the hands of President Assad, bears no comparison with Clinton's measured and calculated performances on Blair's own doorstep in Northern Ireland.

Blairism in power talked the talk but failed to walk the walk. Why? Part of the answer must be that New Labour in power post-1997 was frozen in the headlights of a parliamentary majority of 179 – a curse for New Labour not only in terms of the loony-tunes fringe candidates that were never supposed to be elected to its backbenches, but more vitally because it demolished any prospect of a deal with the Liberal Democrats. This was the component of The Project that was supposed to form an axis of the social democratic soft-left that would keep the forces of Conservatism out of power for generations, if not forever. With such a sun-eclipsing parliamentary majority, Labour had no need of an alliance and Lib Dems could not tolerate the prospect of junior partnership. Paddy Ashdown, who under different Labour circumstances could have sat at the Cabinet table, made a premature exit from politics.

In the absence of a unified front of the Left, New Labour embarked on a policy by default of protecting its own overweening power. It was born as a Government with a mission to retain power, rather than to do anything with it. And in the absence of The Project, what was left? Along with education and the euro were ranked the impossible Northern Ireland, Cool Britannia, the Dome and the devolution of local government in Scotland, Wales and London. In short, New Labour was left in government with political issues it could not or would not resolve and the baubles of a new-millennial image. It's little wonder its spin-doctors so soon became popular pariahs; little wonder Blair embarked on a presidential journey, looking for a role on a grander, global stage. And no wonder Campbell attempted to move upstairs to a more strategic policy role at the 2001 election, away from the grubby business of spin. Blair's admission before select committee in July 2002 that he hadn't realised the difference there was in opposition and in government between announcing something and doing something just about summed up this sense of frustration and emptiness.

But there is more to the popular reaction against spin-culture than New Labour simply being a victim of its own success at the polling booths and immobilising itself with the size of its parliamentary majority. There was also felt to be a vacuity in its politics, a vortex in New Labour's political ideology that drove popular contempt for the political process – a contempt that manifested itself in the easy condemnation: 'It's all just spin.'

It's to do with the move to the plain-vanilla centre of politics. New Labour had been forced into the centre-ground of politics in order to make itself electable after the Foot/Benn/Healey debacles of the early Eighties that did so much to provide Margaret Thatcher a free reforming run at the electorate. The alternative was to stay radically left and remain unelectable. Nevertheless, Labour has abandoned comparative politics for comparative management – we no longer distinguish between methodologies for managing the economy, but between relative competencies for custody of it. There is no ideology – and what is left is spin.

A simple test, by way of illustrating how indistinguishable are the ideologies of modern politics: Below are two passages from separate books. Can you distinguish between the politics of the writers?

> *'Britain's national affairs are reaching explosive levels of stress. The individualist, laissez-faire values which imbue the economic and political elite have been found wanting – but with the decline of socialism, there seems to be no coherent alternative in the wings.'*

'We should spend more energy establishing a workable and lasting framework for the relationship between government and industry, and less on the foredoomed attempt to breathe life into the economics of State Socialism on one side and laissez-faire on the other.'

The first passage is from Will Hutton's *The State We're In* (Vintage, 1996), which was to New Labour popular-economic philosophy what Stephen Hawking's *A Brief History of Time* was to astrophysics – it simultaneously benchmarked and popularised the subject matter. The second passage is taken from *The Tory Case*, by Chris Patten (Longman, 1983), the intellectual Tory grandee who was forced to go and give back Hong Kong to the Chinese when he lost his seat in Bath and is now a European Commissioner. The comparisons are remarkable for their similarities throughout their books – minutes of harmless fun can be had asking dinner guests which is the Tory and which is the New Labour acolyte. In many instances, what Hutton in 1996 and Patten in 1983 had to say are interchangeable – in other instances one says what you would expect the other to say. If that's the case with the designers of policy, how much more is it likely to be the case with the policy minions and, indeed, the voters? The Third Way is not so much a path as a static meeting place in the middle of politics. Ultimately, then, the trouble with a Third Way is not that it simply pushes all politicians into a mélange of compromise between a bit of this policy and a bit of that economy, but that it makes politics indistinguishable. And when that happens, the only differentiators are soft qualities of stewardship. The arguments are consequently not those of substance but of style.

That wearies voters. Because it's all spin, innit?

New Labour: Naïvety and insecurity

Vacuity at the heart of the Government's policy-making machine may have encouraged a spin-culture in politics post-1997, but it can hardly be blamed for the public antipathy with which spin has become imbued. The absence of substance, in a person or a government, can be ridiculed, but it hardly of itself justifies a role as a central tenet of political opposition. An opinion poll, conducted by YouGov for the *Daily Telegraph* in April 2002, found that those who believed that Blair relied 'too heavily on PR men and spin-doctors' had risen from 52 per cent to 71 per cent – but this is not the stuff that brings down governments. We may have discovered through market research in the late Eighties that Margaret Thatcher relied too heavily on hairspray and sycophants, but it was the Poll Tax and Europe that brought her down.

The absence of policy can have its appeal to an electorate. In its early years of government, New Labour benefited from simply not being the Tories. Blair himself articulated the appeal of a political environment in which there was no longer a 'Big Idea', but rather a number of small, managerial tasks to be performed in the running of the economy, public services and social provision. In this scenario, it is plausible that, after an economic experiment conducted by Chancellor Nigel Lawson in the late Eighties that precipitated a bitter economic recession in the early Nineties and after the profound vacuity of the Major years, there was a case for sound and sensible stewardship rather than Thatcherite Big Ideas or the petty-mindedness of the Major regime.

So it was active symptoms of a spin-culture, not the absence of a policy platform, that became most apparent during Blair's first term. There were behavioural characteristics, rather than a simple absence of substance. These have been referred to by detractors of Blairism in terms of presidential style – again alleging a provenance for New Labour's style in the US – as well as arrogance, deceit and even a post-ironic reprise of Tory sleaze. These are the weapons of Her Majesty's Loyal Opposition, chiselling away at the edifice of Blair's personal popularity rating. But they are not the causes and conditions that give rise to those symptoms. One does not need to be a qualified clinical psychologist to arrive at a diagnosis of the cause of these symptoms. All those symptoms associated with the presidential style and the smoke-and-mirrors culture presented themselves as the result of two core conditions within the political body of New Labour that were to traduce it in the body politic. These were *naïvety* and *insecurity*.

These are close cousins in the family of human weaknesses. Consciousness of naïvety undermines self-confidence, generating insecurities that are often concealed deliberately or unconsciously by arrogance and self-delusion. We are scratching the surface of New Labour's first-term psyche here. For fear of trespassing too far into the marshy territory of the armchair celebrity shrink, it may be as well to cite two specific examples of these root conditions within New Labour.

🖐 NAÏVETY

Shortly after Robin Cook ensconced himself in the ornate marble-and-mosaic halls of the Foreign & Commonwealth Office and made his hotlink call to Madeleine Albright in the US, he announced that New Labour would be exercising an 'ethical foreign policy'. In part, this would have been a measured implication that Tories were unethical in their foreign affairs. Not only had the likes of former foreign-office minister Jonathan Aitken, Cook liked to imply, enjoyed relationships of too cosy a nature with Arab arms dealers and the Thatcher and Major governments shown an unseemly enthusiasm for financial support from dubious sources, but Tories also liked to exploit the Third World, strip developing economies of their natural resources, intervene only where there were vested interests and abandon countries to their fate where no such interests existed. More kindly, it might be added that Cook acted with good, if naïve, intentions in attempting to put human rights at the heart of the new Government's foreign policy.

It took Lord Carrington, in late 1999, to expose what was, at best, the naïvety and, at worst, the hypocrisy of his position. Carrington, so far as the casual condemnations of New Labour were concerned, was one of the Tory tainted, a relic of a discredited era in which the dispossessed of the world were left to fend for themselves, unless they happened to eke out their existence in oil-producing areas. As it happened, Carrington was nothing of the sort. Carrington was a pre-sleaze politician. Or, rather, he was from a political era in which sleaze existed – it always had; look at Profumo, Wilson or Gladstone – but in which politicians exercised choice. It hadn't as yet become associated in the minds of the public with a whole government, as it would in the stub-end of the Thatcher government and through Major's tenure. Carrington, it should be recalled, resigned against Thatcher's wishes at the outset of the Falklands conflict in 1982 for no stronger reason than he felt that the Foreign Secretary should do so under those circumstances. No claims, far less evidence, of any wrongdoing and no attempt to hang on in office. This would look like curious, even eccentric, behaviour within a decade. But what Carrington was able to do nearly two decades later was to disassemble Cook's aspirations to an ethical, human-rights-driven agenda in foreign policy. Carrington could do so, perhaps, because he understood ethics – Cook understood the assertion of them.

What Carrington did, writing in the *Daily Telegraph*, was to present three foreign conflicts of the late Nineties and examine Nato's – and by extension the British Government's – response to them. In Kosovo, where there had been brutal attempts by Serbs ethnically to cleanse the territory, Britain led the drive to take the war into Serb heartlands precisely, and only, because a major armed conflict with Serbia was unlikely. In East Timor, by contrast, where the Indonesian Government had put down democratic attempts at independence, the United Nations only entered the country with Indonesian permission and there was no suggestion of British participation in any bombing of Jakarta, in the manner that Belgrade had been bombed. But then, you understand, Indonesia occupies a vital British and western trading position in Southeast Asia. Finally, when the Russians rolled tanks into Chechnya to quell an uprising, the UN did nothing at all, other than a few somewhat hand-wringing declarations of concern for humanitarian issues. Here again, the overriding factor was not one of ethics, but of pragmatism. Russia was, and is, a nuclear power with vast armed forces – there could be no question of intervening in the manner of our intervention in the Kosovo crisis. To have done so would have risked a world war, whatever the humanitarian considerations.

The *Telegraph* reported with glee that Cook's moral selectivity by location for his ethical foreign policy exposed him as a hypocrite. I'm not so sure. I believe that what the early years of New Labour exposed was a naïvety. Things could only get better because these were nicer blokes (and women) who cared about people – unlike brutish Tories. But with very few exceptions – such as Jack Cunningham, whose star burned brightly at Agriculture, and as New Labour's firefighter before imploding – New Labour's ministers had not been in government at Cabinet level before. They had no direct experience of governmental realpolitik. On the foreign stage the lesson has not been learned. In response to the Arab fundamentalist terrorist attacks on New York of September 2001, Blair first and unilaterally threw British support behind George W. Bush's war on terrorism, wherever it occurred and however it was defined (by the United States). He subsequently embarked on a role as world ambassador for peace – possibly out of frustration with the lack of opportunity for statecraft at home, other than with Northern Ireland. This led Blair to commit to grandiose and ill-defined plans for peace in Africa, to a poorly received tour of the Middle East and a humiliating public exposure of his ignorance in Syria. Finally, he was to find himself caught between the rock of the US and the hard place of Iraq.

There have been political naïveties on the domestic scene – one thinks of the Millennium Dome, hospital waiting lists, instant fines for yobs and withdrawal of family benefits from hooligans – but these can be and have been spun as the faults of 'a pretty straight kind of guy'. On the world stage, such naïvety is both more dangerous, in terms of our national security, and more starkly apparent as the manifestation of inexperienced politicians wading out of their depth in strong currents.

❧ INSECURITY

Mandelson's greatest talents had never been of the intuitive kind – his lack of intuition would soon be apparent in his utterly naïve assumption that his eccentric mortgage arrangements with the Paymaster-General, Geoffrey Robertson, on a house in Notting Hill in some way didn't matter. Mandelson was always a gritty scientist – the sort who becomes so wrapped in his experiments that, one imagines, his car is towed away and his dog wees on the kitchen floor for lack of exercise. At Millbank, the image of Mandelson as the spinner of half-truths, the underminer of Tory reputations and the spontaneous creator of lines of New Labour policy is also wide of the mark. At any rate, it is only a half-truth. Mandelson's greatest strength was as the cool and analytical scientist. The deployment of Excalibur, a database that identified hot election issues in key marginals, is testament to this. Though Excalibur held as mystical a threat over its owner's enemies as the original, one was never sure if the magic was real or imagined. Nevertheless, there was reportedly a clinical exactitude with which issues were identified on a local basis and communications resource devised to address them. Transferred to Downing Street, it is little wonder that this psychology, nourished by the nutrients of governmental power, should manifest itself in the centralisation of communications. This was to become widely known among the dispossessed of Whitehall, and the media that they fed, as 'control-freakery'. The control freaks of Downing Street were to be most exposed, both in terms of visibility and vulnerability, during the set pieces of regional-government devolution during their first term.

A paraphrase of Mandelson's advice to Blair when the idea of a directly-elected mayor for London was first floated would be: 'Don't do this unless you know who you want to be elected.' The implication is clear: Go for a free election by all means, so long as our man or woman is elected. The 'one of us' rubric of Thatcherism – those who are one of us are 'sound'; those who are not are our enemies – is one of the inheritances of quality that is less celebrated by, but no less apparent within, Blair's Camelot. Preparations for a Welsh Assembly, for these reasons, degenerated into the kind of unfortunate loss of parental control within the Blair family that was to lead to an adolescent son being found paralytic by police in the West End. As all parents discover, you can't allow teenagers a developing freedom without them making mistakes. Furthermore, you cannot expect them instantly to develop the kind of responsibility that goes with those freedoms. As the schmaltzy American movies have it: 'Let them go – if they love you, they'll come back.' In Wales, Blair's children studiously contradicted, embarrassed and abandoned. First Ron Davies, the favoured Blairite candidate, was forced to stand down from the leadership contest to be Wales's first First Secretary after salacious details of his private life became public. Then Alun Michael was imposed by Blair's corporate centre on the Welsh Labour Party, against the wishes of party activists who favoured maverick left-winger Rhodri Morgan.

At this stage, as the new millennium approached and New Labour sought to make it its own with the cavernously empty imagery of the Dome in Greenwich, Morgan stood as an early incarnation of the Beast for Blair's regime. The fight was more symbolic on a national scale than the mere fight for the Welsh Assembly. When Morgan spoke of spin-doctors – or 'masters of rotational medicine' as he called them – he meant more than to abuse the Prime Minister's spokespeople. For Morgan, it was second nature to abhor the vacuum within New Labour. Opposition to Michael grew so strong within Wales that, within a year, he was forced to resign as First Secretary in February 2000, to be replaced, ironically enough for a New Labour regime that had claimed and exploited the title often since 1997, by the people's choice, Morgan. If, for the forces of the one true way at Downing Street, Morgan had been the first manifestation of the Beast, then Ken Livingstone was to re-emerge in London as the incarnation of the anti-Blair, to fight what appeared to be, given the seriousness with which New Labour met the threat, an Armageddon for the heart and soul of politics.

Again, as in Wales, the Blairite corporate centre at Downing Street sought to impose its favoured candidate on the process – or, more obviously, to block its least favoured candidate. To the astonishment of ministers and MPs, the party machine ruled out a one-member, one-vote ballot in favour of an electoral college of members, trades unions, MPs, MEPs and London assembly candidates. The corporate centre endeavoured to keep Livingstone off the candidates' list, grudgingly included him and then tried to drown him out with His Master's Voice. Blair backed a number of anti-Livingstone statements from his ministers – or perhaps confirmed what they were told to say – and then addressed Labour meetings, describing Livingstone as a potential 'disaster' for London. He even went so far as to suggest that a vote for Livingstone was a vote against the progressive momentum of New Labour, that Livingstone would be a return to the Eighties and would jeopardise the Blair Government's prospects at the next general election (how laughable that seems now).

Frank Dobson, Labour's official burnt-offering to the London electorate, was duly elected to – or manipulated into – the candidacy, evidently against his better judgement. Livingstone pretended to ponder, stood as an independent, was excommunicated from the see of New Labour and swept all before him in a mayoral contest that wanted to kick Downing Street's despotic butt. Poor Dobson, a genial but obsessively committed politician who had always offered journalists fantastic copy – once the expletives had been deleted – during Labour's dark wilderness years before New Labour had been invented, grew irritable and sarky during the campaign. In fact, much like the beleaguered Alun Michael in Wales during his brief tenure as First Secretary in Wales. He was, of course, trounced at the poll, but Livingstone's victory was not just over Dobson and a process that had conspired against him, but also over the control-freakery, born of Mandelson and Campbell and nurtured in the artificial, autocratic atmosphere of New Labour's Number 10.

It wasn't just in Wales and London that this was apparent – the Scottish parliamentary elections had been manipulated to keep left-wing candidates out and there were allegations of stitch-up levelled at Millbank over the way it effectively imposed Labour candidates on the 1999 elections for the European Parliament. The wonder is that they were able to get away with such ham-fisted manipulations. Their favoured candidates were defeated, one way or another, by electorates that refused to be spoon-fed their leadership. But Labour candidates of one sort or another were still elected (if, as we should, we count the Labour-expelled Livingstone in that line-up). It wasn't as though control-freakery forced voters into the arms of other major parties.

This was partly to do with the weakness of alternative candidates. With not the slightest hint of irony, Jeffrey Archer remarked of the mayoral contest from which he had been expelled on historical perjury charges that would also lead to prison: 'If the Archangel Gabriel had stood with the name of Winston Churchill, Ken would still have won – there's such a myth out there.' Leaving aside Archer's own contributions to mythology, there is a truth in his observation, if not the one he intended. So hopeless, so untrusted and untrustworthy had the Tories become, with no real opposition alternatively offered by the Liberal Democrats, who snatched humiliation from the jaws of honourable defeat, that local-assembly elections in Scotland, Wales and London became battles between Labour candidates, rather than battles between Labour and any meaningful opposition.

The greater wonder, then, is why Labour's corporate centre bothered with all his control-freakery at all. One answer clearly has to be that Labour remained at battle with itself, the Blair Project being a constant struggle not just against the 'forces of conservatism', Blair's catch-all targeted enemy, within the Tory Party, but also within Labour too. New Labour's Project was not to be held back by its own Luddites. But that doesn't explain the degree of time, energy and commitment that was invested in devolving regional government, while simultaneously centralising control of the candidacies in those elections. New Labour's agenda – in broad terms and in so far as it can be perceived, the adoption of Tory wealth-creation economics and their co-option to support of public services and the dispossessed – could not have been de-railed because Rhodri Morgan is First Minister for Wales or Ken Livingstone is Mayor of London. This is not the kind of smug observation that comes with gin-clear hindsight. With the kind of parliamentary majority that would have enabled New Labour to donate Hampshire to the Conservative Party as a reservation for distressed fox-hunters, without doing itself any real damage, it is inconceivable that the political resource invested in control-freakery was in any sense worthwhile.

To some extent, the Government acknowledged this. During the summer of 2001, it became apparent that Millbank had backed off its autocratic and authoritarian position and was prepared to recommend a 'one member, one vote' system of candidate selection for the European Parliament and Scottish and Welsh assemblies. But the paradoxical desire to devolve power with an instinctive urge to hang on to it still requires explanation. It is not sufficient simply to label such dichotomies as control-freakery. That may offer a sufficient explanation for the centralisation of communications resource in Number 10. It is not difficult to conclude that what worked in Millbank before winning power might work in Downing Street after winning it. But it simply isn't sufficient to explain away the hobbling of a major plank of New Labour policy – devolution – as a desire to control all theatres of power. This is not about the processes of communication, as was the meeting of Campbell and Mandelson with civil service heads of information shortly after the 1997 election, but about the exercise of governmental power itself. Nor is it satisfactory to offer naïvety as an explanation in the way that the starry-eyed Cook took up his Foreign Office brief with a promise to place human rights at the top of his policy priorities. The devolution debacle is about something related to naïvety, but that has grown as a separate symptom of another disability.

What the New Labour Government demonstrated through its cack-handed management of devolution is its innate insecurity. It is an almost unbelievable charge to level at a new government with such an unequivocal mandate that it should be insecure, but its instincts for self-protection and autonomy during elections for local assemblies can only ultimately be ascribed to a lack of self-confidence. Perhaps it was the lack of an opportunity, with such a parliamentary majority, to pursue The Project through alliance with the Liberal Democrats – perhaps more experienced and self-confident parliamentarians – that left the governmental new intake with a sense of vulnerability. But the point is that, for all its alleged arrogance and self-satisfaction, New Labour may well have been as frightened as a suddenly over-promoted army officer, needing to look self-assured and in command while feeling unsure about commanding the respect of those for whom it has responsibility. This would not matter – people grow into the role of command – but for two important consequences of New Labour's innate insecurity. The first is that it needed to cover it up. This means that it had to act with authority without feeling that it had it; to attempt deliberately to have image and style triumph over reality and substance. It becomes turbo-charged spin – spin on speed. It is toxic, noticeable and provides a justification for those who would use 'spin' as a casual pejorative.

The other consequence is that, sooner or later, your supporters, as well as your detractors, start to see through you. It is exhausting to keep up an act of self-confidence, as both Blair's and Campbell's wearinesses with the communications of government demonstrate. It is impossible indefinitely to invite those you represent to believe in you, if you do not wholly believe in yourself. The act of command will no longer suffice as a virtual reality. They can smell your fear.

25th June 2002 – Robert Harris, in his column in the Telegraph, *has joined the game of comparing Blair's premiership with the Third Reich. A former civil servant, Sir Richard Packer of the Ministry of Agriculture, started it last week. What is going on? I never knew Harris, but he was political editor on my shift as Industrial Editor at* The Observer. *We both used to get in to the office early on Saturday mornings and, there being no one else about, greet each other stiffly at the coffee machine. He swept into the car park in an XJS and wore a spotty silk hanky wafting out of a thornproof pocket. He went on to write hugely successful novels, such as* Fatherland, *and live in a small mansion in south Berkshire on the proceeds, where he'd hold fashionable house-parties. This is my kind of lefty, I thought. He was, in fact, an early symptom of New Labour – a bit rentier-than-thou before Labour got the middle-class habit. Mandelson is godfather to one of his children. Harris was with the Blairs on election night 1997. But then something went very wrong. Harris had written startlingly for the* Sunday Times, *preparing the Third Way. But Mandelson was out of government – twice – and, in the minds of his coterie, had* been shockingly treated. Harris switched to the Torygraph after the millennium and started penning Blairo-sceptic prose, disappointingly reverting to type as a sort of Colonel Bluster. He could still write, though. When Downing Street dismissed Sir Richard's Hitler comparisons by calling them 'colourful' and 'out of date', Harris noticed this was a curiously limp denial: 'Oh yes, we used to do all that Hitler stuff until around 2000, but then we decided to stop.' Harris has a mild literary obsession with the Second World War, but the question is not – obviously – whether Blair is a genocidal maniac, nor even whether Blair's bureaucracy 'works towards the Fuhrer' (you might as well say 'Oh look, the Khmer Rouge had a leader and so does New Labour. Therefore ... '). The question is: Why is Blair suddenly being likened to the Fuhrer by clever people?

The answer is not because there are similarities. The answer will ultimately tell us more about those who make the comparisons – not because they're nasty or distasteful (Harris and Sir Richard appear to have no track record in either of those character traits), but because they feel the time and the public mood is right to make such parallels. Harris, in observing that there is a Hitleresque similarity in subordinate creeps producing policy initiatives that are half-baked, is careful to add: 'Heaven forbid that one should seek to draw too close an analogy here ...' Yes, heaven forbid. But would Packer or Harris have felt able to make any such analogy during Blair's first term (irrespective of the fact that they were both, in separate ways, 'in' with the regime for much of it)? Of course not. All the centralising of power, all the sucking up to the Fuhrer was well under way, but no one would have felt comfortable with making a public comparison with the Third Reich. They may have thought it, or observed it privately in a Berkshire library well stocked on the subject, but the public would not have tolerated it and the Press would not have supported it.

So, again, the question must be asked: What has Blair's government done to deserve this? Part of the answer lies in that limp disclaimer to the Nazi charge from Number 10. Alastair Campbell – 'heaven forbid' that we should compare him with Goebbels, though nothing should surprise us or him anymore – emerged chastened by the belligerent engagement with the right-wing commandoes of The Spectator, the Mail on Sunday and The

Standard over the Queen Mother's lying-in-state and his subsequent abortive PCC complaint. Quite the right thing to have done, as I record elsewhere, would have been to ignore charges of Blair's alleged 'muscling in' on the ceremony; the coverage would have been widely interpreted as the rantings of the marginal right, the contempt for such charges would have been palpable and the issue of Blair's vanity, whether perceived or real, could have been addressed over time. Somewhat belatedly, Campbell's communications or propaganda machine – call it what you will – was learning its lesson. 'Colourful' and 'out of date' were far more effective dismissals of Packer's eccentric comparisons with a fascist mode of government than, say, 'this is as offensive as it is untrue' (Blair on lying-in-state-gate) or, for that matter, 'we will hunt him and his kind down and wipe them from the face of the earth like the sub-humans they are – *sieg heil!*'

Now, I can trace no one who has received a response quite like that from Campbell's office, even when Burnley FC has lost at home. Even Bernard Ingham confined himself to 'bunkum and balderdash'. But there can be no doubt that Number 10, after its centralisation of communications after 1997, garnered a reputation for bullying. Protracted over five years, producing a number of incidents that would justify parents of media children going straight to the headmaster, a zeitgeist has been created in which polite, middle-class professionals feel no compunction about likening Blair's once effete and metropolitan set to the nastiest bunch of hoods, incompetents and industrial mass-murderers in modern history. It's not that Packer and Harris said it, it's that they felt able to say it without embarrassment – we had come to accept the centralised, bullying regime for what it was and to tolerate attacks on it.

This is partly down to Campbell's abrasive, news-room style. But only partly. Campbell, though as an old hack giving as good as he got with a news-room style in the Lobby, expressed concern about the haemorrhage of GICS civil servants after New Labour's accession, aware that the Lobby would not respond well to the loss of old mates. Cabinet secretary Sir Robin Butler shared his concern, though for different reasons. Losing good GICS operatives meant they had nowhere else to go within the service, meaning more outsiders had to be brought in – such as Martin Sixsmith at the Department of Transport. Furthermore, another Downing Street source claims that Campbell 'never turned down proposals from senior civil servants' and – here's a departure from conventional Lobby wisdom – 'was assiduous in making sure that Blair couldn't misuse his communications resource'. Campbell, apparently, recognised the value of having a permanent – and consequently consistent – communications resource.

Furthermore, the charge of bullying may be laid at Campbell for getting things done – an unusual talent in Whitehall, but much sought after on the diplomatic scene. A friend reported having lost touch with him after 11th September because he was 'saving the world' – shorthand for running the Coalition Information Centre out of Islamabad, Washington and London. The time-zones involved tend to make for long nights, but that's the point. The Kosovan war had demonstrated the Serbs were dictating the communications game by the simple expedient of starting the day 10 hours before Washington. As any journo knows, when you're ahead of the story you tend to stay there. This extraordinary observation was only apparent to Campbell, who took the Serbs on in their own time-zone. Similarly, he 'bullied' the other members of the coalition in the new war against terror (otherwise known as the Taliban in Afghanistan) by ensuring that the West's response and rebuttal was in real-time. The Taliban's media ambassadors noticeably gave up shortly afterwards. By the summer of 2002, a similar tactic was being played out towards the United States, the United Nations and Iraq.

Campbell can do this because he has greater direct media experience and greater authority invested in him by his national leader than any equivalent role to be found in the US. This is not to do with any mysterious dark arts. It has everything to do with the relatively simple structure of democracy in Britain compared with the States. Unhealthy as it may be deemed to be in other contexts (such as unelected power), Campbell has none of the checks and limits of a federal system, so could push the coalition into working together simply by being assertive. Old hacks are assertive.

There is clear water between being a bully and being assertive. But those who prescribe reputations aren't fussy. Nor is Campbell, come to that – old hacks are thick-skinned too. And old hacks are cunning. Here's an example: Cabinet Secretary Sir Robin Butler established a review of the Government's communications in September 1997 under Robin Mountfield, at that time permanent secretary at the Office of Public Services.

Shortly after Mountfield reported, Campbell abolished the old Lobby conceit that the Prime Minister's Press Secretary is never attributed – only 'Downing Street sources' and weaselly variants appeared in the Press. Campbell became 'the Prime Minister's official spokesman'. This seemingly innocuous piece of glasnost, in the style of 'call me Tony' or the renaming of GIS, in fact had a greater significance. Early in Labour's first term, the question of Britain's membership of the euro had pitted Number 10 against Number 11. While Campbell briefed on behalf of the PM unattributably, another 'Downing Street source', the Chancellor's Charlie Whelan, was holding court at the Red Lion, across the way in Parliament Street. So Campbell went on the record. Whelan was left briefing unattributably against Downing Street's official spokesman – until it all went horribly wrong for him. Similarly, when the Lobby went on the web, someone remarked that 'a reporter in Scunthorpe' had access to the same information. 'Exactly,' replied Campbell.

But, again, these are not the initiatives of a bully, nor of a shadowy master of manipulation. They are the street-wise actions of an old hack. The reputation of Campbell either as a bully – pity the poor flowers of the press corps, whence he emerged – or as some kind of Machiavellian stalker of the corridors of power nevertheless developed. Perhaps it was the centralisation of communications through Number 10 – very much in the style of the opposition disciplines that New Labour had learned and, as the former minister himself has conceded, very much driven by Mandelson – that supported this perception. Communications systems such as The Grid, a forward-planning matrix adopted for the whole of the Government, may further have contributed to the atmosphere of sinister control-freakery.

Whatever the causes, as the Government approached its re-election year in 2001, there was more than an intangible feeling out there that New Labour was spinning a threadbare yarn. With a massive mandate from the British people, New Labour had still managed to lose its way. The mood was caught in a leaked memo of Phillip Gould, the focus-group guru, to the Prime Minister's office just ahead of the May 2000 local elections. Extracts convey the sense of panic:

> 'Our current situation is serious. There is absolutely no room for complacency ... There is currently now a chance that our majority will fall dramatically, following the pattern of 1945 and 1964 ... for much of the past 18 months, the Government has been drifting and growing almost weaker and more diffuse ... we are suffering from disconnection; we have been assailed for spin and broken promises ... we are disliked on the left wing for being right wing, on the right wing for being politically correct ... Perhaps worst of all ... the New Labour brand has been badly contaminated. It is the object of constant criticism and, even worse, ridicule ... undermined by a combination of spin, lack of conviction and apparently lack of integrity, manifested by the [London] mayoral selection process ... PM [Peter Mandelson] said the other day: "Something has gone seriously wrong – but what is it?"'

One of the most intriguing phrases is that New Labour had become 'the object of constant criticism and, *even worse, ridicule* [my italics]'. Constant criticism might imply an examination of policies that are found wanting – ridicule is simply a case of gags at New Labour's expense. But apparently the latter is perceived by this senior and influential figure within the New Labour camp as more serious than the former. As an indication of the triumph of style over substance, it doesn't get much better than this for the Government's detractors – even in a lather of panic, New Labour's priority is to manage the image rather than the issues. In the event, we know the panic was misplaced – the Government was returned in June 2001 (thanks significantly to the Tory leadership of William Hague who bored the electorate with Europe and jumped on any passing right-wing Little Englander bandwagon) with an almost unchanged majority of 167.

But spin was no longer a casual insult to be thrown at New Labour from the outside – it had been identified from within Camelot as the enemy. It had begun its journey to being New Labour's public enemy number one. Maybe it was the communications centralisation of the first term. Maybe it was perceptions of bullying by a Prime Minister's unelected Press Secretary getting too big for his boots. Maybe it was, as Mandelson himself later identified, a case of continuing to behave in Government as they did in opposition. Yet these factors on their own cannot have generated the opprobrium and contempt in which the Government's communications function was held within a year of that Government's return in 2001 – a spin-culture so despised that casual comparisons with the Third Reich had become routine for educated people such as a former civil servant and a successful novelist and columnist. In the event, it was nothing even vaguely Machiavellian that did for the political spin-culture with which New Labour had become associated. As so often in affairs of state it was the banal and the bungling that tipped the balance. Two communicational events knocked the last bolt from the slurry gate over the Government's head – one in which Campbell was not directly involved and so was unable to recover the situation and another in which, whilst this time he certainly was involved, there was little he could do to remedy once the wheels of events had started turning. The first was the Jo Moore affair; the other was the debacle of the Queen Mother's lying-in-state.

We know the facts: On 11th September 2001, just after two jetliners hijacked by al-Qa'ida terrorists are crashed into the World Trade Center in New York, killing some 2,800 people, a Department of Transport special adviser, Jo Moore, dispatches an email memo suggesting that 'this is a good day to bury bad news'. The memo leaks on 9th October and in the subsequent furore Moore provides a doe-eyed television apology. Her boss, Transport Secretary Stephen Byers, stands by her and so does the Prime Minister. On 14th February 2002, reports allege that Moore tried to release bad rail statistics on the day of Princess Margaret's funeral, but was stopped by communications director Martin Sixsmith, the BBC reporter turned civil servant, though the evidence this time is less than patchy. Moore resigns the following day and Sixsmith's resignation is announced. Sixsmith subsequently claims he never resigned and it is mooted that his scalp was required in some sort of deal with Moore. Meanwhile, Byers is mishandling the administration of Railtrack and alienating the City in doing so. He is also causing embarrassment on the euro and when discrepancies in his accounts emerge over his role in the Sixsmith affair he is branded a liar by the Press. On 28th May, he resigns, being granted the honour of doing so from within Number 10. After he has gone, it emerges that a transport official, Dan Corry, has used emails to ask whether the Paddington rail-crash survivors group were Tories. Byers says he's sorry about that too.

Byers conceded at his resignation that 'with hindsight' it would have been better to have disposed with Moore's services after she sent her fateful email. Had he done so, he might not have become such a media target and may have survived, though his handling of the railways may have done for him without the assistance of Moore. So why did Moore survive 11th September? It has been suggested that Blair, who said that Moore shouldn't have to go for 'one mistake', was anxious, on the advice of Campbell, that she shouldn't be hounded from her post by the media. They feared where it might end if a precedent was set. This is not just ironic, given that this decision led substantially to a Secretary of State being hounded from office by the media some seven months later. It is also risible, considering with what unseemly haste Mandelson, a close friend of Blair's as well as a senior member of the Government, was dropped just as soon as allegations of impropriety appeared over the Hinduja brothers' passport application – allegations subsequently dismissed by the Hammond inquiry's report, which vindicated Mandelson; meaning he was hounded from office for nothing.

It is fair to say that Sixsmith is not alone in refraining from joining the Jo Moore fan club. Moore was popular with Byers and was protected by permanent secretaries at the DTI and subsequently at Transport, because looking after the Secretary of State is in their job description. But amongst her colleagues she was said to have been widely resented and unpopular and when the media went for her she found her trench empty.

Perhaps the real reason Moore survived the initial 11th September memo to become a much greater liability for Byers was fear of another precedent it would set – not that it would lead to further media-inspired sackings, but that burying bad news in the shadow of greater world events would have become a sackable offence. And governments do that all the time. The bald fact is that there wouldn't be a Press Officer left in Whitehall if every one that did it had to go. Moore's crass and 'terrible error of judgement', as she put it, was not to seek to bury bad transport news on 11th September, but to commit her suggestion to email. It is one of the unpalatable truths of working life – like the retention of organs after autopsies – from which the public are protected. It has been a practice in the Government information machine as long as governments have been obliged to communicate with their electors.

The Blair Government's mistake was to allow this unedifying, but necessary, practice to be seen in the light of day. And to allow a spat to develop between Moore and Sixsmith. These, remember, were communications 'outsiders' – Moore as a spad (special adviser, although in this instance the alternative transport-department usage of 'signals passed at danger' serves just as appropriately), Sixsmith as one of the new breed of civil servant recruited to replace those who had left the service post-1997. When older hands in the civil service murmur 'it would never have happened in the old days' they don't mean the practice of slipping out bad news in public holidays, alongside Budgets, during royal events when any other major news event is dominating the news – they just mean that they wouldn't have been caught. It is, perhaps, ill luck that the New Labour Government should have been the one to be associated with the practice, when it has been around for generations, but it brought at least some of that ill luck on itself by bringing into its service those who were untutored in the ways of government news management. The consequence is that it is New Labour that will always be associated with one of the spivvier examples of news management. So much for 'raising their game', as Campbell put it.

> So to lying-in-state-gate – or lying-to-the-state, as the Government's attackers would have it. Unlike the Jo Moore case, the facts are less clear. But a sparse synopsis runs as follows: Peter Oborne, Political Editor of The Spectator, runs a column in the 13th April 2002 edition claiming that the Prime Minister's office had tried to 'muscle in' on the arrangements for the Queen Mother's lying-in-state at Westminster Hall. The essence of the story is that Number 10 had badgered Black Rod, the member of the Royal Household responsible for the arrangements at

Westminster Hall, for a more prominent role. The Spectator *story is gleefully followed by pieces in the* Mail on Sunday *and* The Standard. *Number 10 goes berserk, outraged that questions to Black Rod from one of its officials on matters of protocol have been presented as manipulative, and refers the incident to the Press Complaints Commission. It appears subsequently that Black Rod declined to corroborate Number 10's version of events – he is said to have submitted a 'killer memo' to the PCC – and Number 10 withdraws its complaint, claiming satisfaction that it has been demonstrated that Blair had not personally sought to enhance his position at the ceremonies. The right-wing stables of the Telegraph papers (including* The Spectator*) and Associated (*Mails *and* Standard*) continue to worry the bone by stating that they had never claimed that Blair was personally involved, that it was a humiliating climb-down for Blair and Campbell and that they stand by their original stories. Senior editors of national newspapers are very excited by this – but it's hardly Pulitzer prize-winning stuff.*

Before assessing whether any of this matters or not, it's worth examining some of the personalities involved. As with the Jo Moore debacle, an examination of the nature of the players helps to explain what went on and the significance of it. First off is the author of the original piece, Peter Oborne. This gentleman journalist is something of an anachronism, a sporting Edwardian figure who once settled a spat with a colleague on the City desk of the *Evening Standard* by taking him on for three rounds in a boxing ring above a bar in Blackfriars Road. He will often simply judge people as to whether they are a 'good egg' or not. He attaches great value to being a good sport – he wins and loses with equanimity at the bookies and, when at a Cheltenham Festival his friends served his portion of steak and kidney pie with tinned dog-food, he declared it delicious. Lest this be taken by Oborne's detractors as proof that he will swallow anything, he wears his learning lightly, but is no patsy. He will allow his friends to the left of him – which, depending on his mood, can be all of them – to wind him up in the back bar of El Vino and will run an informal book on who will take offence and flounce out first. But, for all this sport, it's worth remembering that he took a first in history from Cambridge and started his career with N.M. Rothschild in the City and worked widely in financial journalism – including a stint as the *Telegraph*'s chief City reporter under Neil Collins – before embarking on political journalism. He is no one's stooge and to swallow the Colonel Blimp act is dangerously to underestimate him. And he has written a not entirely flattering biography of Alastair Campbell.

Claire Sumner is the young civil servant at Number 10 who is alleged to have bombarded Black Rod with mobile-phone calls, pressing for a more significant role for the Prime Minister – though her version is that her guidance notes stated that the PM would greet the cortège at Westminster Hall, Black Rod's was that he would not, to which Sumner declared 'fine'. Her claim is that the liaison with Black Rod was procedural, not negotiational. Sumner is described variously by colleagues as bright, ambitious, hard-working and tough. She is consequently respected in the service as 'a class act'. She originally entered the GIS as an Assistant Information Officer, but in the months before the 1997 election became involved, as is customary, in the preparation of briefs for incoming ministers. Sir Robin Butler was retiring as Cabinet Secretary after the election, so permanent secretaries and their officials were effectively writing their job applications. Butler's eventual successor, Richard Wilson, was at the Home Office, needing assistance with the briefs, which are enormously comprehensive and demanding documents. Sumner was known as a good drafter, so was seconded to Wilson's private office. Her brief was a triumph, which set her up with the incoming Jack Straw. Off this springboard, she was fast-tracked to Number 10, where she worked initially alongside Bill Bush, a former head of research at the BBC and, at that time, a spad in Number 10's Research and Intelligence Unit. She was doing a parliamentary questions (PQs) job as one of the Prime Minister's private secretaries. As such, she would see at least as much of the PM as anyone else. This is important, because it gives private secretaries great authority with regard to the PM's wishes. She would have known what Blair would want and would take initiatives accordingly. According to one colleague: 'She has a reputation for knowing the way things are going to be and will brook no argument'. Possibly Robert Harris would have it that she was working towards the Fuhrer. More prosaically, we can safely assume that she may have come across as a little bossy for a young woman to a senior military man such as General Sir Michael Willcocks, Black Rod.

Willcocks is reported to have become particularly exasperated when he took a call on his mobile as he stood at the north door of Westminster Hall awaiting the Queen Mother's procession, advising him that the PM was considering walking to the Palace (Jack Straw has subsequently declared that the walk was his idea because it was a sunny day, but that it was rejected on security grounds). Willcocks is described as 'incandescent' at this stage, saying: 'This is completely crazy and will backfire badly.' Lord Falconer, a friend of Blair, sought to calm Black Rod by remarking: 'It's not Tony – it's his advisers.' Much subsequent argument has focused on 'Tony and his advisers'. There is the Harris/Packer view that Blair's advisers 'work towards their leader', anticipating his will. Oborne takes the less extreme view that a Prime Minister and his representatives are indistinguishable as organs of the state. This view has been deployed by those journalists on Oborne's side as a means of suggesting that they never implied that the PM himself engaged in an exercise of self-aggrandisement (and that, therefore, the PCC's apparent 'settlement' was meaningless). But this is somewhat disingenuous; Oborne's piece in *The Spectator* was not only headlined 'How Tony Blair tried to muscle in on the mourning', which just about might be argued to refer to the whole corporate office of the PM, but went on to state 'The Prime Minister ... was unhappy ... he felt that the arrangements did not recognize his importance and he wanted them changed'. When the request was rejected, Oborne wrote that Blair 'accepted all this with good grace'. It is difficult to see how it can be claimed that the PCC's settlement statement – that Number 10 withdrew its case because it was satisfied that the newspapers accepted that Blair was not personally involved – could be construed as irrelevant because that claim 'had not been made in the first place'. A reasonable reader would construe that Oborne had written that Blair had himself sought an upgrade.

Oborne himself sought to dissociate himself from this inter- pretation on *Newsnight* on 14th June. I felt for him. Oborne is a highly intelligent and able writer, but is not a broadcast performer. On television, you have to talk quickly and concisely – this is the world of the pseud's soundbite, not the considered view. A more experienced TV performer, Andrew Rawnsley, was making the running and played it for laughs as Oborne said that there was no right-wing press conspiracy against the Blair Government, that he was a simple hack working on his own and temporarily elevated to celebrity status by this story. But Oborne was right. Anti-Government conspiracies require proprietorial co-ordination and, with the stand-offishness of Lord Black at the Telegraph group and death of Associated's fiercely involved Lord Rothermere, there is no concerted anti-Blair campaign, as former *Guardian* editor Peter Preston wrote in *The Observer* at the time, just a disparate collection of right-wing journos taking pot-shots at Number 10.

So how do such clever and powerful people come to be having an argument, involving a complaint to the PCC and acres of newsprint, over whether or not the Prime Minister, or his representatives, sought a bigger role at a state event? The Blairs were censured for 'glad-handing' at a state opening of Parliament, allegedly upstaging the Queen, and for looking glum (and, in Cherie's case, hatless) at the Queen's Golden Jubilee celebrations. They can't win – if they play the crowd or look downbeat on these occasions, they get it in the neck. Campbell's view is that the media thinks he is obsessed with spin and that he thinks the media is obsessed with trivia. He has a point on the second count.

There is a fashionable view that the right-wing press has to provide Her Majesty's loyal opposition because the Conservative Party is too weak and disorganised to do so. Maybe it's an indictment of the lack of quality of modern politics that opposition, in the parliamentary sense, amounts to sniping and personal attacks. But the media can only blame themselves for adopting the style. The quality press does, of course, tackle issues such as the euro, education policy and public services. But disproportionate space is ascribed to the trivia such as the role of Campbell at an interview, or the role of Blair at a lying-in-state. For his part, Campbell doesn't always help. The Queen Mother story would have been confined to what he could have cast as the Conservatives' barking tendency in *The Spectator* and the *Mail on Sunday* had he not complained, on weaker grounds than he anticipated, to the PCC. But perhaps Oborne should cut him some slack. As Oborne said on *Newsnight*, he was just a hack thrust into a celebrity role. So is Campbell. And journos, as Oborne knows all too well, are prone to react emotionally and irrationally to attack. Oborne might not unreasonably rejoin that Campbell is far from an old hack now – as some would have it, he is the second most powerful person in the country. But Campbell is no longer a political editor, with all the responsibility of influence that entails – the circulation of *The Spectator* may be tiny, but Oborne's story reverberated through the readership millions provided by the *Telegraph* and Associated papers. Oborne wielded similar power on this occasion.

On balance, Oborne and Campbell probably deserved one another on the lying-in-state story. But the Government probably has a greater issue to address in the wake of it than do the media. It isn't good enough to declare that the media are obsessed with trivia. Chancellor Gordon Brown isn't dogged by trivial matters. Perhaps if he were next door in Number 10 things might change – but it's hard to visualise. There is something about the Blair court that attracts a fascination with the trivial. That must be a longer-term worry for the Number 10 communications machine, because eventually trivia sticks and the PM himself will look trivial despite his minor stance over Iraq. That may be what some quarters of the right-wing press are after – making Blair an icon of trivia. At that stage the big issues will be irretrievable. But, worse than that for Blair, the middle-classes that gave him such a commanding majority will be heartily sick of the game.

> 25th June 2002 – *The Fabian Society's summer drinks party on The Terrace of the House of Commons. I bump into a friend and sometime client who is a Labour-supporting industrialist. 'This Queen Mother business – it's a shame, but it'll be iconic for Blair, the sort of thing he'll always be remembered for,' he tells me. 'It could do for him eventually. It's very sad, but every Prime Minister has one – a defining event in their administration.' He glances over his shoulder in the direction of Gordon Brown, who has just spoken to us. 'I hope he gets it,' he adds.*

INSTITUTIONS

Establishments of Truth

The thrust of this book so far has been to suggest that developments in politics, particularly the emergence of New Labour, but also the presentational premises which preceded it and on which Thatcherism prospered, were symptomatic of a developing spin-culture, rather than the causes of it. What was happening alongside politics in the media, in the business world and the City community that financed it and in startling info-technological advances meant that spin-culture was a zeitgeist, rather than a politician's trick of the light. This argument only stands up if the development of spin-culture can be traced in a broad swathe of public life. If it is confined to politics, business and the media that report them (however exciting have been the technological developments in the latter process), then it is perhaps broader than New Labour's circle, but still very far from all-pervasive. I will come later to the effects of spin-culture on private lives – and the consequent social ennui of the power of style over substance – but I want now to examine three bastions of what used to be called the Establishment for the presence of spin-culture. Traced here, in walks of public life touched by, but supposedly independent of politics, the evidence for a spin-culture should be incontrovertible. The arenas to be examined for this evidence are the Law, the Monarchy and the Church.

April 1992 – Monday. Temple. The defence team for David Reed, the erstwhile County NatWest corporate financier, is having lunch ahead of his sentencing, alongside his five fellow convicted defendants in the epic County NatWest/Blue Arrow conspiracy-to-defraud trial. There are sandwiches on the table, but the only person with any appetite for them seems to be Reed's silk, the boyishly combative Anthony Hooper QC. Nor does anyone think it's really appropriate to have a drink, though Reed thinks it's a 'bloody good idea to have a gin and tonic', which is his prerogative, given where he may be going later this afternoon. Reed is keeping his spirits up, aided by the booming interjections of his solicitor John Hume. Maybe it's partly relief that, after more than three years of inept prosecution since the now notorious £837 million rights issue for Blue Arrow in 1987, it's nearly all over. Even Mr Justice McKinnon has been showing signs of strain in the latter stages of this marathon trial. It hasn't been a picnic for those in the dock either. Before we walk in a morose crocodile up Chancery Lane to the specially enlarged courtroom in Chichester Rents for the last time, Reed is relieved of his cufflinks, watch and pen and given a couple of vast books – if he's taken down into custody, this is the last family contact before prison. As it turns out, sentence is suspended and Hoops has all the convictions quashed on appeal. In what feels like a final gibe from the judiciary system, the appeal is heard in a courtroom in the Strand up several flights of spiral-stairs. Hume is in a wheelchair, but we get him there anyway, wheeling himself in like a triumphant Ironside. What has been the point of all this litigation? That's rhetorical. But for me there is a big lesson learned. They were convicted, against the odds, on the Friday and sentencing was deferred to Monday. We hit the phones to the newspapers, putting the case against custodial sentences to the columnists. I'm unsure as we leave Chichester Rents quite what we've achieved. But one senior lawyer is in no doubt. He stops me and tells me that he's quite certain that what appeared in the papers over the weekend is what kept the convicted out of jail. If that's so, there's a new and very potent media power about.

I'm not going to claim that the media influences the entirely independent minds of the judiciary, far less is able to alter the outcome of a civil or criminal prosecution. What I am going to say is that what happens outside the court in the public eye in the interpretation of the case has grown to match in importance for many plaintiffs and defendants what happens inside it. For those – and there remain territorially possessive lawyers – who claim that the media should be ignored, that there is only one process that matters and that is the process of law in the courtroom, I have two words: the first is 'Jeffrey' and the second is 'Archer'.

Archer won his libel case against the *News of the World* in 1986 over allegations surrounding his undisputed gift of £2000 to prostitute Monica Coghlan. But the half-a-million that Archer – later Lord Archer – won in damages was as nothing to the ultimate cost to Archer imposed by those who watched from outside court. And, whatever the fragrance of Mary Archer inside court, the stench remained on the outside. It was a smell that was going to take 14 years to clear – when, in 2000, media eager for vengeance fell on the revelation of a former Archer friend that he had been asked to lie in the witness box. Archer paid with his London mayoral candidacy, the last vestiges of his reputation and credibility and, finally, his freedom when he was jailed for perjury. Whatever the jury had decided in court in 1986, there was a wider public jury that remained dissatisfied and waited 14 years to be vindicated.

For companies, too, there is a critical balance to be struck between what can be won in a courtroom and what can be lost outside it. The media can turn in a company's favour. When George Michael sued Sony to release him from his recording contract in 1994, the story was originally cast that a brave young artist was taking on the faceless corporation. By the time the case finished, Michael in the media eye was the spoilt and misguided popster who threatened to spoil the nurturing system for aspirant young artists. Or the media can play against the litigant – when McDonald's litigated against two unemployed eco-warriors for distributing the most outrageous libels in leaflets, the penniless 'Helen 'n' Dave' were always going to win more media mileage than McDonald's was going to win justice. Similarly, when British Airways took on Richard Branson's Virgin in what became know as the Dirty Tricks case, BA chairman Lord King self-confessedly underestimated the commercial PR prowess of 'the grinning pullover' in Branson's libel case against the airline in 1992.

Something had changed. The courts were no longer remote and rarefied institutions, handing down judgements unsullied by external influences which might be criticised or applauded, but never challenged by anyone other than lawyers, far less leveraged for commercial purposes. Partly, the change had found its genesis in the political climate of the Eighties. Thatcherism was getting into its anti-establishment stride and, sociologically as much as anything else, the closed-shop of the Law was a target for deregulation. The Law Society, for example, was obliged to introduce market forces in the form of law firms, for the first time, being allowed to market themselves, to advertise and to compete for business.

Another cosy mystique, like that of the City, was disappearing. And, again, like the City, restrictive-practice single capacities were eventually to be abolished. The hegemony of the Bar, with solicitors required to instruct counsel, was to be swept aside with the introduction of solicitor-advocates. With major law firms – such as Freshfields, Clifford Chance and Linklaters – operating on a global scale and increasingly organising their own advocacy, it's difficult to see how the medieval Inns of Court, such as Middle and Inner Temple and Lincoln's Inn, will, under the Bar's stewardship, last long into the new millennium. It is not inconceivable that they will be town-houses for the American investment banks' top executives within a generation.

Developments in the City – the abolition of the floor of the Stock Exchange, globalisation of markets, the delegalisation of insider-trading and the sheer greed of the boom years of the Eighties – brought a sharp media focus on to the performance of the courts. This was driven harder by the incompetence with which alleged insider-dealers were prosecuted. In 1987, I scored something of a scoop by securing the first newspaper interview – albeit a spontaneous one outside a hotel lavatory – with Geoffrey Collier, the former managing director of Morgan Grenfell Securities. Collier had been charged, after a Department of Trade & Industry investigation, with insider-dealing in the American market in the shares of AE Holdings and Cadbury-Schweppes. When eventually his case came to trial at the Old Bailey, he was defended by Bob Alexander QC (later Lord Alexander, chairman of NatWest), who had just taken on the chairmanship of the City's Takeover Panel but gamely saw through Collier's case – while Collier's wife performed a worthwhile impression of Mary Archer in the witness box. At lunch in Mother Bunches, the journos' bar under the old railway arches at Ludgate Circus, I bet a rival reporter £5 that Collier wouldn't serve time. Back in the courtroom, Mr Justice Farquaharson duly informed Collier at the top of his sentencing speech that he wasn't imposing a custodial sentence. Collier visibly sighed with relief and we attracted only an imperious glare from the Clerk of the Court as a fiver was passed along the press bench.

Collier, ruined and disbarred by the Stock Exchange, had probably suffered enough. But the case was typical. Despite considerable political pressure from the Tory Government, the Serious Fraud Office and the DTI could rarely score convictions and, where they did – as in Collier – they couldn't get custodial sentences. Top City traders could afford the best briefs, such as Alexander. Where there were juries, these could be infused with 'reasonable doubt' by highly technical financial evidence and the new laws against insider-dealing were sufficiently vague to make the burden of proof often intolerable.

At one stage in the Eighties, Jeremy Warner, then a reporter with *The Times* and subsequently City editor of the *Independent*, faced a spell in jail over Christmas for declining to reveal his sources for a story of an insider-dealing ring he had uncovered. He was found, as a consequence, to be in contempt of court. We faced the hideous irony of the first person to do porridge under insider-dealing legislation being, not an insider-dealer, but a young journalist who had managed to identify insider-dealing where the authorities had failed. High-profile insider-dealing cases have since disappeared, but one suspects that insider-dealing hasn't. In July 2002, we witnessed the ludicrous spectacle of David Sandy, a lawyer with Simmons & Simmons, touring newspaper offices to serve orders on editors to reveal the source of documentation revealing a possible prospective bid for South African Breweries by Belgian combine Interbrew. Admittedly, Interbrew's case – supported by the Financial Services Authority – was that the documents had been doctored as part of a share-ramp scam. But, nevertheless, the vision of authorities fearlessly prosecuting financial crime by reading the newspapers and taking them to court does nothing to enhance the public image of the Law.

So, the effect of these and other fraud cases – such as the failure of any prosecution in the Maxwell pensions scandal – was to devalue the legal process in its dealings with big business in the eyes of the media. When it came to big business being in the dock or witness box, the media as a consequence became increasingly spinnable. There are other factors. One is the climate of reform in the legal system. The Lord Chief Justice, Lord Woolf, reviewed civil litigation exhaustively during the Nineties and produced Civil Procedure Rules in 1999 that take much of the previously protracted and expensive procedures out of the courtroom and into snappier systems such as Alternative Dispute Resolution (ADR). Reforms that remove the advantage in civil litigation from those with the deepest pockets and most time make for more limpid and faster justice. The role and demand for the media alongside this system is clear. Media enhance the system by testing it and recording it. The further reforming initiatives of Home Secretary David Blunkett announced in 2002, such as the limited abolition of trial by jury, may have similar effects in enhancing the role of media. The appetite for doing so among the media appears sharp and a consequence is the development of 'litigation PR' as a communications practice.

Stephen Lock, who quit a job in one of the major world-wide communications groups to start a litigation PR practice and has subsequently retired to Guadeloupe to write his own book, kindly credited me in the *Independent* with being a founder of this 'profession'. From County NatWest onwards, I record immodestly that there has been some truth in that. And I would conclude by saying that the social climate for this faction of spin-culture is set fair. There will be further reforms to the criminal justice system to come. We have a New Labour Government that seems able to combine legal talent – Tony Blair and Cherie Booth having started legal life in Lord Chancellor Derry Irvine's chambers – with a desire to bring the British legal system into the vanguard of advanced democracies and, of course, a high level of media sensitivity. The media and the Law are embarking on a fruitful and mutually dependent marriage together.

31st August 1997 – We're getting up in a hotel near Laon, just north of Paris. I'm taking a shower, when my wife calls from the bedroom. She's switched on to CNN and there's some talking head with a ticker-tape running under her saying something like 'The Death of Princess Diana'. The children pile in from their rooms and we stare at the television. Then I'm wondering why we're trying to take it in. It happens. I don't recall it seeming so unreal when a friend of mine, someone I knew well, died in a car crash. But this is weird. The view from the veranda, looking down over the swimming pool to the boating lake, where we'd played the previous evening, looks different, from a previous time. And why am I writing like Lynda Lee-Potter? We drive to the coast, picking out what we can on French news; then we're in Kent and the BBC news is on a loop, repeating the details of her death again and again, like some purgative mantra. In the days that follow, we do visit the sea of flowers at Kensington Palace and, yes, we do leave our own little posy. We sign a book of remembrance outside the pub in Dulwich Village. Watching the funeral on TV, my daughter suddenly loses it during the Miserere. I sit in front of her on the floor in an act of solidarity, but also so she can't see that I'm tearful – as I suspect are many of the roughy-toughy journalists who subsequently write pieces about how nauseated they were by all the sentimentality. What's happening to us? What did this woman do to us while we were looking but not noticing? Why, above all, do I feel guilty?

The debate over whether Britain should have a royal family is a fairly vacuous one. The Neo-Roundheads claim that they're an anachronism, a relic from an age of deference that shackles Britain to its class-ridden past rather than letting it embrace its classless future, a constitutional anomaly that still grants a head of state, by virtue only of his or her genes, considerable (if dormant) powers through the royal prerogative and that, in the final analysis, they're rather nasty and stupid. The Neo-Cavaliers claim that they provide constitutional continuity during passing parliamentary fads, that the monarch heads the state from beyond grubby politics, providing Britain with the best of its past as it faces the future, a symbol of British stature, that a president would be a good deal worse and that they do a great deal for social continuity, charity and tourism.

This has never been the stuff of high intellectual debate. The royals are at the slapstick end of politics, precisely because there always seem to be more important things to be done than to have them dragged from the Palace and guillotined. The NHS, the economy, the welfare state and Europe are all issues on which politicians can make progress or regress, be tested on and be found wanting or score some points. On the royal family, politics suddenly become banana-skin and whoops-a-daisy. When Mo Mowlam, a woman who, as Secretary of State for Northern Ireland, could bring together hard-line Unionists and Republicans at Stormont Castle and tactically remove the wig she had to wear after treatment for cancer, casually remarks that the royal family might move out of Buckingham Palace into something more modern, she has to appear on television (at Number 10's instigation) to apologise.

It is precisely because politicians in government become timid and/or obsequious about the royals – there remain too few votes in republicanism – that this kind of hand-wringing deference has survived. During the Eighties, however, in the period following Diana's ill-starred marriage to Prince Charles, the royals turned from being something simply anachronistic to being something altogether parallel to real life. As such, they have, unwittingly as well as consciously, made a considerable contribution to spin-culture.

Their conscious efforts are the least interesting: the television documentaries when they deigned to grant access to suitably deferential crews, from the toe-curling early efforts around barbecues and Christmas trees to the equally stilted and epiglottis-curling apologia for Prince Charles by Jonathan Dimbleby. They employed legions of PR people, from old-style courtiers to those from the more practical world of corporate communications – whether they listened to them is a different matter. Prince Charles has made a major contribution to spin-culture, if spin is to be defined as advocating a position without the backing of substance. In his contributions to issues such as genetically-modified foods, architecture and alternative medicine, he has been described as being like a tennis player who will countenance only one shot – his own ace serve. He is not a debater, but a maker of statements. Where there is no dialectic, there is only spin. The Prince of Wales remains his own spin-doctor.

Simon Lewis's secondment to the Palace from British Gas followed Peter Sanguinetti's mission to the Prince's Trust from the same place. Why BG should have such a commitment to the royal line is something of a mystery, as is what they are able to achieve. The Duke of Edinburgh, with his heritage of casually racist public remarks (*vide:* 'Looks like it's been put in by an Indian' with reference to some shoddy electrical wiring; 'you'll be getting slitty eyes' to expats in the Far East *et al.*) and his dismissive, casual nick-naming of Lewis as 'the gasman', would seem to suggest that he's not listening. In any event, it's probably too late for Prince Philip or his family to be rescued by the image police.

Their unwitting contribution to spin-culture is more interesting. It can be traced to a hot summer's day in July 1983, when the Prince of Wales married Lady Diana Spencer. I lived on the Portobello Road and we had walked into Hyde Park the night before for the fireworks, in much the same place that much the same crowd would gather to weep 15 years later for the televised relay of Diana's funeral. We were at the gates of the Palace when the hapless couple left for honeymoon the following day, helium balloons on the back of their landau. As we dispersed, a dark Mercedes swept out of the Palace, with an elegant female thumbs-up from a back window, later identified as belonging to a Hambro. A dewdrop fell from an old man's nose at the Victoria Monument and hissed on the end of his roll-up. Police officers led an obscene sing-along outside my sister's flat in Hyde Park Gardens.

I recall these things vividly because, as everyone said then and since, it was the start of the fairy-tale. But why anyone should believe that fairy-tales are happy is beyond me. They are full of witches and trolls, wicked kings and queens, curses and spells, ugly sisters and princes turned to frogs. And this fairy-tale was to be no exception. It may not have had a happy ending, but then what fairy-tale does? Unless you call marrying a prince a happy ending. What Diana did to the royal family – with some assistance from Fergie as a walk-on part – was to move it into a cruel fairy-tale dimension and, with the connivance of a press that can spot a good fairy-tale when it sees one, blur the edges between reality and unreality. With Diana's amateurish manipulation of the tabloids, this was where spin-culture met Dynasty.

The kindest interpretation of the tears of the millions that had never met her when she died is the sudden and truly tragic realisation that here was a real young woman, whose life had been destroyed by real people who had used and abused her, not some character played by Stephanie Powers in a pot-boiler. And we had shared voyeuristically in her doomed journey, through the pay-per-view red-tops. While we had watched the drama played out for entertainment, as a thousand press sentimentalists had recorded in and at her wake, no one had reached out to the real woman in the real story. Now she was dead in a Paris underpass. And we were sorry. Please forgive us.

The unkinder interpretation is that we had lost the capacity for distinguishing between the real and the unreal story – as Diana may have done herself. This requires that the outpouring of national grief was an ersatz emotion, in the truest sense sentimental, a substitute for real emotion. We had become bit-players in the soap ourselves, so that the tears and the sea of flowers provided an out-of-body experience, a chance to cast and see ourselves in the movie. This is the view that, extended, means that when there is a real disaster, such as a plane crash, or a real human tragedy, such as a child's abduction and murder, we have lost any notion of a real response and indulge in the formulaic cards with 'Why?' written on them and the catharsis of a mild and manageable mass hysteria. The grotesque possibility emerges that we enjoy ourselves a little too much.

Either way, royalty is probably where the demarcations between reality and unreality became most blurred in British society. The media have helped, but it is the Queen's subjects that have gone along with it, or even demanded it of the papers that they have read and the television they have watched. Nowhere other than in royal circles is it more appropriate to apply the damning verdict 'it's all spin'. If you're a Neo-Cavalier, or a disinterested observer who wants to test the validity of that verdict, ask 'what is the royal family for?' and see how quickly the conversation degenerates into the abstruse, the emotional, the sentimental and the insubstantial. Arguments both for and against the royals are antitheses of substance. And without a tangible thesis from either side, there can be no substantial synthesis. Again, as we're fond of saying: It's all spin.

Further evidence was the Queen Mother's centenary in 2000 (put aside the response to her death two years later, which precipitated heartfelt national mourning). Again, we entered a parallel dimension, where truth is a bendy thing. It was widely reported that she hadn't given an interview since a bad experience with the media before her wedding in 1923. Then we saw her on our screens, sitting on a chaise longue and answering questions in the (and her) Seventies. Whatever the qualities of this venerable lady, the media never sought to identify them beyond a general, gushing emotion about what is 'glorious' and 'majestic' about her. She was inspirational during the Blitz in the Second World War and that, apparently, was more than enough to secure her for the nation as a treasure into the new millennium and beyond. Yet Winston Churchill arguably did as much for the war effort as the King's wife and he was kicked out of office in 1945. The position of Queen Mum was something quite different and inviolable. But quite what it was was indefinable. Had it not become such a pejorative term, even the Neo-Cavaliers might have agreed that it was all spin.

A telling moment in the summer of 2000 was when *The Sunday Times* ran its special supplement on 'A Hundred Glorious Years'. Across the first double-page spread ('Magnificently, Majestically Mum') there were three appreciative rag-outs from people of consequence. Who were these statesmanlike commentators? Previous Prime Ministers? Archbishops? Foreign royalty? Ambassadors? No, they were Tim Bell, Max Clifford and Bernard Ingham. The courtiers chosen by *The Sunday Times* for the Queen Mum's birthday were PR men, spin-doctors and publicists. No wonder she was said to have been jealous of the media attention that Diana had commanded.

June 2002 – The Queen's Golden Jubilee. I take my sons up to Fleet Street and the youngest, Charlie, sits on my shoulders and waves his flag as the golden state-coach passes. A number of things stick in my mind long after this Bank Holiday is over. Such as compere Ben Elton, at the pop concert in Buckingham Palace's gardens, asking self-reverentially whether his gags are 'a bit close to the edge'. And a float passes the Royal Family's podium at the endless parade in the Mall with huge cut-outs of iconic figures of the past 50 years, such as Wimbledon-winner Virginia Wade. One of these figures is Princess Diana. Have we really become so inured to the feelings of royals, because we don't believe them to be real people, that we parade a huge celebrity effigy of their dead mother past two teenage boys and their father? But the most revealing aspect of the entire celebrations is the behaviour – and the response to it – of the monarch herself. I am convinced afterwards that she had set this Jubilee as some sort of target, after which everything else is a bonus. She visibly relaxes and looks human. Prince Charles begins his speech on stage at the concert 'Your Majesty ... Mummy ...' She may not be dropping the royal prerogative, but she is dropping the royal pretence. The most enduring image of this is when, at midnight, she rides down the Mall and, with a flaming torch, fires a rocket at her own palace, which explodes. It's only fireworks, but she has a huge grin on her face, as if blowing up Buckingham Palace has been a long-cherished ambition.

The Golden Jubilee may well serve in future history lessons as the marker of the end of an era. Not that the Queen showed any sign during it of abdicating or slowing down. Eventually, her own demise will mark the most striking end of an era. The royal succession, whoever it is, cannot and does not hope to maintain the trappings of imperial majesty and Britain's unwritten constitution will find a default position in some more informal version of monarchy. But the Jubilee of 2002 nevertheless marked the end of pretence, a closure on the phoney monarchy and a celebration of its passing. That was the atmosphere – not so much a celebration of the past 50 years, with its ghastly fashions, decline of empire and many an *annus horribilis*, but a celebration of their passing.

The key importance of the human face of the Queen – and that of her family – at the Jubilee was that it marked the passing of performance as a royal obligation. The Queen started her reign in that black-and-white time, in an austerity born of a world war in which Britain and its empire and dominions had triumphed – through duty and deference and unquestionable authority. That reign developed through the colourful social liberations of the second half of the twentieth century, with the monarch still required to present the impassive face of someone remote, ethereal and mysterious. Latterly, that act sat more than awkwardly with the fairy-tales and soap-operas of the new-generation royals and their chosen spouses – fairy-tales and soap-operas, most obviously incarnate in the sorry lie-story of Diana, that were no more part of real-life in millennial Britain than the old imperious and remote act.

Now, at the 50-year mark, there was an opportunity to say goodbye to all that and the Queen looked like she was doing so. Goodbye to the protocol that meant she couldn't embrace her young son in public when they were reunited after months of a royal tour. Goodbye to the pretence that they were some kind of different species by virtue of royal genes and goodbye to having to maintain that pretence while their progeny behaved like spoilt Sloanes – not unnaturally, because that's what they were. The penny – or perhaps golden sovereign – dropped at the Jubilee: The royals, under the Queen, weren't adopting the modern spin-culture, they were giving theirs up. The Royal Family has existed in a bubble, with its own spin-culture, for as long as the Queen has known it. For years, they have been subject to that spin-culture, the fabric of which has been the spell of deceits and fabrications that has supported the image that they are in some way separate from the world, occupying their own sphere of monarchical authority. It was a mystique that the late Princess Margaret struggled to equate to modern living – the mystique of Mustique. But there could be a fresh start, free from these peculiarly royal spin-cultures.

The strain must have been enormous. And the parallel universe in which they have been confined has not served their subjects well either – it is not satisfactory to have a head of state and her heir separated from the harsh realities of the end of the twentieth century and of the start of the twenty-first. The Prince of Wales visited St Bride's, the journalists' church in Fleet Street, in March 2002 to deliver a speech to newspaper proprietors, editors and worthies, including Rupert Murdoch. The gist was that newspapers have the opportunity to report what is good in life, in public services and in national achievement, but squander that opportunity in favour of criticism, cynicism and coverage of what is widely known as bad news. After a lifetime under the lens of the world media, with possibly more experience of handling them than anyone else in British public life, Prince Charles still didn't understand. That's what newspapers do. It's their job. It's why people buy them. This other-worldliness can only be the result of the royals' separation from society, supported by their own spin-culture in which a mostly adoring public have conspired. Without the usual means of navigation through the pressures and idiosyncrasies of life, they have understandably from time to time lost their bearings. One can only feel for them. But if he is willing to do so, the heir to the throne is not too old to learn to live outside the spin-culture of his own peculiar life.

May 1998 – It's just after 7 pm and I'm in the dark womb of an ITN studio on Gray's Inn Road for Channel 4 News, struggling to spot a monitor through the hardware and cables. I'm on to talk about debt forgiveness for the Third World, ahead of the G8 meeting of economic leaders at Birmingham. On my right is Dr Vincent Magombe, an intensely generous-spirited man who runs Africa Information International in London. He has been painstakingly patient in explaining the urgency of debt relief to me in the Green Room and I can tell that he's grown used to glaze-eyed western suits like me. In the past fortnight I've become an easy airtime filler on this issue as, apparently, the only person, bar Clare Short, who doesn't believe that whole-sale debt forgiveness for the Third World is necessarily a good thing. I have recorded this view in a column I write for Marketing Week, *a shrine of capitalist enterprise. I haven't quite been spat at in the street, but the view makes me something of a pariah in liberal circles. It's one of those issues you don't argue about, like whether Spike Milligan was really funny. So broadcasters seem grateful for someone who will – last week it was with the redoubtable former Bishop of Birmingham, Hugh Montefiore, on BBC's* Business Breakfast, *but since we were only allowed a couple of soundbites each battle was hardly joined. The news-magazine style of Channel 4 is giving it altogether more space and, with some effort, I spot the package that's running ahead of the studio discussion. There are the most harrowing shots from Niger of the starving which, whatever the nature of the report that's going with them, will be cast in the public eye as a direct result of western debt. I know I've not been deliberately set up, but I'm bound to look like the monster who's come to defend that situation. Christ, I advise multi-nationals on how to deal with circumstances such as this and I'm completely unprepared for a change of position – this cobbler's child is barefoot. Jon Snow turns to me and I manage something about 'crimes against humanity' and the importance of selectivity in debt relief. Africa wins this little spat with western capitalism. Snow, Magombe and I part amiably enough on the pavement outside. At home, my local Church is distributing cards to sign, by way of lobbying the Chancellor to push for debt relief to save the starving of the world.*

The issue of Third World debt is worth examining here, because whatever the merits of the arguments of those concerned with it, it also represents the degree to which Britain's Christian churches have been drawn into, and participated in, the development of spin-culture. It is also an issue that Tony Blair can ill-afford to leave to his Chancellor, having committed himself to the pursuit of a solution to the African problem at the Labour conference immediately following the 11th September atrocities. The argument to date, developed by a lobby group called Jubilee 2000 and supported by Christian Aid, has been that lesser-developed economies, particularly those of sub-Saharan Africa, were drawn into western industrial exploitation as a consequence of the explosive development of oil production in the Seventies (too much cash was chasing too little investment opportunity).

The Third World was consequently saddled with western debts which, subsequent experience demonstrates, are impossible to repay. It is further claimed that this situation has developed into an economic repression that may not be overtly as barbaric as the slave trade, but is certainly up there as a crime against humanity. As I hurriedly conceded on Channel 4, television pictures of starving people must constitute proof that a crime against humanity has been committed by someone – the question should be, by whom? The politically correct answer to that is western lenders, but my argument would be that this assumption has to be tested, not for the selfish interests of the west, but for the sakes of the starving peoples of the sub-Sahara too.

Only a few extreme radicals would claim that the western loans of the Seventies were cynically granted with deliberate repression in mind – though I have met Christians who have argued that the very principle of charging interest is anathema. They would have it that interest is usury. I think this takes us down a very dark road – when Christians start to talk of the evils of money-lending, anti-Semitism may not be far behind, whether they mean it or not. But the fundamentalist wings of Christianity should not be allowed to contaminate the views of Christian liberals. Their consensus, so far as I can identify one, is that world economic circumstances over the past 20 years have conspired to make investments in the Third World a burden rather than a benefit to the economies to which they were applied.

While gross domestic product (GDP) per capita has typically doubled in developed economies such as the UK over the past two decades, according to the International Monetary Fund GDP has halved in Kenya and in similar economies, partly because of the collapse in the price of commodities. There are fantastically persuasive statistics from the debt-relief activists: The 63 poorest countries in the world, for instance, pay some $80 million every day servicing their debts, which is calculated to be the equivalent of enough healthcare for a year for 5 million people. The bottom line is that continually rescheduled Third World debt drives the poorest countries of the world further into penury, while the developed economies prosper like never before. It follows that we can easily afford to consider such debt a gift from the rich to the poor of the world. This conclusion comes not only with sound, practical Christian credentials but is also broadly millenarian in the secular sense of a new start.

But the issue that should be raised, to satisfy even the most basic dialectical test, is whether wholesale write-offs of debt is the way to relieve human suffering in Africa. Because if it is not, then the exercise will resemble a macro-version of the kind of western self-flagellation and guilt-relief that was Bob Geldof's Band Aid exercise in the Eighties. The drumming up of public hysteria in the past 20 years has produced the sort of sentimentality that not only delivers a sea of flowers in Kensington Gardens and sobbing in Hyde Park for Diana, but also brightly-coloured Band Aid lorries up to their axles in sand, their goods being looted by Sudanese soldiers.

A solution for Africa is not to be found in western financial aid – and debt-relief is another form of aid – but in politics. The Sudan, for example, from which some of the most heart-breaking television footage has emerged, is wracked by long-term civil war. And there is one straightforward reason why hundreds of thousands of people are starving to death in the south of that country: the north wants them to.

Sudanese history shows that when western colonialists arbitrarily carved up northeast Africa in the nineteenth century (for which Britain must accept its share of shame), northern Sudan was left with sovereignty over a southern Sudan, whose peoples were essentially a mixture of east African tribes. As a result they had Sharia law imposed upon them and were considered sub-human slaves. As one twentieth-century consequence, relief aid has had a job on its hands getting past Khartoum.

Agricultural land in northern Sudan is called the Bread Basket of Africa, so fertile is its Black Cotton soil. The awful truth is that the Sudan could feed its own people with ease. But it grows cotton instead as a cash-crop for export. When it does grow sorghum, a maize-like grain, it exports it for further cash from Saudi Arabia and elsewhere. This gives rise to the sort of grotesque situation of the past decade, when imported grain from the likes of Band Aid was being matched by exported grain from the domestic market.

Furthermore, one of the causes of the Sudanese civil war was the southern rebels' understandable fear that an oil pipeline from El Muglad to Port Sudan would be used to enrich the north at the terrible expense of the south. Oil companies, such as Chevron, had to give up on the development in frustration, which in terms of averting further bloodshed may have been a good thing.

The Sudan did not feature in *Forever In Your Debt?*, Christian Aid's tract on behalf of the eight poorest nations on earth, which it called P8, in order to lobby eight of the richest in the shape of G8. But the Sudan's political barbarity and corruption is replicated in many countries within the developing world. Within the P8 list, Ethiopia is recovering from the ravages of the Mengistu regime, of which Pol Pot would have been proud; Bolivia has a dubious record on corruption and Jamaica has one of the most disgusting penal systems on earth. Even relatively benign and reformist regimes, such as that of the late Julius Nyere in Tanzania, have not created economic systems capable of managing any form of advanced financial structure.

Against this background, those most likely to benefit from wholesale national-debt forgiveness by the west are the oppressors, rather than the oppressed, of the Third World. With their bullet-proof Mercedes and motor-cycle outriders, the tin-pot dictators, gun-runners and drug-dealers of Africa have been dubbed the M'benzi tribe by aid-workers and those who can still manage satire under the boot of those who funnel Africa's potential wealth into their own pockets and Swiss bank accounts. It is these ogres who will welcome debt-forgiveness above all others, not those who starve at their hands, for whom bank loans are the remotest of concepts, way off on the other side of the barriers to humanity erected by their oppressors.

The trouble with raising these issues is twofold. Firstly, one is accused of drafting a charter for capitalist complacency, for doing nothing in the face of appalling suffering. Secondly, it is interpreted as a kick in the teeth for Christian Aid, whose efforts to reach out to the world's poor is a heroic demonstration, in contrast to widespread apathy, of the messianic faith from which it arose.

Both accusations may contain more than a grain of truth, particularly the accusation of western complacency. But complacency isn't an argument for 'doing something, anything', especially where the something is in the best interests of evildoers and, consequently, the status quo. Yet throughout Britain, Sunday School children produce presentations for how the world's poor will miraculously be fed if only we release what passes for their governments from the yoke of the evil western bankers' debts – and the congregation signs cards to petition our Government to see to it.

Anyone with access to a moral framework, Christian or otherwise, must agree that to do nothing about starving humans is an evil. Just as evil triumphs over Kosovans, Albanians and Kurds where the good people of the United Nations do nothing. But the long-term solutions are about politics, as well as remedial charity. They are real politics that intervene where there is human suffering and where there is no political imperative beyond that suffering being wrong, and doing nothing about it being even more wrong. They are the kind of real politics that inspired foreign secretary Robin Cook's post-election commitment to an 'ethical foreign policy' before the realpolitik pressures obliged him to differentiate between human suffering in Indonesia, Serbia and Chechnya. Blair reiterated the issue at his first party conference, speaking of Africa as a stain on the conscience of the developed world. If politics are to mean anything in these circumstances, they are about applying pressure to brutal regimes to improve the lot of the people at the mercy of such regimes. They do not require that the effort be confined to well-meaning charity workers putting pieces of silver in Christian Aid envelopes and signing cards supporting debt write-offs.

In this regard, the Christian churches have made a considerable contribution to spin-culture. There can be little more tangible example of the substitution of substance with style, of action with gesture and of dialectic with vacuity than the churches' responses to human suffering with their campaign for Third World debt relief. To repeat: The practical responses of Christians themselves, individually or collectively, are invariably beyond reproach. To quit preaching at home to comfort and to heal and to relieve in the front line of starvation or Aids infestation is thankless this side of heaven and revelatory of the divine servant-humility that is the Christian faith's inspiration. But to adopt an unthinking, Pavlovian response is an affront to that professed faith, more about appearance than reality, about salving guilt than about salvation.

This is why politics should not be kept out of the Church any more than the Church should be kept out of politics. They operate in the same fields of human welfare, suffering and fulfilment. The currency of politics is life before death (interestingly, however, also Christian Aid's catchline) and that of religions tends to be life after it; but there remains a symbiotic relationship between the two arenas of human endeavour. Christianity has historically abandoned the notion that eternal life is earned by actions during mortal life, in favour of faith in the grace of God, but the promise of His eternal kingdom still informs humanity with the divine in practical ways, if we are not to be as entirely otherworldly as a bunch of hermit monks.

This must mean seeking to alter the human condition where it affronts our glimpses of divine purpose, however these are interpreted. There have been some astounding examples of this endeavour over the past 20 years despite and possibly because of the visibility of declining church membership. The death of Mother Theresa of Calcutta in 1997, so soon after the events surrounding the demise of Diana, Princess of Wales, focused the world's attention on how serving the dispossessed in apparent humility can exert political influence. How else to explain world leaders falling over themselves to pay homage? Less theatrically, perhaps, the erstwhile Bishop of Liverpool, David Sheppard, found he could exercise a considerable political power without apparently compromising his churchmanship by standing up to the remorseless materialism of Thatcherism in the Eighties with tracts such as *Faith in the City*.

Elsewhere, the Church was rapidly becoming a monument to spin-culture, if the triumph of style over substance was anything to go by. This is the more remarkable because of what the Christian Church is offering. There could be a competition for encapsulating this offer in as few words as possible, but it is as simple as this: There is a God, who loves humanity unconditionally and to prove it became incarnate in Jesus Christ, who expiated human sin through his death and offers eternal life through his resurrection. That sure beats the latest mobile-phone special offer or equity-linked savings plan. As Blaise Pascal had it, this is either the most important thing that ever has been and ever will be, or the greatest con-trick perpetrated on a gullible humanity. Either way, in media terms, it's a great story. True or not, you can't ignore it.

The trouble starts when it is marketed. Here is The Gospel – literally 'the good news'. Through Christ, Christians believe, you can know God and have eternal life. That is news that is so good that even the BBC's Martyn Lewis, self-appointed arbiter of good news, would approve. This is about a personal relationship with God, one through which he will reveal to you His purpose for you and through which that purpose will be fulfilled. It is unlikely that you will want to keep this divine revelation to yourself, so if you so wish you can go to church to share it and celebrate it with others. This would, at first sight, seem to be beyond the reach of marketing, with its brand management and sales gimmicks.

If only. Spin-culture knows no bounds and turns up in religion as it does in politics. I'll offer two examples. The first relates to the Alpha course that emanated from Holy Trinity, Brompton (HTB for short), in the late Eighties, under the driving force of a charismatic preacher called Nicky Gumbel. The Alpha programme is an introductory, beginners' course in Christianity and has done incredible – some might say miraculous – work in stemming the decline in church numbers by providing an accessible, user-friendly guide to Christian faith and the salvation it offers. In itself, Alpha is a sound and simple guide to Christianity and in gentle, exploratory hands it is of enormous benefit and interest to church-newcomers. An accurate guidebook to the Christian faith could hardly be dangerous in itself. The same cannot always be said of the hands that hold it. It's never the gun, it's the gunner.

The problem with Alpha is precisely that it emerges through the cultural reredos of HTB, which being in Knightsbridge and an unravelled turban's length from Harrod's, attracted the post-Eighties, post-conspicuous-consumption Sloanes, celebrities and City professionals disillusioned with shallow materialism. Nothing wrong with that – God must have a plan for them too. Where it forms less of a tenet of faith than a pillar of the spin-culture is when its apostles disperse from Knightsbridge to spread the word with evangelical fervour.

Bright-eyed and shiny, they will appear in a church near you offering Christianity as a mountebank cure-all. Just take one Christ and everything will be all right. At one level, this is in the apostolic tradition. It is certainly evangelical. But its weakness is in selling Christianity as a package-tour, or as a club. In joining the club, you join Christ and in joining Christ you join God. But, if it is all to mean anything, in joining God you give up clubs. In the context of eternity, the only club is a humanity from all time united in the divine. As one of the greatest Archbishops of Canterbury, William Temple, put it, the Church is the only organisation that exists exclusively for the benefit of its non-members. What HTB and Alpha sell, in common with much of the evangelical Church, is not so much access to faith as a lifestyle choice. Never has a point so comprehensively been missed. And never, outside politics, has spin-culture enjoyed such a success. Nearly four million people around the world had done an Alpha course between its inception in 1993 and 2001. Yet overall church attendance continues to fall. The question that is seldom raised is whether these two factors are in any way related. Is it just possible that HTB-style Alpha, with its away-weekend in the Midlands where course-members are invited to greet the Holy Spirit in circumstances that border on mass hysteria, repels those for whom the most evident and visible acts of evangelism in the Christian church appear to embrace cultism and psychological abandonment? You can recruit huge numbers to a sect, but it remains a sect.

My second example demonstrates the evangelical Church's confusion between advertising and PR, which further feeds the vacuity of spin-culture. The Churches Advertising Network (CAN) in the late Nineties represented the mainstream Christian Churches in the UK with poster campaigns aimed at delivering the gospel message as though it was a brand of lager. Thus the Virgin Mary ahead of Christmas was zanily cast as having a 'bad hair day' because she was giving birth to the Messiah in a stable with oriental kings in attendance. For the Easter of 1999, CAN launched posters that featured Christ in a pastiche of the iconic Che Guevara student posters of the late Sixties. The crown of thorns replaced the beret and the catchline read: 'Meek. Mild. As if. Discover the real Jesus. Church. April 4.'

Predictably enough, the treatment led to howls of protest. Christians claimed it was unfair to Christ who, as God incarnate, is somewhat above politics. As for politics, the CAN offended the entire spectrum. The Tories' Christian voice, Ann Widdecombe – no stranger to the media; witness her invitation to the media to attend her conversion to Rome – remarked thoughtfully that we shouldn't be modelling Christ on ourselves, so much as ourselves on Christ, while unreconstructed Marxists remarked that it was all a bit unfair on Che. Widdecombe is considerably more serious a politician than spin-culture allows. Her views on the illiberalism of New Labour – on issues such as the abolition of trial by jury, for example – are often lost in the ridicule that spin-culture generates as a substitute for dialectics. But, in intuitively pursuing a theological point, she missed the more prosaic commercial one. Was this an advertising or a public relations campaign? If it was the former, then it was about a sales effort (bums on pews) and experience shows that it was a failure. If it was a PR issue, then it was (or should have been) about managing the Christian issue, which is a theological aim. On this count it would have failed too, because it focused attention on the outrage of the image, rather than the revolutionary content of its message.

If marketing is about identifying and satisfying a demand in the market, then its communications can be identified as being about creating the demand. The CAN didn't appear to know what it was doing beyond making a noise, which is a characteristic failure of spin-culture. The CAN efforts on behalf of the Christian Churches was about opportunities to see (as marketers rate poster-campaign effectiveness) rather than having anything to say. Which in terms of the potential import of the Christian message must count as another of the greatest communications-missed opportunities of all time. In any event, the CAN proved all too mortal and faded away. It was not ever thus. The apostles, albeit closer to the event of the resurrection but without recourse to modern communication beyond the spoken and written word and with little concept of image, spread the gospel throughout the Hellenic and Roman world and converted the emperor Constantine early in the fourth century. In those days you could get thrown to lions for your evangelism. In a spin-culture two millennia later, the potency of Truth is subsumed beneath image, style and effect. The result, for far too many who explore the nature of their faith, is that those who appear to be in charge of its propagation are, as one 13-year-old put it in research for this book, 'cheesy'. In seeking to make Christianity more exciting, perversely its new evangelists make it more boring. The result is that the Church is failing to communicate with the most potent of messages. In spin-culture it falls victim, as has politics, to the desire to be admired and seen rather than heard. And the Church doesn't see that. But for Christ's sake it had better start looking.

ISSUES

Abandon Your Positions

The search may be on for a new dialectical substance to fill the vortex that has drawn the trivial and inane into it. Tony Blair conceded as much before select-committee chairs in July 2002, indicating that there were three issues on which his Government was committed to make substantive progress – transport, pensions and housing:

> 'I think there are three issues ... on which I think there is a lot of long-term thinking ... One is transport, one is pensions, one is housing. I think in all three of these areas it would be better if we were able to have some cross-party consensus that would survive individual governments in dealing with them because they are really tough long-term issues. The political pain for any government dealing with them in my view is enormous, whatever government is in power. I do not have the exact answer or solution to this but I do think they are areas where it is worth in some way trying to establish some broader political consensus.'

This indicates that, again, politics is following business management techniques – in this instance, adopting the disciplines of issues identification and management. Issues management is a communications discipline, specifically identifying the issues that threaten prosperity and reputation and devising communications solutions for them. To trace the development of this management resource from the early stages of PR-style communications we need again to take a step back to trace developments in communications. I want to start in the Fifties with a political instance, because it best demonstrates where the idea of issues management emerged.

Close behind 'You've never had it so good' as Harold Macmillan's most famous aphorism comes 'Events, dear boy – events'. The latter has been cheated of first place in the lexicon of Macmillan clichés because – as with many of the greatest quotations – Macmillan never said the former. What he did say, in a speech in Bedford reported in *The Times* in 1957, was 'Let us be frank about it; most of our people have never had it so good', but that was altogether less catchy. It is reminiscent of Nicholas Ridley's comment at water privatisation, 'They can drink Perrier', being translated into the altogether more Antoinettesque 'Let them drink Perrier'. Incidentally, 'You Never Had It So Good' had been the Democratic Party's campaign slogan during the 1952 US elections, which shows that nicking campaign techniques from the States is far from a new phenomenon. It's as well to remember too that our great national newspapers' capacity for spinning a line is far from a modern phenomenon.

'Events' was said in reply to a questioner asking what was his biggest problem. That, anyway, is one attribution. Macmillan had a fatalistic view of the fickleness of fate and the futility of mortal attempts to control divine chaos. At the height of the Suez crisis, he sought to soothe a fretful permanent secretary by asking him if he knew what made God laugh. He didn't. 'People making plans,' explained Macmillan. It's pointless to judge previous generations by subsequent standards, but, compared with the events for which today's politicians have to plan, we know now that Macmillan, at least in terms of mass communications, never had it so good nearly half a century ago. A still largely obedient press, a respectful BBC and enough time during the prime-ministerial working day to enjoy a glass or two with colleagues and advisers out of sight and beyond scrutiny – all this still echoed the deferential Edwardian age in which Macmillan grew up. Accountability to Parliament may have waned latterly. But accountability to regulators and the legislature, the transparency of business dealings, whether in the public or private sector, and the demands of 24-hour media with a degree of access that would have been vulgarly intrusive to our political predecessors bear testament to 'events' being an infinitely greater problem to the modern politician than they were to Macmillan's generation.

Macmillan's tenure at Number 10 ran into the Sixties, but wasn't of the Sixties. It is a matter of continuing occasional debate the degree to which dissemblance over the affair of his war minister, John Profumo, with Christine Keeler holed Macmillan's administration below the water-line. Anthony Sampson quotes Macmillan as saying of Keeler and her friend Mandy Rice-Davies 'I was determined that no British government should be brought down by the action of two tarts'. But the aristocratic Macmillan and his patrician successor Sir Alec Douglas-Home were giving way to the dawn of an egalitarian and progressive age of Harold Wilson. Contraceptive pills, hallucinogenics, the Beatles, comprehensive education and the white heat of the technological revolution (a popular misquote of Harold Wilson) had arrived. With free love, flower power, the white heat of technology and the storming of the establishment came the assumption that government information was of the people and for the people. The alternative as well as the establishment press proliferated – both *Private Eye* and *The Sunday Times* were born in the Sixties. The Canadian communications guru Marshall McLuhan declared in 1964 that 'the medium is the message'. The mass-media were a market in which the commodity traded was information.

As with any free market, it attracted its brokers and agents. By the late Sixties, the press agent was a common accoutrement for the successful. The independent press agent was about message delivery, a simple agency role between client and media – the mechanism through which press statements reached their media, through which the target audience itself was eventually reached. This was also how the dissemination of government information worked. As the market for information grew more sophisticated – as the derivatives market was developed, as it were – the press agent evolved into the introducer/networker, the charm and self-confidence of the ex-Army officer suiting the role nicely. By the Seventies, the roles were fragmenting into specialisms.

Financial reporting in the stock market developed its own City practice with pioneering City editors such as Patrick Sergeant of the *Daily Mail* and Patrick Hutber of the *Sunday Telegraph*. The great corporate communications consultancies that grew out of the US – Burson-Marsteller and Hill & Knowlton – developed the business of long-term corporate reputation management. The great national and global brands were to demand the same service from consumer agencies. And, of course, political lobbyists were developing parliamentary and public affairs practices, taking those 'events' to the government machine, endeavouring to bring some self-interested order and management to the inheritors of Macmillan's semi-ordered chaos.

The mistake is in thinking that this developmental process of communications disciplines has a natural or forced conclusion. It has its watersheds – the 1987 meltdown in global equities markets brought temporarily straitened times to the financial PR industry – but it is a continual development of evolution, a survival of the fittest so long as there are communications channels to be managed. These channels, for the four decades since Macmillan identified his problem, have offered a means by which 'events' can be managed. In the Macmillan sense, communicators have been, for half a century, in the business of events management.

This is, however, an unsatisfactory term for modern communications management, although entirely appropriate for the organisation of corporate entertainment. The management of 'events', in Macmillan's sense, is what communications management had become by the mid-Eighties. Whether it was the management of a privatisation share-issue, a contested takeover bid, a general election campaign, an environmental initiative or a reference to a regulator such as the Monopolies & Mergers Commission (now the Competition Commission), communications management had become the management of complex events. It became increasingly inappropriate to demarcate the communications specialisms in this management process. Without indulging in organograms, in the argot of the management consultant who prospered during this period, the development of discrete communications functions post-Seventies (when the fragmentation of specialist functions had its genesis) goes like this: The early stages show demarcated communications functions, addressing particular audiences through specific media – and deploying specialist communicators to do so. This model was to serve PR groups well in the Eighties – and, from 1990, when Tim Bell and his colleagues bought out Lowe-Bell Communications (now Bell Pottinger, part of the publicly-listed Chime Communications group) from Lowe Howard-Spink and Bell – as they charged separate budgets for financial, corporate and public affairs communications.

It became increasingly apparent even to the most profligate client and the most departmentalised communications group that there were both synergies and economies of scale to be struck in merging compatible and complementary communications functions. The mergers most likely initially to occur were between financial and corporate communications and between parliamentary and public affairs. The development of common cause in communications continued until the skills within communications functions, whether in-house or consultancy, began to look holistic from where the client was sitting. Since communications solutions of all disciplines were now being provided from within a single resource, focus began to switch from the specialist natures of the communications function themselves to the nature of the communications challenge itself. The process of message delivery to an audience became the management of the audience itself.

At one level, this is perhaps the most significant contribution of professional communications to spin-culture. One person's management of an audience is another's manipulation. Done in a heavy-handed manner in the political or corporate spheres, voters or shareholders are going to resent such prescription of thought and action. At another level, the communications function was becoming significantly more sophisticated, because the focus was no longer on the communications function itself as a means of message delivery, but on the nature of the issues themselves – financial, corporate, political, environmental, whatever. Significantly, this would often reverse the established directions of information flow.

Message delivery depended on information generated passing through relevant media to an identified audience of choice. The model more recently under development required an understanding of issues affecting target audiences and the identification of communications solutions that could appropriately be brought to bear. In the Eighties, this generated explosive growth in quantitative and qualitative research resources, as communicators sought more to understand the audiences they were addressing – this was to take on a political dimension with the research of potential shareholders for privatisation issues. More recently in politics, the emergence of the focus group for more accurate definition of vote-winning policy is a symptom of the same reversal of the communications flow – or, more accurately, the dual-carriageway of issues management, compared with the historical one-way street of message delivery.

Issues management had appeared on agencies' service rosters before its development in the Nineties, but only as a somewhat hubristic attempt to cover the services waterfront – the one-stop shop was the promised land for marketing services groups on the acquisitions trail and nothing was to be left out. If there was a function defined, it was stuck in the brochure, alongside design and direct mail. Issues management was a professional service and this was the professional services industry – so in it went. Only very rarely was issues management identified as an entire professional service in its own right, a management discipline from which all other communications functions could be deployed as appropriate. This was a radical thought to emerge in the early Nineties – that possibly the communications functions could be subordinated to the identification and analysis of issues that offered the potential to enhance or undermine corporate or political reputation or prosperity. If the growth of professional communications functions was and is organic and progressive, then it followed that the coalescence of communications specialisms and the two-way traffic of information in the process of issues management wasn't an end in itself, but suggested a further progression. The natural evolutionary process was pointing to the relatively radical notion that the process would not ultimately be between communicator and audience, but between the audience and the constituent parts of the issue itself. The communicator – the corporate client or political party – could stand outside the matrix of communications flows and achieve strategic aims by managing the issue. Communications had become a management function. Again, this generates claims for the communications function, or PR, taking its place at the boardroom table – we have seen already that this claim is founded on a mistaken premise.

Media have developed to match the communications models that they represent. The early, fragmented audiences and discrete communications functions that reached them were served by the emergence of specialist trade and professional publications – Michael Heseltine founded his fortune on this industrial development in the Seventies with his magazine enterprise Haymarket Publishing. More recently, the granular development of communication, in which the communications resource is the constituent part of the target market itself with the identified issue managed by interested parties, is served most effectively by the internet, more of which later.

If the issue, rather than the medium, became the message in the Nineties, it took a while for those in the business of communication to catch on. The political stage, during the wilderness years of John Major's grey premiership, was being prepared by the architects of New Labour, who were working around what turned out to be the caretaker leadership of John Smith towards a system of policy-making that replaced the ideology and dogma of the Thatcher years with an identification of what British voters wanted – or what issues they wanted managed on their behalf. This was the system on which the focus group, subsequently much derided when Labour won power, was established.

The tide was turning among commercial communication professionals, with a new holism demanded in corporate and public affairs, but the shift towards an integrated application of communications disciplines, as previously described, was a slow one. This was partly because traditionally established PR firms had grown accustomed to taking several fees for allegedly separate communications functions. Their shareholders had grown accustomed to them doing so too – there can be no doubt that the PR industry underwent some years from the fall of Thatcher in a state of denial that there wasn't some mystical or technical difference between communications in Westminster, the City or anywhere else. The progress towards communications holism was also hampered by the uncomfortable but increasingly apparent fact that a great many, if not most, communications professionals were not very good at communication. There was still a legacy of the booming Eighties that those who could, did – and those who couldn't went into communications.

The simple reductionism that had adequately served the political and corporate climate of the Eighties was unlikely to be replaced widely by more sophisticated models of issues management until communications resources had matured. For most of two decades, complex issues – such as the levels and nature of government policy on the earning power of corporations – had been understood in the limiting analysis of their constituent parts. It would take a while for holism to emerge in communications practice – and for some of the dimmer communications practitioners to realise and accept that there was a critical relationship between their clients' spheres of influence.

A kinder interpretation was that professional communications needed time to evolve. The *modus operandi* of those engaged in financial communications may have differed significantly from those applying public affairs programmes. The conditional tense is significant – the differences between communications functions were largely exaggerated by instincts of self-protection and territorial sensitivities. Evolution is still required where genetic differences are trivial, but where social and behavioural character-istics are nevertheless entrenched. As significant was the evolution in communications practice required of those on whose behalf communications were being conducted. Corporate clients of those engaged in PR had long established separate relationships for communications functions, with diverse reporting structures and fragmented budgets – it would be a long and arduous task to consolidate both the discrete strategic thinking and the systemic separations of those who paid for communications.

Meanwhile, the development of communications practice would increasingly focus on the marriage of its separate disciplines and a concentration on the identification of relevant issues and commu-nications solutions to those issues, rather than on the simple delivery of messages from communicators to what they perceived as their audiences. The symptoms of this development were a growing apparent examination of issues that held the potential to affect, for good or ill, the prosperity and reputation of organisations and the application of more imaginative and widely resourced communica-tions solutions to those issues. It's as well to examine some examples of the application of issues management in commercial circumstances through the integration of otherwise separate communications disciplines. The examples that follow are from my own and my colleagues' direct experience, for which I make no apology – they offer the benefit of first-hand experience. What they are meant to illustrate is how communications disciplines can be brought to bear on delivering solutions to complex issues.

***

Looking back to the early Nineties, it's not easy to conceive now that the British pop music industry was having a tough time. Since then, we have had the re-explosion of Britpop and the resultant Cool Britannia with which Tony Blair's new regime allowed itself to be associated. Not since Harold Wilson had tried to ride the wave of Beatlemania in the early Sixties has a Prime Minister so assiduously courted the pop scene, allowing Oasis's Noel Gallagher and others carefully to stage-manage impertinencies at Number 10.

It is a sign of how seriously the Government grew to treat the pop industry that a Deputy Prime Minister, in the not insubstantial shape of John Prescott, should allow himself to be exposed to a mild assault at pop's prestigious annual awards ceremony, The Brits (he had a bucket of iced water thrown over him). Pop spent the Nineties being high profile and prosperous. But it started the decade from a low base. It had little or no political or industrial influence and was facing a competition inquiry over the pricing of CDs in Britain, which largely for differences in economic structures were relatively more expensive than equivalent units in America.

The British Phonographic Industry (BPI), the record industry's trade body, embarked on a communications programme to establish British music as a vital foreign-exchange earner in the political environment, ahead of the industry's referral to the Monopolies & Mergers Commission (MMC). In media terms, the industry had been consigned to the ghetto of arts pages, where arts correspondents had (and have) little or no commercial agenda and even less practical political awareness. The BPI's task was to shift coverage of the CD pricing issue from the arts pages to the business pages. On the old message-delivery model, the objective had been simply to devise messages representing the industry's case on CD pricing and convey those messages to their traditional and well-worn audiences. The BPI was making its case through the wrong media and the consequence was that the relevant departments of Government knew nothing about the industry. The BPI undertook direct communication to the DTI and the Treasury, as well as reaching them through more appropriate media.

By the time the MMC inquiry was convened in 1993, business media and relevant politicians were keenly aware both of competition issues and the economic importance of the industry to the UK. This was no ramshackle peripheral industry run by ageing hippies for teenagers with more money than sense. It would be wrong to suggest that the British competition authorities (like judges, when it comes to litigation PR) are anything other than independent, but regulators have to glean their information from somewhere – and they weren't restricted to the arts pages and the *New Musical Express*. Nor were those who do the Exchequer's sums. When the MMC published its report in April 1994, its introductory sentence ran: 'The UK record industry is large and internationally important.' The report concluded: 'Given the strong competition in the market we believe this pricing policy is justified.'

Within weeks, an independent report from trade body British Invisibles concluded that the record industry was Britain's third most significant generator of foreign earnings for the UK. Chancellor Kenneth Clarke addressed the BPI's annual meeting in 1994, praising the industry's economic achievements. In 1995, opposition leader Tony Blair did the same. When it came to power, New Labour, for whom hanging out with revenue earners has always seemed cooler than Cool Britannia, convened the first meeting of the Music Industry Forum, an industry panel that advises ministers on policy.

The experience of the British record industry during this period demonstrates rather more than refreshed creativity on the part of artists. It's also symptomatic of the developing awareness in New Labour, as it approached government, of the relationship between media and policy-making. This was properly becoming a two-way process. In the twilight years of their Nineties Government, the Tories regularly whinged that there was fundamentally nothing wrong with their policies – they were just 'failing to get the message across'. While Tories saw the media as means of message delivery and, to a degree, message receipt, the music industry's experience was that the actual substance of policy could be developed by media. The Music Industry Forum, and the high regard in which the music business was held post-1997, is testament to that, because it had its roots in the development of properly integrated communications. This was not, as some of the old school of communications would have it, a government affairs programme with a bit of media support. These were the early indications that government affairs and the media were becoming indistinguishable. It was a trend that few were identifying, but one that was redefining communications processes.

***

Michael Heseltine was not in the best of moods on the morning in early spring 1997 as his personal Jag whisked him to the less than glamorous Port Greenwich Peninsula for the ground-breaking ceremony for the Millennium Dome. He may not have been in a very good mood for some time. He was Deputy Prime Minister and the Tories were heading towards a general election that they may not have been so certain to lose had Hezza not had 'Deputy' before his job title. But he seemed especially irritated that morning. At the last moment, his office had tried to alter the date of this event so as better to accommodate some of the potential sponsors. The vendors of the site, British Gas, had politely to explain that everything was set up for the contractors to start – they weren't going to wait for a better photo opportunity.

Heseltine strode about the industrial wasteland in his hard hat, rather keener to be photographed with BA's Colin Marshall, who had his fingers on purse strings, than with the managers of British Gas Properties, which had sold the site to English Partnerships for the Millennium Exhibition site. A twisted old sign, marking the Greenwich meridian, had been a symbol of the site in the newspapers. A JCB dug it up and dumped it on a flat-back for the cameras. Heseltine left abruptly. What a parable for our times it had turned out to be. We had wandered around in a wasteland, making symbolic gestures about a fresh start, but the open spaces still felt useless and empty. Little did we know that, three years later, it would feel much the same as the Blairs linked arms with the Queen to sing 'Auld Lang Syne' at the millennium.

The Millennium Dome turned out to be a symbol of all that could be wrong with modern communications, from the internet to the subsequent fragilities of what came to be known as New Labour's spin machine. It was impressively engineered and packaged, but there was nothing in it. Or, rather, there was not much in it that anyone wanted. It was the embodiment at the millennium of the triumph of a lack of style over a lack of content. The stage that triumphant Prime Minister Tony Blair was meant to bestride like a Colossus just ahead of his second election as leader was to become a downstream millstone, a drag on credibility, a south-estuary bubble, concurrently a white elephant and an albatross. It consumed much money and little imagination, suffering temporary remissions and dashed hopes until in 2002 it would be 'sold' by the rather more inflated figure of Lord Falconer for nothing but a share of future revenues.

It's difficult to see who emerges from the Greenwich escapade with any credit – it's a bit like asking who benefited from the Royal *It's a Knockout*, Prince Edward's most counter-productive project in a highly competitive field. But it is worth citing the role of British Gas in this context. Whatever else the butt of fat-cat hysteria and privatised-utility horror stories got wrong, its decision to sell the Dome site for £20m and relinquish its liabilities for remediation and decontamination beyond statutory requirements to the new owners (plus a handy 7.5 per cent of the market value at the time of the sell-on) was, with perfect hindsight, a more than sound one. There had been alternatives, ranging from continued ownership and total remediation of the site, through to actual co-ventures with The New Millennium Experience.

British Gas Properties, later to form part of Lattice Group in the break-up of BG, was in the business of reclamation and regeneration of former gasworks sites. It was emphatically not in the business of flag-waving, Millennium celebrations, New Labour theatricals or visitor attractions. There were companies that stuck to the Dome project like flies to sticky paper – or worse – for purposes of ingratiating themselves with the great and good (many of whom were ultimately left out queuing in the cold on Millennium night) or, funnily enough, out of fear of being left out in the cold.

It would be wrong to suggest that British Gas Properties had any privileged prescience of what a turkey the Dome would turn out to be. But it knew its job and what it was good at – the business of brown-field development. It and its successor company enjoy a strong reputation in a relatively low-profile field that is nevertheless of considerable public interest in terms of urban regeneration. It can't afford to be distracted from its endeavours. While the flies stuck to the paper, British Gas Properties stuck to what it was good at. There are lessons offered for politicians and for industrialists in confining activity only to what they're good at, managing the issue in which they have an expertise, rather than associations with wilder aspirations beyond the remit of that expertise, where the only attraction may be the dubious baubles of publicity and profile.

***

The stories heralding a hi-tech Armageddon at the Millennium really gathered momentum during 1998. In the event, the only hi-tech Armageddon occurred in the financial markets a little later, when the dot-com bubble burst. The Millennium Bug turned out to be snug in the Government's rug, rather than the killer virus that would sweep through global computer-land like a millennial Black Death, killing national and international communications infra-structures, rendering public and private services powerless and driving panic-stricken populations into the sea.

The avoidance of worldwide catastrophe – well, the avoidance of unnecessary panic caused by ill-informed and well-nigh hysterical media reports – was largely down to the dedicated Government office for Millennium Bug communications, the Y2K Media Co-ordination Unit (MCU) at The Cabinet Office. The work of this unit has already been addressed elsewhere, but the purpose here is to describe what it did and how it did it.

Its aim was to temper the wild surmises of potential Bug damage with direct communication with those potentially affected, so that public and corporate behaviour was predictable and rational. There were real fears that systems and infrastructural collapses could occur, not as a result of the Bug itself, but through unpredictable and irrational demands on those systems by contingency-planners and stockpilers. The communications effort of the MCU was research-based. Tracking research identified hot-spots of concern or unpreparedness, which were addressed in a highly-targeted and direct fashion. A combination of media-monitoring and rebuttal, combined with rapidly deployed practical information, served vulnerable peer groups, such as pensioners, before public fears built their own momentum. This communications technique bears comparison with the identification of critical voter issues through Labour's computer systems in Millbank Tower, ahead of the 1997 election.

There had been some anticipation that media coverage and public concern would feed off each other as the Millennium approached. In the event, as public awareness of the Bug was raised, tracking research indicated that public concern was falling. Those with political, mischievous, fanatical or theatrical interest in Armageddon – the doom-watchers – concurrently lost the power to make a mark. By the second half of 1999, concern about the Bug registered lower than awareness of it. Government confidence was such that it felt able to invite the media to broadcast live from the Government Millennium Centre through New Year's Eve and into the Millennium.

There is nothing astonishingly sophisticated or novel about this operation. But what it does represent is an instance in which the Government has addressed and managed the issue itself, rather than concentrate solely or principally on management of the communications process. The discipline is replicable in other spheres of government – or corporate – activity, if those with responsibility for communications have the wit and gumption to adopt it.

**

The instinct to take direct action after acts of cruelty, abuse and violence to children is primal and atavistic. We see it when vigilantes march on neighbourhoods that house paedophiles. Less dramatically and less frighteningly, we see it in well-meaning legislators in the wake of dreadful crimes. When two-year-old Jamie Bulger was abducted and murdered by 10-year-olds in 1993, Liberal Democrat MP David Alton's proposed amendment to the

Video Recordings Act emerged in an atmosphere in which a public desire for retribution was reflected by media demands for a crackdown on the video industry – the boy-murderers were said possibly to have been influenced by the depiction of a monstrous puppet called Chucky in a video called *Childs Play 3*. The prosecution offered no evidence to this effect and the Police were moved to deny it, but the story had its own momentum. The *Sun* ran with the front page 'For the sake of ALL our kids BURN YOUR VIDEO NASTY'.

'Video Nasties' were not the only issue for the British video industry, represented by the British Video Association (BVA). The proposed legislative amendment was directed at videos that potentially 'cause distress to children'. There were clearly separate issues to be addressed that, in the heat of anger and frustration, were being conflated – the classifications for violent videos and the desirability or otherwise of blanket censorship. In relation to the latter, it became apparent that 'distress to children' could plausibly encompass Bambi, the shooting of whose mother in the eponymous Disney movie could be interpreted as deeply distressing at a formative age – it was so interpreted by mature and ostensibly balanced individuals during debate in the House of Lords. The movies of Quentin Tarantino would undoubtedly become below-the-counter items.

The BVA implemented a major programme of education for parents – those who hold the real power of access to video material – while addressing the concerns of MPs directly and involving them in the process of classification standards. The proposed legislative amendment resulted in no further censor-ship, while the mainstream British video industry cast itself as the executor of standards and classifications in leading, rather than responding, to the debate. Heritage Secretary Chris Smith in the BVA's 1997 Yearbook: 'The British video industry is already a proven and increasingly successful business. But [its] importance ... goes further than just a thriving business, providing employment to 43,300 people. It is also an important cultural force within this country.' Again, the exercise demonstrates the potency and desirability of managing the issue itself through the communications process, rather than simply participating in and attempting to influence the communications process at the media level.

***

These brief case studies are not intended to be definitive demonstrations of model performances in communication. But what they are intended to demonstrate is that, during the past decade or so, the process of formal communications has developed from ideas of message delivery in discrete forums, where Parliament, industry and 'society' have separate identities addressed by means peculiar to each of them, into a practice in which the issue at hand is not just addressed by communications but is managed by it. Audiences are not islands to be reached by separate journeys, but wholly integrated elements of the culture in which we live. To be a specialist communicator in this environment is to miss the point massively – you might as well try to be a specialist human being. This further supports the view that communications can and should never be a specified management function at board level.

The development of professional communications practice at this level amounts to little more than a recognition that government affairs are more effective if the communications effort is aimed at addressing the issue itself, rather than at simply conveying a message. Detractors of the PR function may rejoin that all walks of life are engaged in the processes of communication in a holistic way on a daily basis. MPs, doctors and nurses, teachers, journalists, cabbies and lawyers and tarts are addressing their varieties of audiences on a daily basis. All the professional communicator is doing is co-ordinating these processes where there is a suitable commercial opportunity to do so. Exactly so. But where the commercial opportunity is seized only in order to convey a message, then the opportunity to manage the issue is missed.

Message conveyance in itself achieves little of significance for the long term. Governments in their twilight months discover this. So the development of the practice has further to go than that – organic evolution only leaves the extinct behind and, since communicators appear to be surviving alongside the fittest (whoever they may be), it's likely that the evolution of professional communications continues. The next stage may be to discover that the issue is not only the message – it may be the medium too. This acknowledges the role of communications in the management of the super-issue. One such super-issue is the development of a single European currency and we should now turn our attention to it.

May 2001 – My business partner, Charles Stewart-Smith, is enjoying some corporate hospitality at the Chelsea Flower Show. He gets to a good deal of other people's client events as the spouse of Kirstie Hamilton, at this time City Editor of The Sunday Times. This intensely annoys some other PR firms, but Charles compensates them by sportingly turning up under-briefed on their clients. It's for this reason that he asks the American he is seated next to what he does for the huge American investment bank he works for. 'I'm president of Europe,' replies this incredibly important man, apparently occupying the job that Tony Blair covets. Charles pays closer attention. The incredibly important banker is very pro-euro and hopes that Britain will join the single currency at the earliest opportunity. 'Why is that?' asks Charles. 'Because I don't want to have to go and live in Frankfurt,' replies the banker.

It is as important as that. If Britain stays out of the euro-zone, major American and other global companies will move their headquarters and investment to a country that is in it, even if the prospect of knackwurst for breakfast is less appealing than Cumberland sausages. And it is as important to recognise what this means: Britain's entry into a European monetary system will be decided by business and the prices that their consumers have to pay, not by politicians. This is not to imply that, in some way, industry would seek to circumvent a plebiscite on the issue, or to rig it in some way. Nor does it suggest that voters will not remain suspicious of the commercial world's desire to rip them off – research shows a widespread expectation of a rounding-up of prices at euro entry. It is simply to say that voters will be most influenced by issues of economics and that, in relation to costs and a sense of well-being and wealth, corporations have the most effective lines of communications.

Business people know this. They know that they have communicational power and influence of which politicians can only dream. The Labour Party has come to this realisation relatively late – it's what the Tories have known and exploited for generations – but, having realised it, they have worshipped at Mammon's altar. It's why Labour has garnered a reputation for being love-struck with Big Business. It's not just about lining campaign coffers – it's about power over and influence of an electorate that not only decides the Government's tenure, but decides whether we adopt the euro. Prices, not sovereignty or Brussels or stories of EC-regulated straight bananas, will decide Britain's euro-fate and both the Government and industry know that. The following story illustrates it.

In the spring of 2001, a delegation of 15 FTSE company chairmen and chief executives put together by Britain In Europe, the lobbying organisation launched in 1999 through an 'historic coalition' of europhiliacs from all the major parties, went to make their views clear to Prime Minister Tony Blair. As you would expect, Blair made all the right pro-Europe noises before facing a test of humility. The message was: 'With respect, Prime Minister, you're not the one we want to see – he's next door.' Within 10 days, a meeting was arranged with Chancellor Gordon Brown.

Again, I paraphrase, but the message from pro-European industry was unequivocal: 'Chancellor, Britain has to join the European single currency. If it does not, we will take all our investment out of the UK.' Then came the core message: 'Furthermore, we will hold you personally and publicly responsible.' Those present report the colour draining from Brown's face as he absorbed the implications of what was being said. Students of political coincidence should note that, by the autumn of 2001, Blair was making explicitly pro-European speeches. He intended to address the Trades Union Congress (TUC) on the subject on 12th September, but events the previous day blew it away. His draft read:

> 'On Europe I want to make it clear. This government believes Britain's proper place is at the centre of Europe as a leading partner in European development ... Tell me what other nation anywhere, faced with such a strategic alliance right on its doorstep, at the crux of international politics, would isolate itself from that alliance, not out of accident but design? It would be an absurd denial of our own self-interest. It's not standing up for Britain. It's sending Britain down a road to nowhere.'

Fairly unequivocal. By 23rd November, he had turned the 9/11 atrocities into support for a unified Europe, when he addressed the European Research Institute in Birmingham:

> 'The instability of the world today makes a successful Europe more necessary than ever. The aftermath of 11th September demonstrates the power and importance of nations working together, not in isolation ... Britain's future is inextricably linked with Europe ... to get the best out of it, we must make the most of our strength and influence within it ... to do so, we must be whole-hearted, not half-hearted, partners in Europe.'

Blair's Chancellor, the man that had been told in the spring that a significant proportion of British industry would hold him personally responsible for a failure to join a European single currency, said none of this. But Blair and Brown had a plan. Those who watch them within Whitehall claim that Brown has played bad cop to Blair's good cop on euro-policy. The strategy has been that Brown's apparent euro-scepticism will be all the more powerful in its conversion to support for the euro when he deems that the time is right for euro-endorsement. Brown's seemingly statesmanlike U-turn could, when it comes, put as much as 10 per cent on the 'Yes' vote. His perceived canniness, not to mention stern, Calvinistic manner, his well-managed budgets, his sleaze-free image and his apparent non-participation in the spin-culture (Charlie Whelan is history in this regard as much as the reputation of Campbell at Number 10 is not) put his stock high in the public's market for information on the euro. The belief of euro-campaigners is that there is a great deal more latent support than has yet become apparent that will emerge behind Brown's endorsement. All the more reason for it to be stage-managed properly.

Brown's conversion to the euro will, naturally, coincide with an announcement that the five woolly economic tests that the Treasury requires are fulfilled in a 'clear and unambiguous' manner for entry to have been satisfied. It would help if the five criteria themselves were clear and unambiguous. It's always worth reminding ourselves what they are: sustainable convergence between Britain and the economies of a single currency; sufficient flexibility to cope with the economic change; the effect on investment; the impact on our financial services; whether it would be good for employment. It was never going to be too hard to persuade oneself that these subjective criteria were fulfilled, just as soon as the moment seemed right to take the euro to a British referendum. The more important issue, from the Government's point of view, has been that the British public becomes inured to the euro. This process of softening up voters started in earnest in the New Year of 2002. The media always struggle over the thin Christmas-holiday news period. Luckily for print and broadcast media this time, there was the launch of a single European currency to fill space and airtime. Media-watchers wouldn't have been surprised to hear of one of the large retail chains opening a special counter for journalists trying to buy things in euros, so they could inform viewers and readers how easy/hard it was (either result served the purpose of europhiles – if it was easy, we were as good as in it already; if it was hard, we were making unnecessary difficulties for ourselves).

Thanks to an incessant bombardment during that January of pointless live-links to solemn reporters saying banal things like: 'There's no doubt, Anna, that the euro is here and it'll take some getting used to', British consumers were bored rigid by the euro within the month. This very much served the purpose of the euro's supporters within government and industry. The best way to manage the euro issue was to make sure that it wasn't an issue, beyond a general feeling of isolation and a sense of nuisance at the thought that we seemed to be the only people on holiday who had to make currency conversions. The softening-up process – a form of obfuscation of the political and economic borders of the euro issue – was developed in part concurrently at this time by Leader of the Commons Robin Cook and Labour Party chairman Charles Clarke, who claimed that there was a political imperative for joining. Treasury official Gus O'Donnell also chimed in, asserting that it would be a political decision. These interjections might have been seen as undermining the Government's declared position that economics alone would decide a recommendation for euro entry, but really they amounted to little more than the Government endeavouring to demonstrate that it did have a position on the euro. A Government that claims not to be making political decisions may not unreasonably be asked what it does for a living.

But the truth of the matter is that the euro is an entirely economic – rather than a political – issue. There will be those who claim that this is an unnecessarily fine distinction. The Chancellor's budget speeches are embodiments of the symbiotic relationship of the two disciplines. But the point must be that the Government can reasonably be assumed to enjoy dominion over politics – which is why apparatchiks such as Cook, Clarke and O'Donnell were busy claiming the issue for politics in early 2002 – while the economy, for all the tinkering of the Chancellor and the Bank of England, is run by business. That is why British industry was in Number 11's parlour in 2001, telling the Chancellor which way was up. And that is why the Chancellor was discomfited – he knew that they could.

Britain In Europe is a powerful body. Anything that draws Blair, Brown, Michael Heseltine, former Chancellor Ken Clarke and Liberal Democrat leader Charles Kennedy to share the same platform must be. Not because such statesmanlike individuals make it important, but rather that their presence confirms that this is where the action is. It is chaired by Lord Marshall, chairman of British Airways – among his deputies are former BP chairman and chief executive and sometime Labour minister Lord Simon and Merrill Lynch vice chairman Adair Turner. The advisory board is as long as the VIP queue for the Queen Mother's lying-in-state, featuring industrial figures such as Unilever chairman Niall Fitzgerald and WPP chief executive Sir Martin Sorrell. Oh and there's Peter Mandelson.

This is not an organisation to be messed with. And yet there has been some frustration expressed in pro-Europe quarters that Britain In Europe has not been visible enough in the campaign that defines it. This is completely to miss the point of the strategy developed by Britain In Europe, led by Simon Buckby, who was recruited from the upper echelons of the Millbank team that put New Labour into power. This strategy has been one of deliberate delay of engagement with the issue on a public basis. It is far better for the electorate to be bored by the subject in the sense of becoming familiar with the euro – for it to become part of the fabric of European life, to feel it and to use it on holiday and to witness that those who have adopted it have not relinquished their sovereignty (whatever that is thought to mean), have not become puppets of 'faceless Brussels bureaucrats' and have not been forced to eat straight bananas by them.

It would be quite another matter for the British electorate to be bored by the arguments in favour of the euro by its protagonists, rather than bored by euro-usage itself. Euro-supporters saw the mistake that the Tories had made during their last parliament and during Thatcher's last parliament – and, indeed, during Labour's first parliament – by banging on about the euro's solar-destructive properties to the extent that voters were bored to tears and the Tories' election death by it. Britain In Europe plays a longer game – encouraging acceptance of the euro by custom and practice. The europhobes recognised the strategy early on, dubbing it 'eurocreep' or adoption of a single currency by stealth. As a consequence, Tories belatedly adopted Britain In Europe's tactics for their own purposes – there followed a protracted, post-Hague moratorium on the shadow cabinet discussing the euro publicly unless it's inescapable. A Tory front-bencher privately concedes that the Tories went too early on their euro campaigns.

Careful timing of debate on the euro issue allows space for planning for when the campaign starts (some six months ahead of a referendum should be about right). As with the shadow communications committee that Mandelson chaired ahead of the 1997 election, there is a pro-euro communications committee that meets under the aegis of Chris Powell, of Labour advertising agency BMP DDB Needham and one of the political triumvirate of Powell brothers, along with Charles (Thatcher) and Jonathan (Blair). This committee is supported by research directed by Leslie Butterfield, who is to Europe what Philip Gould has been to focus groups for Labour.

The research generated demonstrates that, whatever Planet Right would wish to be the case and whatever antipathy is expressed towards the euro, the British electorate is far from concerned about matters of sovereignty, Brussels bureaucracy or straight bananas. The populisms of European football, continental clothes designers such as Armani and Benetton and German car engineering has pushed euro-awareness deep into the consciousness of the politically coveted C2D2 Middle England. The campaign for the euro is consequently to be conducted on the basis of prices – British shoppers are being ripped off in 'dear Britain' by being outside the euro-zone.

What Britain's eventual entry into Europe's single currency will demonstrate is the potency of addressing the issue itself, compared with the relative futility of conveying political messages about it. While opponents concern themselves with questions of sovereignty, macro-economic threats and the trivia of Brussels scare stories, the real power lies in the hands of those who know whether life on the outside will be more or less expensive for the British as a consequence. The task is to handle British industry's desires in relation to the real concerns of British subjects. That calls for skills in management of the issue itself, rather than simple communication of position, as well as sound empirical research. Without such research, politicians are playing on imaginary fears and desires within the electorate.

The rubric must be: Manage the issue – don't just communicate position. Blindingly obvious, maybe, but so is the injunction not to tell lies in politics, because they'll always catch up with you. Because it's a truism doesn't make it any less true – as politicians across the spectrum, from Jonathan Aitken to Stephen Byers, have discovered. The temptation to adopt a position, rather than to address the issue, is an intense one. You can bet that conversation within Number 10 after Cherie Blair spontaneously appeared to sympathise with the Palestinian cause on the day of the murder of 18 Israelis at the hands of a suicide bomber (June 2002) had more to do with message-delivery than with management of the conflict itself (hardly surprising, when the original comment was about taking a position, rather than addressing the issue).

Similarly, the fracas over Blair's role at the lying-in-state of the Queen Mother ultimately had little to do with the issue itself – whether Blair sought to 'muscle in' on the state arrangements – and a very great deal to do with a communications department vendetta with some mischievous right-wing publications (and possibly vice versa). If the issue itself had been addressed, hindsight would direct that by far the better course of action would have been to ignore the allegations, which would have been soon forgotten, and to have addressed the issue of Blair's apparent vanity over time. In this regard, Blair has demonstrated a greater sure-footedness on matters of state diplomacy than on domestic issues. The progress of a peace process for Northern Ireland has had far more to do with the management of issues than the adoption of position – aside from some appalling expressions of spin-culture, such as Blair's 'the hand of history' soundbite and the treatment of Northern Ireland Secretary Mo Mowlam. In the Middle East, Blair has at least endeavoured to address the issues on his diplomatic tour, even if it has cost him media humiliation in Syria, when President Assad in effect publicly told him he didn't understand the conflict.

For all the apparent concentration at home on education, public services, the economy and employment, there remains a pervading sense that the issues are not so much being addressed as being said to be addressed. Some issues show indications of being ignored altogether. Take the projected pensions crisis. Western economies with prolonged bear markets in equities are increasingly likely to harbour investment systems that cannot afford to meet their pensions liabilities. Company pension schemes and their investment managers blame the markets; unions blame the pensions holidays enjoyed by companies during better times. Final-salary schemes, to which employers typically contribute 11 per cent of earnings, are to be replaced by less remunerative defined-contribution schemes, with 6 per cent employer contributions. Governments face a potential pensions tab that they cannot afford.

What is happening? Are new European reporting requirements (the fearsome FRS17) being used as an excuse by incompetent investment managers? What do the most vulnerable group – the under-35s – know about this and what, if anything, are they prepared to do? Is there a case for recouping private-sector cash saved during the pension holidays? Is there a public-sector solution? Are the days of equities-linked pension schemes numbered in favour of fixed-interest instruments? We are not likely to learn the answer to any of these questions so long as the Government, company pension-scheme managers and investment institutions adopt positions and state the problem. The Pickering Report on pension reform in July 2002 seemed to concentrate on how to make the future work for pension schemes rather than for pensioners – perhaps no surprise from its author, Alan Pickering, a former chairman of the National Association of Pension Funds. Similarly, the almost simultaneous Sandler Report, from Lloyds of London chief executive Ron Sandler, on related issues in the financial services industry called for school-age education on financial planning. This missed the central point that people don't properly plan their lives financially because retail financial services are anaesthetically boring to the vast majority of the population. Money lessons would only institutionalise that boredom. The management of solutions to this is going to be complex. But empirical research of the issue as it really exists and the subsequent identification of a range of options would seem to be the way towards solutions. Again, it requires concentration on the issues, rather than just the communication of blindingly obvious messages that support positions.

Easily said. And simple enough as an aim. But the challenge of achieving this transformation in our approach to corporate and political communications is mammoth. The corporate psychology of defending and promoting one's own position, whatever the wider consequences for the market in which one operates, is a deeply entrenched one. To raise consciousness of a better and more effective approach to issues amounts to more than encouraging some ephemeral idea of co-operation. It requires an appreciation that more efficient and effective markets generate greater wealth for participants in the process. The runes are not favourable that any such transformation of purpose can be achieved in the short-term – there is not the imagination nor the will in industry or in politics. The game has been played for so long in a manner that encourages the concept of competitive advantage as the benchmark of success, that it is almost impossible to envisage a circumstance in which the players will raise their eyes to a horizon, on which there may be discerned the coastline of a promised land whose fruits can be plundered in whatever way we decide. To look at politicians and industrialists in hope of this vision is too often to despair. But it has to remain the aspiration.

The mould needs to be broken. Issues such as the euro and pensions are too important to be left to soundbites and the impenetrable technical language of equally impenetrable institutions, populated by actuaries that are convinced that they are right but are doing nothing by way of solution other than arguing their companies' books. It needs a concentration on issue over communication. It demands a more intelligent use of research. But it also invites a degree of candour, trust and honesty that has been absent where it matters. To achieve that requires a new attitude to doing business. This doesn't mean new ways of doing business – it means establishing what the nature of new business is going to be. As Labour re-invented itself to match the new environment, so must the commercial community. We need New Business.

NEW BUSINESS

CAPITAL OFFENSES

If assertion had become the principal characteristic of spin-culture in politics by the late Nineties, it had already been the main driver of equity markets for most of the decade. The economic recession of the early Nineties enjoyed its farcical apotheosis when Prime Minister John Major allowed his Chancellor, Norman Lamont, to use interest rates as a stick with which to beat the pound into the exchange rate mechanism. Even a base rate of 15 per cent, raised five percentage points on Black Wednesday, 16th September 1992, couldn't achieve that and Britain made its excuses and left the ERM, to enjoy a free period of unbridled prosperity for the rest of the decade.

The subsequent protracted bull market of the Nineties was variously attributed to relatively low interest rates, consumer spending, a buoyant housing market and the American boom. So far as the runaway economy in the United States was concerned, it may have been a bit rich, frankly, for the chairman of the Federal Reserve, Alan Greenspan, to attribute the record-breaking heights of the US equities markets in December 1996 to 'irrational exuber-ance'. The degree to which the Federal Reserve itself discreetly participated in the US futures markets to support the economy remains a moot point. There was certainly a political imperative on the part of the Clinton regime to keep the feelgood factor alive among voters by ensuring that the deeply entrenched culture of US share-ownership was not poisoned. The scale of the US boom was awesome in the Nineties. In the second half of the decade, the US

economy grew some 3.5 per cent a year, fuelled by an unprecedented fall in domestic net saving encouraged by the bull market.
Americans were simply so brimming with confidence in their
economy that they were investing flat-out in equities and running
up credit to do so. The numbers didn't – and still don't – work.

Wall Street's over-valuation of US equities may have been as
high as 50 per cent by the end of 1999. Without this over-valuation
bubble, annual economic growth may have been a more modest
2 per cent. A decade previously, Britain and Japan, along with
Finland and Sweden, had also floated their economies with asset
price bubbles (in the case of the UK, a hugely over-priced domestic
property market) with sharply falling levels of private saving. All
these economies suffered severely when asset prices finally
collapsed and the populace reverted to correspondingly high levels
of personal saving. At the millennium, the US was facing a quite
implausible future in which its family budgets would either have to
devote nearly a quarter of their income to servicing their debts, or
Wall Street's bubble would have to inflate further to corporate over-
valuations of 70 or even 80 per cent. The alternative – to manage
the USA's prospective switch from investing to saving without the
economy collapsing – would have required massive tax cuts and a
devaluation of the dollar, initiatives that did not immediately
present themselves in the year before a presidential election, with
the budget running in surplus.

This was the USA's economic situation before the technology
bubble burst, pushing the Nasdaq down 25 per cent in a month in
spring 2000 and – before the far greater blows to US confidence
that came out of the sky in September 2001 – the Nasdaq would be
down 60 per cent within the year. It was much to the credit of US
resilience that it did not suffer economically as it might have done
in the early years of the new millennium. But it was, nevertheless,
an achievement of smoke-and-mirrors, hardly sound economic law,
that built the US economy in the last ten years of the twentieth
century. The US economic miracle was, in effect, an act of spin, a
symptom of the global spin-culture. It couldn't be made to last –
unless a political imperative emerged in which it became
impossible for the US economy to show that it could be rocked
for anything other than the most temporary of bear markets. Such

an imperative emerged on 11th September 2001. The economy had started its retrenchment ahead of the terrorist attacks – after them, it could not be allowed to deepen too sharply and quickly for political reasons. The economy had to be spun out of despair, so the downturn had partly to be manipulated. The Federal Reserve embarked on a series of interest-rate cuts that may have been patriotically, as well as economically, driven.

By comparison, the British economy was a boring little sideshow. But there were similarities with the US nature of economic management by hype. By the mid-Nineties the growth in the British economy had become similarly self-fulfilling – markets boomed simply because they boomed. The financial markets of the Nineties were to resonate to the aspirations of Thatcher in the previous decade – they would, investors claimed, go on and on. We were, argued the City's wiseacres, in a new economic paradigm, a model that didn't respond to the traditional economic cycles and – short of cataclysmic world events (such as, perhaps, a worldwide war on terror) – could be expected to continue indefinitely. We were to discover that we were in an economic morality tale that would lead to the dot-com balloon, a parallel universe in which, in retrospect, it seemed that any kind of economic model could be justified if you willed it.

One of the formulae developed to give an impression of science to a market in psychological denial of the laws of economics was a magical acronym that would soon be chanted reverentially at the City's altars to Mammon. This was Ebitda – or earnings before interest, tax, depreciation and amortisation. In short, this was a means of measuring a company's performance and value, without taking into account some of the most significant cost factors in its management. It was a device that, unsurprisingly, became popular for the measurement of performance in the telecoms industry – one of the triple towers of the TMT (technology, media and telecoms) sector. Again, Ebitda was a child of assertion – the mentality in which the economy is post-rationalised and the facts are made to fit what we will to be the case. Some wags held, in the wake of the Enron and Worldcom collapses, that the 'a' in Ebitda stood for 'auditors'. But before these harsh reminders of the excesses that protracted bull markets could bring, Britain's economy, like the USA's, was being spun rather than managed.

We know now that the reckoning was to come with the evaporation of billions of dollars of investors' cash in a Lilliputian world in which a company defied all known rules of return simply because it employed an on-line means of reaching its customer base. But, at the time, it seemed perfectly plausible that the markets would support any notion of prospective earnings for a company, simply because it asserted that those earnings were realistic. These self-fulfilling markets witnessed the pre-eminence of the indexed or 'tracker' investment funds. These institutional vehicles thrived on the principle that no degree of investment skill – whether gritty, scientific analysis of prospective value or simple punter's hunch – could match over time a basket of major stocks that reflected the inherent growth of the market. This view was axiomatic in the rising markets of a protracted bull market. It also relied unduly upon assertion, with no underlying premise other than its own self-evident truth, that it worked. A moment's examination of this assertion exposed its flaws. For one thing, those FTSE stocks that made up the index and were, therefore, the market that was 'tracked' saw their share prices rise precisely because the trackers were invested in them. This growth endorsed the tracker's confidence and saw further money rush after the tracking principle, further inflating the shares and so on. Companies watched market capitalisations balloon and their share prices flourish simply by virtue of having joined the FTSE100. Likewise, companies that dropped out of the size-oriented FTSE watched their share quotes plummet as the trackers abandoned them.

The tracking principle was also a mirage. Most trackers were covert stock-pickers, in order – perversely – to do better than the next tracker fund. In theory, all trackers should have performed to a uniform standard. If they were truly following the index of leading stocks, then there was no competitive advantage to be had over rivals. The index couldn't lie. But tracker-fund managers could. So if they fancied the prospects of a particular stock, they would weight their investment there. Similarly, they would underweight their position in leading stocks that they believed to be prospective dogs. The growth investor was a closet value investor. But so far as much of the investment market presented itself to its clients, index-tracking was the only game in town. Cash – as in money uninvested in the equity markets – and fixed-income instruments were for cissies. At one level, this simple system worked – the index attracted investment, it rose and attracted further investment – but it took no account of what might happen when the music stopped playing, nor what would happen to over-inflated share prices when it did.

Meanwhile, the financial public relations industry saw one of its principal functions – investor relations – largely emasculated. Investor relations had, until the Nineties, largely depended on communicating the relative value of investment in its clients' shares against the market and against its direct rivals. At the top end of the market, the tracker funds largely confiscated that responsibility. If you were part of the basket, you got tracked. It was as simple as that. There were no arguments about relative value to be had. There was certainly little or no point in clients investing time and energy in briefing and lushing up institutional investors if they weren't going to be tracked anyway. And you can't spin a company into the FTSE100.

There was a communications case to be made for those below the threshold of FTSE entry – the mid-cap market – but only on the basis that they might offer potential value as tomorrow's FTSE constituents and that was of no interest to the trackers. For the heavy investment guns, it was a case of coming back when you'd made it and they would assist you to make it some more. Many mid-caps grew disillusioned with the public markets, with their regulatory demands and responsibilities to grow earnings per share quarter by quarter with no noticeable advantage unless you were big enough to be tracked, and sought to de-list into the private-equity markets. The financial communicators continued to make their fees through a flourishing takeover market, as listed companies sought to grow their earnings to the satisfaction of shareholders, particularly those trackers who would reward their increase in size with further weighting. But it wasn't the merger mania of the Eighties, when there was a highly opportunistic, not to mention highly leveraged, smell in the air. Thatcherism had encouraged the mid-caps and the leviathans sought to consolidate power as much as earnings. The Nineties was about size, not for market power or even its own sake, but to justify over-weighting from the trackers.

Financial PR became a far more prosaic, mature and patisserie-like activity. The recipe called for some stodgy cake of financial calendar reporting, a rich icing of lucrative but dull merger activity laced with a marzipan layer of investor relations activity – which amounted to keeping the large clients in touch with the trackers and everyone else from the frustrating feeling that the investment institutions took no notice of them. The large financial PR shops, themselves consolidating to satisfy the expectations of share-holders, started to resemble the accountancy and auditing firms before they discovered management consultancy – large and morose and, in the most part, operating on wafer-thin margins that worked for them because of the sheer volume of business that they shifted. The quality of service was to suffer, but the publicly-quoted markets of the Nineties weren't looking for quality advice – the investment markets didn't demand creativity or consultancy services. They demanded reporting structures. And that's what they got – agency functions, not consultancies.

There would be fun – if that's what it could be called – to be had during the dot-com bubble of the millennium. But that, too, was to serve to strip financial public relations down further to its most functionary motor. Those who became over-excited at the prospects of a new industry that was allegedly to re-invent the way the corporate world communicated would take equity in lieu of fees from their fledgling clients. The new paradigm was not to be. This episode would re-establish financial PR, if anything, more firmly in the mode of prosaic, functional activity, expanding only on an international scale, with a global clientele that demanded a plain-vanilla communications service in all trading locations with capital markets attached to them. An expansion of the quality of communications service was not on offer. All would be well, however, if equity markets held up. They didn't. By the high summer of 2002, the stock markets on both sides of he Atlantic knew what it was to be low and were trusting that they had found the bottom. Wall Street had seen 45 per cent of its equities value disappear – London was similarly off its peak. Equity markets that had been driven by hype were no longer responding to it. President Bush tried to stem the sell-off, but a new kind of hype was driving the markets down – the hype surrounding bogus auditing at those prize long-horns of the bull market, Enron and Worldcom, was proving as potent at pushing markets artificially low as the dot-com nonsense had proved in pushing them artificially high.

But there was more to the stock-market collapses of 2002 than mere panic that some of the new-wave auditor-consultants had got a little carried away imaginatively during the boom years. An 18-year party was drawing to a close. According to research from Schroder Salomon Smith Barney, the investment banking arm of Citigroup, as early as May 2002, the disinflation, rising corporate profitability and lower political and economic risks that had fuelled a bull market that had lasted as long as or longer than many lucrative City careers, was over. World share prices had held their upward trend throughout the 18 years until 2000, despite the short bear-legs of 1987, 1990 and 1998. The adjustment had come. Many in financial services had grown accustomed, like Thatcher in a political context in the Eighties, to prevailing circumstances going on and on. Investors had developed their perceptions of their markets during those 18 years – few had any recollection or appreciation of the 17-year period of negative real returns that preceded it. Western economies remained essentially sound and the prospect of recovering stock markets was eagerly discussed during that torrid summer. But the party was over. For the financial spin-culture that had developed since 1980, this was of greater significance than they cared to admit – though the downsizing and sudden availability of financial PR executives on the books of headhunters told their own story. The trouble was that 'traditional' financial PR – investor relations, stock-exchange announcements, some takeover activity to feed earnings growth – only enjoyed a tradition that went back as far as 1980 and the start of Thatcherism. In its present guise, it only knew raging bull markets. It knew of no existence other than the equities up-trend. It was left with one of two options before it – deny the existence of change or find something new to do. The first was not a long-term solution and the second required them to be something they were not.

THE NAME'S BOND

The financial markets caravan had, in any event, moved on by the turn of the millennium, unnoticed by the dogs of the financial communications market, who kept barking at the fading bonfire of the UK equities market, the dot-com sparks from which were fading fast. In what had become systemically a low-interest-rate environment, the rhythm of the new music was being provided by the debt markets. The shareholder was being usurped by the bondholder. By 2001, the global bonds market had hit a record annual issuance level of $2.7 trillion – close to 10 times the size of the equities markets. One explanation for this explosion in the fixed-income markets is the sheer range of institutions that were able to access them in a manner wholly compatible with the prevalent fashion for globalisation. There were the supranationals in the shape of the World Bank, the European Investment Bank or the Council of Europe. Sovereign states, too, were already familiar with fixed-income instruments. Financial institutions from government agencies to the commercial, investment and mortgage banks were driving the market and, of course, corporations were increasingly flattered by the borderless markets for bonds as they coat-tailed the gods of globalisation.

The shareholder had once held British management in the palm of his hand – now bondholders held the power to dictate strategic direction. In 2001, Boots (the Chemist, as we must no longer call it) switched its entire £2.4bn pension-fund assets into the bonds market. By 2002, BT was carrying net debt of £13.4bn, against a market capitalisation of £16.2bn. Even more striking and highly geared was France Telecom, with a market capitalisation of €16.3bn against net debt of €63bn. Elsewhere, Swissair, Marconi and NTL all demonstrated that major companies could no longer rely solely on rating reviews and investment banks to manage their capital markets. A more flexible range of financing options was available than through the geographically fixed and relatively pedestrian equities markets, from plain-vanilla Eurobonds to globals, foreign bonds, medium-term notes, asset-backed securities and convertibles. The credit derivatives markets further enhanced the options available for issuers, borrowers and bondholders.

Like all significant market developments, once a new regime is in place it's difficult to comprehend why it took so long to appear. Part of the reason must be that, unlike the equities markets, bonds have traditionally been considered and treated as a commodities market, with prices set by a sovereign ceiling and credit-worthiness simply set by the hegemony of the debt ratings agencies. So only very limited opportunities were traditionally available for issuers of debt to add any value to their offer through advanced communications. Such promotional activity as existed was conducted through the market's niche media, such as *Euromoney* magazine, the industry's flagship publication presciently founded by former *Daily Mail* City Editor Patrick Sergeant in the Seventies, and financial events, such as debt summits in Vienna and the Global Borrowers and Investors Forum in London.

The development of this huge but undeveloped financial market into the global mechanism that would start to eclipse the equities markets was properly underway by the late Nineties. It was partly driven by the European regulatory environment, with the prospect of greater disclosure and transparency requirements driven by the innocuous sounding European Commission instrument FRS17 – as dry and as explosive as dynamite in the corporate governance world. This was said to have triggered the iconic move by Boots. But FRS17 is a symptom of the equities-to-bonds paradigm shift, rather than an essential motive for the shift itself. Indeed, there was a view approaching prevalence in the fund management industry that FRS17 represented an excuse, rather than a prime motive, for the switch of market emphasis from equities to bonds. While it's true, in a wider context, that the drive by European governments to reform their pensions systems has increased the pool of capital available to institutions and, in order to meet their long-term liabilities and yield targets, these institutions are diversifying their assets to include a wider range of securities from a more eclectic choice of issuers, the development of the market is far from driven by pensions alone. For principal motivators of the trend, we need to look elsewhere and deeper into the changing nature of debt markets and what drove them to new levels of sophistication and competitiveness.[7]

In Europe, a major motivating factor has been the development of monetary union. The euro has been a principal factor in generating competition and transforming the debt markets. The removal of exchange and interest-rate risks that it represents has shifted the focus to the purity of credit research as the most significant differentiator of issuers. The effect on nation-state governments and quasi-government issuers is a keen appreciation of the requirement to be at least as pro-active as the commercial private sector in marketing their debt and competing for capital – or face an economy-threatening and electorate-alienating hike in their funding costs. At the corporate level, the pressures further to embrace the bond markets go far further and deeper than the stick of FRS17 goading global corporations towards the carrot of the bond markets, with their cost-effectiveness, predictable return projections and relative lack of volatility. The late Nineties surge in mergers and acquisitions activity may have offered something of a last hurrah for the traditional equities-obsessed financial communications industry – their star, perhaps, burning brightest before its implosion – but much of the growth in bond markets was provided during this period by companies demanding a wider range of funding requirements. To some extent, this syndrome has characteristics of the addictive personality – the more debt a corporation runs up, the more it will need to service or refinance that debt at low points in the economic cycle. The debt market – as loan sharks on sink estates know – is self-perpetuating once borrowers are substantially committed. The more finance raised in the market now, the more will be required in the future.

---

[7] I am indebted for insights to *Financial Issues*, established in 2001 and the first dedicated communications service for the fixed-income markets.

As a consequence of the growing debt habit, the credit analyst has assumed a far greater status in investment banks and institutions and, as a consequence of function or ambition and empire-building, has further developed the pattern of debt's hegemony. There are today analysts of all grades of borrower and across all sectors of the economy, mirroring their counterparts in the equities markets. As a consequence, credit ratings are now simply one factor in the gamut of influences on analysts and investors in the fixed-income markets – reflected by the burgeoning media coverage. Similarly, the relationship between issuer and bank has changed. During the debt markets' wilderness years, issuers relied on their banking book-runner to offer marketing advice and lead the roadshow for deals to key accounts. This process amounted to a communications exercise – or, more literally, a public relations exercise – for which the banks were ill-equipped once the markets started their exponential growth. Within that growth, the investment banks had a greater and more limpid interest in transactions than in marketing and communications. Transactions represent a volume business – banks understand that. Communications, by contrast, are a low-volume, value-added activity – demanding a new breed of communicator.

If it's a new breed for the debt markets, it represents a new species for the financial communications market. This is because the evolution of the fixed-income markets has occurred in both a different era and a different geography to traditional financial communications. Financial PR, for all its developing sophistication and professionalism, is born of an era of the bow-tied ex-hack – not necessarily from journalism; from the armed forces too – who established a profession on the basis of a latter-day, Johnsonian coffee-shop discourse, depending on established personal relationships in a fixed location, most obviously the parlours of the City of London, peddling share-tips.

The genetic construct of the fixed-income communications professional is different, if no more complex. Probably out of the global financial markets, this creature is not of the environment of personal relationship, at least not one fostered in a fixed location. Relationships are likely to be screen-based and remote. The 19th-hole, word-in-the-ear that served equities communicators in

London for a generation is replaced by the e-presentation and, if necessary, the wine-bar is usurped by the airport lounge. If financial communications developed a spin-culture during the Eighties and Nineties – the smoke-and-mirrors of the subterranean drinking den to rubber-necking at the power-tables of the Savoy Grill – the nature of market developments in general and the fixed-income markets in particular will change it forever in the Noughties. That would seem strongly to suggest that corporations are likely to change, for it was only the early capital markets that drove incorporation in the merchant-venturing seventeenth and eighteenth centuries. The capital markets define companies, not the other way around. With the capital markets changing beyond recognition, it's worth asking what companies are now for. What is their corporate function and what do they stand for?

WHAT ARE COMPANIES FOR?

One of the least heralded incongruities of the dot-com debacle of 1998–2000 was a paradox in the corporate constitution of the pony-tailed entrepreneurs who, in all senses, blew up the bubble. It's perhaps not surprising that this paradox went almost universally unremarked, because too many important people in the investment communities were embarrassed. There was more than enough to be embarrassed about in the absurdity, admittedly with hindsight, of experienced investment bankers and venture capitalists falling over each other to sink hundreds of millions into enterprises that made no profits and were 'valued' on multiples of notional hits on websites. The paradox is that, while the internet promised – and still promises – to be the most democratising communications and distribution conduit from, and route to, market for the individual, the dot-com pioneers formed traditional companies to deliver its promise. At one level, this is wholly credible – the route to the capital markets was though incorporation and flotation on one or other of the tradeable exchanges. At another, it was quite absurd. What the internet was doing, and what many of its proponents claimed as its mission, was the replacement of traditional corporate structures with a looser global regime of interconnected peer groups and individuals, many of whom for the first time could exploit their own intellectual property rather than have it exploited on their behalf by the company for which they worked.

It didn't work – dot-commery bit the hand that fed it financially – which is why becoming part of the corporate structure that it aspired to destroy went unrecorded. But the question that the dot-commers, had they by some quirk of natural selection survived the unfittest formulae for return on capital invested ever devised, would soon have been asking is this: What are companies for? More specifically, what are companies for that carry permanent staff, overheads, headquarters and, for that matter, boards of directors? The internet apparently offered a looser and liberated confederation of trading interests, in which services and intellectual property could be traded without the strictures of registered company status, limited in imagination as well as liability. The historical answer, dating back to the roots of incorporation in the seventeenth and eighteenth centuries, is that companies pool endeavour and capital, with a view to sharing the value of growth in earnings with the shareholders (owners) of that company, while limiting the risks of the individuals. This definition has latterly had to be extended to encompass the value and ownership of brand value. More recently in the twentieth century, with the development of education and the liberation of labour, an alternative definition can more cynically ascribe a social purpose – to provide identity and purpose for the individual and, most specifically, a place for men to go during daylight hours, in uniform, to play displacement war-games and latterly for women to find a post-liberation fulfilment beyond the rearing of children (ditto the uniform).

But on the traditional definition of a company, its purpose is to generate value for its shareholders. The essential effort of the financial communications industry has been to convey the relative incremental value of its clients' shares over those of its competitors. It is consequently seeking, in a large part of its activity, to position clients above the index (it's a mathematical law even the most innumerate will appreciate that only half of them will succeed). But modern stock theory, as originally enshrined in the Efficient Market Hypothesis of the Sixties, states that no one can know a stock will rise, or even reliably predict that it will rise. Every single trading day, in every single stock market of the world, is a random process of selection in which half the stocks quoted will, by definition, do better than the index, while half will under-perform it. No one has been able to date – nor, one might safely venture to predict, will anyone in the future be able – to predict the pattern of these performances. If they did, their period of Croesus-like riches would be short-lived – it would be the end of publicly-traded equities markets and, very possibly, the end of post-industrial capitalism. So, on the existing model, fund management remains a process of calculated gambling and the selection by asset-owners of fund managers becomes a straight bet on their relative skill in stock selection. This, again, fuelled the rise of index funds during the Nineties, as fund management firms tacitly admitted that to endeavour to out-perform the index in the long term was pointless.

In terms of trying to establish what is the purpose of companies, this has some significance. Because if a highly incentivised, sophisticated, educated and experienced City equities analyst, with the most revealing databases and learned economists at his or her disposal, can't know the most worthwhile application of invested money, how possibly can the manager of a company know how to invest shareholders' money? There is simply no empirical measure by which a company manager can know whether the £100 invested in lunch with a customer or the £100m invested in building a new factory is the best application of that money, compared with junk bonds, diversification through acquisition or the staff Christmas party. He can make an educated guess – like the fund manager – but self-evidently it is a punt as to whether his strategy is going to work out more or less successfully than the average of corporate efforts, which amounts to the index. Naturally, there will be more skilled managers than others. But for every wealth-creating manager, there will be thousands who lose money – which tells us something about how exponential is the contribution of the successful and where the index lies in relation to their success (something, incidentally, to be taken into account when executive remuneration is being calculated). And it is in the nature of the index not to lie. Of itself, it represents a 50 : 50 bet that any manager – of business or funds – will exceed or fall short of it.

Such an analysis of the capital markets can be accused of being nihilistic. If it is correct, why are shares traded through stock exchanges (and, therefore, owned) rather than simply backed in betting shops? The answer has to be that the indices – and consequently the stock markets – exist to provide benchmarks against which investors calculate the degree of risk that they want, or are prepared, to take. An investor may covet a higher level of return for accepting a higher level of risk. Asset managers buy the index as a base investment and subsequently weight portfolios with a perceived level of higher risk/return through individual stock weightings. This is not stock selection so much as risk management. Low risk does not equate with low performance or low rating – in the latter category, value investors are active in identifying potential performance in undervalued stocks. Investors, incidentally, who demand lower risk than the index itself offers, combine the index with bonds, as there is no place in a portfolio for stocks offering lower risk than the index, which intriguingly distorts the index in favour of risk. This is the Capital Asset Pricing Model (CAPM).

It follows that, at the investment level, the purpose of the existence of companies is to package the risk of its trading activities and market that risk to appropriate investors. Note that they are not there to know what is the right thing to do, either in investment or trading terms – only to appreciate the nature of risk attached to that trading activity. This is a truth almost universally unacknowledged by the financial PR industry, which will invest endless and fruitless, if lucrative, time in trying to convince investors, and the media that reach them, of the relative merits of their clients' strategies. This may represent another of those managerial choices for the investment of budget that amounts to no more than a 50:50 punt.

It's worth noting too, that this interpretation of the markets and the purpose of companies traded in them presents a particular problem for companies that offer conservative investors returns similar to the index. Clearly, investors can enjoy similar returns at lower risk by buying the index. Investors should not buy individual stocks for low risk – a combination of the index and bonds serves that purpose more efficiently – so companies are obliged to offer managed risk that offers a better return than the index. And we know that only 50 per cent of them can achieve that.

Financial PR began in the late Sixties (though through little traceable relationship with the Efficient Markets Hypothesis) by reporting company results to and through the Stock Exchange. It developed its dialectical edge during the Eighties as a weapon of acquisition. It consolidated to ape the factory-style management consultancies of the Nineties. The truth is that the investor relations component at the heart of its offer is about the communication of industry's risk management in a game where half the players will be losers. All the rest is spin.

If there is a simple answer to the question of a company's financial existence – that it manages risk for the investment community – it still fails to explain why company's exist in the form that they do, as locations of communal labour, with corporate structure and identity, support structures and counselling and crèches. Why do people go to offices? What are companies for, if they have any purpose beyond risk management for the portfolios of current and prospective shareholders? Because they provide employment. Because they are agents of social cohesion. Because they constitute an economy.

These are facetious answers to pretty pointless questions – the most practical observation being that companies exist because they do – but they are questions that the overwhelming majority of those engaged in corporate communications would not bother to explore beyond that practical observation. Corporate communications as a PR discipline would claim to be concerned with the protection and enhancement of corporate reputations. Its country cousin, consumer PR, would offer similar service to the brand and corporate identity, as distinct from the corporation. Either would only rarely explore what business generally is for, or even specifically what their client businesses are for, beyond what they read is required in their commercial briefs.

The next question is whether that matters. Corporations believe, whatever the evidence to the contrary, that they should have aspirations and commercial imperatives to deliver in the best interests of their shareholders – the success of such ventures need to be communicated effectively and failures mitigated. Professional communicators do this, very often to the annoyance of consumers and customers. The public-to-privatised utilities, particularly telcos, have excelled in over-claiming on customer service standards. The lantern-jawed heroes of television commercials and colour press ads bear no greater comparison with reality than movie depictions of a medieval Robin Hood with blow-dried hair and good teeth. But the job is done – if deceit and deception is the job.

Why the question matters has nothing to do with whether the tasks of corporate or consumer communicators matter. Nor does it matter because business managers matter, allegedly, to the management of an efficient economy. The question matters because over the past decade business has been pushed into a new role of social responsibility. It has been here before. The Victorian philanthropists and Christian Socialists of the nineteenth century believed that companies had a social responsibility toward the working families of the industrial revolution. Robert Owen's Co-operative movement of the same century sought to share its earnings with its 'members'. The Fabians sought to apply socialist principles within capitalism, rather than against it. Their legacies are apparent today in the Co-operative Wholesale Society – which resisted a break-up bid from Monaco-based raider Andrew Regan in the mid-Nineties – and the social-inclusion policies of retail group The John Lewis Partnership and the socially-conscious Quaker influence in companies such as shoe-retailer C&J Clark and Cadbury-Schweppes.

But, given the social construct of the day, these reformers of social conditions in and around industry were patrician, patriarchal and colonial in attitude and approach – and not to be judged by modern criteria for that. Companies were to be both exploiters and charities that offered some remedy for that exploitation. It was a system that suited an industrialised world in which working and family lives were given over almost entirely, with the exception of a soul that the Church taught was God's, to the local employer. In grotesquely inhumane conditions by any standards, this combination of social ownership with social care has provided modern challenges of corporate image and perception that have required careful management.

Guinness, for example, has been brewed in Dublin since the eighteenth century. It was overwhelmingly the most significant employer and social provider during the industrial development of the city. Today, it is a global brand, owned by drinks and leisure combine Diageo. In an Ireland that has grown from a net exporter of labour to the vibrant, euro-zone 'Celtic Tiger' economy importing labour, the management of both Guinness the brand and Guinness the company has been a challenge of embracing the opportunities of the new without squandering the values of the old. What has not changed in the course of two centuries is that companies, such as Guinness, are not only perceived to have an economic purpose, but also a social role. Companies, through the generations from Robert Owen to Tony Blair, have been re-interpreted as agents of good and components of social change, rather than simply of social remediation. What is different from the old philanthropists is the standing and motivating force of business in the process of social management. Companies are recognised as agents of socio-economic progress – wealth-creators in the broadest sense, rather than narrowly for their owning shareholders.

Corporate social responsibility – CSR, as it has been universally tagged – at the start of the twenty-first century represents an entirely different and dangerous approach to social conscience from its forebears. Industry can no longer affect to run society – it is considered to be part of society. The socially-responsible Victorians were the same individuals who controlled politics and industry. They were simply in charge. Today, industry and politics are, for the most part, separate constituencies that try to have a relation-ship. But industry is considered to be part of society and, as such, politicians aspire to control it. The result is the imposition of a set of social requirements that politicians seek to impose on industry. The New Labour Government instituted a minister for CSR. In May 2002, the incumbent of that ministry, Douglas Alexander, pub-lished the second of his government's reports on CSR with this statement: 'CSR offers a new alternative to the idea that economic and social goals must always be in conflict. It offers an integrated approach to business in the modern world. It shows the way forward, to achieve economic, social and environmental benefits at the same time ... This is an opportunity for business and society to work together, to create a better society, to make a real difference. CSR should not be for show and should not only be skin deep.'

The Government's detractors surprisingly refrained from the rejoinder that New Labour should not be for show and should not only be skin deep. But the message was clear: The responsibility for social provision lies at least as much with business as it does with government. This has massive implications for the processes of corporate communications that we shall come to later (the integrated combination of public affairs and corporate communications). First, it's as well to acknowledge that Blair's Project contains within it the desire to take on the challenges of social provision with business as an ally. This is significant, because it means that the media's confinement of concentration on Blair's relationship with business – and that of his kitchen cabinet, including Mandelson, not so much minister without portfolio as minister without job, but no less influential internally for that – as a source of funds for the Labour Party is at least in part misplaced. Since 1997, Blair and Mandelson have been variously accused of being in thrall and dangerously close to business people, with (in no way unjustifiably from the media's point of view) stories concentrating on donations from allegedly dubious sources such as Ecclestone, Mittal and Express Newspapers owner Richard Desmond. In reality and irrespective of any lack of discretion in the source of funding, the Government sees social provision and reform as a joint venture with British industry that goes well beyond the Private Finance Institute. That, ultimately, will be of greater significance to business and to Britain than whether anyone bought a political favour.

This is an entirely fresh definition of what business is for. If New Labour succeeds in its intent, no longer will the purpose of a company simply be to reward its shareholders or to manage risk in order to do so, but to be a partner of government in social provision. That begins to make the point that Director-General Greg Dyke has been making at the BBC – that business coverage is at least as important to the public as political coverage. Indeed, the differences between the two are increasingly indistinct. Whether government is entitled to do this or not, the agenda for business produces a set of responsibilities and communications challenges that are entirely new to it. It follows that no longer will it be appropriate or efficient to have strategic and tactical communications addressing government, corporate and community relations – they will be the same thing.

NEW
COMMUNICATIONS

CRUSTIES TO FLUFFIES

There is a whole lot more to a multinational corporation's communications demands than its social responsibilities, particularly as practised by some of the unsatisfactory people who define those responsibilities. The corporation needs to continue to address its investors – though, as we have seen, the capital markets are a fast-moving target. In the modern argot, it continues too to need to address all its stakeholders. But it is worth spending some time addressing the CSR issue, not because it's the only game in town, but because it is paradigmatic of the new communications demands on the corporate body – it embraces such a wide variety of communications targets for complex integration, from staff to activists to domestic, federal and foreign authorities, that it represents the closest affiliation of politics with prosperity that a corporate executive of any current working generation is likely to have to manage. The growth of CSR as a fashionable tenet of corporate faith in the UK owes much to the positioning of New Labour to occupy a middle-ground of British politics, where it could marginalise the Tories by embracing capitalism in a free-market economy, while presenting the soft, caring face of social democracy. Then there is the parallel pressure on companies to get ethical applied by the resistance movements to global corporatism – from riots at an economic summit in Seattle to violent May Day demos in London. The more hawkish corporates would strive to present these as the eternal nihilism of the post-War drop-out – Crusties with dogs on strings. But even comfortable men and women in suits were conceding that Swampy – an activist who temporarily dominated broadcast news by occupying a tunnel to stop a road development – and his friends might have legitimate grievances, even if their standards of debate and personal hygiene were found wanting. Hand-wringing commentators, conservative as well as liberal, became concerned that globalisation was alienating and disenfranchising those excluded from the financial fun, most specifically in developing economies, and was damaging the planet.

The personal style of the Prime Minister in the UK also gave the alternative life-stylists an impetus. He wore his faith on a weekend shirt-sleeve, at the end of which was a mug of tea. His claims to be 'a pretty straight kind of guy' may have rung hollow with the sophisticates of *The Spectator* class, obsessed as they were with matching Labour's corporate funding with the former sleaze of the Tories, thereby rather pointlessly working towards a projected conclusion that Tony's Cronies were every bit as revolting to the electorate as they were. But Blair's personal ratings continued to ride unprecedentedly high in the polls, suggesting that the people bought the product presented as the People's Prime Minister. He had a special breaking-with-emotion voice, first market-tested at the death of the Princess of Wales, but deployed in varying degrees of subtlety wherever his humanity needed to be displayed. The climate was conducive to the flourishing of CSR. Then came 11th September 2001, or 9/11 as it became globally branded in a grotesque, if unintentional, pastiche of an American convenience store. Blair found the world stage on which to perform as an agent of world peace, a reconciler of western secularism and eastern Islam from his own intuitions of high-Anglicanism. At the Labour Party conference in Brighton in October 2001, Blair played to his instincts for the emotive power of his message, making a Gettysburg-style address that made it clear that the distinctions between the global economy and the foreign policies of western governments had to go, if his vision of reconciliation was to be achieved.

He declared that the doctrine of international community must motivate rich countries to take responsibility for the most chronic symptoms of global injustice and poverty: 'The state of Africa is a scar on the conscience of the world. But if the world as a community focused on it, we could heal it. And if we don't it will become deeper and angrier.' It's mischievous to point out that Blair apparently talks about healing a scar on our conscience, rather than the problems of Africa, but we can assume that he meant the latter. Former President Bill Clinton was to make similar points in the 26th Dimbleby lecture at Oxford the following December: 'Don't tell me about the global economy – half the people aren't part of it. What kind of economy leaves half the people behind?'

New Labour was no longer singing that 'things can only get better' – a rather indistinct and parochial anthem that suggested little more than Tories had taken Britain about as low as it could get. New Labour, with the help of enlightened western friends, could now save the Third World. Thoughtful think-tank Demos[8] summed up the implications:

> 'This mighty ambition builds upon New Labour's formative premise that we are living in an era defined not by right and left, but by right and wrong. Motivation towards progressive political outcomes is rooted in morality, rather than, say, class interest. Morality has become the new ideology.'

As we have seen, New Labour was enjoining British and multi-national businesses to form a co-venture to deliver this project. Beyond donations to its campaigning coffers, this was and is the true value of corporate money to modern politicians. To convert major corporations from their roles in the political world as paymasters to an altogether more altruistic purpose as co-venturer, not only in domestic social provision, but also in the creation of global harmony, is fraught with practical and systemic obstacles.

Firstly, the quality of manager employed in CSR functions is not of the highest calibre. The function is at the same early developmental stage that PR or corporate communications was in its formative stages two decades ago, when it was a job for the chairman's daughter and the pleasant, but otherwise unemployable, army officer. CSR is currently and widely in the hands of the earnest-but-dim. If companies are alarmed and threatened by Crusties, they have very often employed Fluffies to take them on.

---

[8] The Moral Universe, 2001.

These are the Alice-bands and polo-shirts who are driven by no more complex motivation than that companies should be 'nicer' – to their people, to their environment and, more than likely, to their CSR departments. They talk of sustainable development and corporate citizenship, set objectives and measure performance and have that performance independently audited in respect of a 'triple bottom line' of the three critical constituencies of social, economic and environmental responsibilities.

The problem here is that the working focus is not on what is being achieved among the marginalised and dispossessed economies of the world – nor even among the marginalised and dispossessed of their domestic economy. Nor is it on greater efficiencies that may be delivered to the CSR-aware corporation, so that it can generate greater revenues and profits, the better to serve the economies in which it operates. No, the focus is exclusively on responsibility for its own sake – they are demonstrating CSR because it is right to do so. The reasons for this are unclear, but there's a lot of it about. As their aunties might have told them, it's nice to be important, but it's more important to be nice. And for all the good they are doing to their domestic and world economies, they might as well be helping old ladies across the road.

These Fluffies then come up against the second problem. Business is, by its nature, exploitative. To corrupt Churchill, capitalism is the worst way to run an economy, except for all the other ways. The capitalist economic model of the West that has triumphed so spectacularly over socialist command economies during the last decade of the twentieth century – leading to aspirations of hegemony, not least on the parts of Blair and George W. Bush, for liberal democracy and, in Francis Fukiyama's phrase, 'the end of history' – depends for its progressive prosperity on exploitation.

This will be the exploitation of natural resources, at competitive prices, to fuel it. It will be the exploitation of labour, in the sense that, unless there is a margin between what a workforce is paid and the value that it adds to the enterprise for which it works, there will be no profit in employing that workforce. It will be the exploitation of markets, by which corporations arbitrage the prices of goods and services sourced in one market and sold at a profit in another. None of this means that the executives of multi-national companies are obliged to behave like nineteenth-century mill-owners, to put children to work down mines or, the more likely modern equivalent, in Asian sweat-shops, or to poison the environment for better profit margins. They do, indeed, have a responsibility to their indigenous populations not to do so.

But it's a question of degree, not principle. It's far from clear that companies in capitalist economies can be partners in social and economic reform, so long as they rely for their own welfare on this principle of exploitation. In short, they can be regulated for purposes of corporate social responsibility, but they can't be regulators of it, at least not efficiently. As such, they are a poor choice of partner by government for the delivery of social responsibility agenda items. You don't use a cat to guard the aviary.

Thirdly, CSR may not work anyway. Work by a former head of the economic and statistics department of the Organisation for Economic Co-operation and Development (OECD) in Paris, David Henderson,[9] for the Institute for Economic Affairs demonstrates that proponents of CSR mistakenly presume that notions of sustainable development and the actions needed to promote it are well defined and generally agreed. He argues that CSR's supporters show as little understanding of society's expectations of businesses – claiming that there is a demand for sustainable development and for work alongside stakeholders in support of the triple bottom line, when clearly society expects no such thing – and even less understanding of the profit-making process. Henderson debunks the impractical ideas of 'global salvationism' and believes that fateful choices have to be made now on behalf of humanity and the planet.

Henderson claims that the effects of the enforced uniformity that CSR promotes damage labour markets:

'The greatest potential for harm of this kind arises from attempts, whether by governments or by businesses in the name of CSR and 'global corporate citizenship', to regulate the world as a whole. Imposing common international standards, despite the

---

[9] Misguided Virtue, IEA, 2001.

fact that circumstances may be widely different across countries,
restricts the scope for mutually beneficial trade and investment
flows. It is liable to hold back the development of poor countries
through the suppression of employment opportunities within
them.'

Taken together, these factors of lack of quality and cohesiveness
on the part of the CSR movement and the incompatibility of its
aspirations with the machinations of a free market economy make
the prospects of a joint venture between public and private sectors
to cure the ills of the world look unlikely. More importantly,
the idea of multi-nationals and NGOs working side by side
with common cause looks increasingly absurd. These doubts
are confirmed by the mutual suspicion with which NGOs and
corporations eye one another. One NGO describes CSR thus: 'A
fashionable PR stunt by politicians to win over sceptical voters, by
showing that capitalism has a caring side. A corporate façade that
should be exposed.'

CSR is consequently never successfully going to be spun as a
concerted effort at global remediation by governments, multi-
nationals and NGOs. It follows that the communications function
for politicians, corporations and NGOs alike is best served by
processes of dynamic tension – debate, engagement, compromise
and, where possible, co-operation. But no pretence that we're all on
the same side. Politicians need votes. Companies need profits.
NGOs need to serve special and vested interests. NGOs know this to
be the case. There are signs, too, that companies recognise as
axiomatic that their role is not one of global benefaction, but that
through increased economic activity human happiness is generated
through raised prosperity. There is at least, in the minds of some
capitalists, the notion that profit-making is of wider benefit to more
than simply the shareholders of the profitable enterprise. In this
context, consumerism is good. As Lee R. Raymond, chairman and
CEO of Exxon Mobil, puts it in an open letter accompanying the
energy combine's corporate citizenship report (2002): 'Energy use
grows as economic prosperity increases. And there is a proven link
between economic development and advances in societal welfare
and environmental improvement – particularly in the developing
areas of the world.' What companies such as Exxon need to see as

their mission is not the development of beach-friendly solvents and successful completion of CSR audits, in support of the triple bottom line, so much as increased prosperity from what they do and the demonstrable social benefits that flow from it as a consequence.

What this means for the way that companies communicate is a complex matter. There is no room for fantasies of common purpose with the proponents of CSR – even those NGOs with whom constructive engagement is possible and desirable cannot be viewed as allies, since the destination and the strategic course for reaching it is at considerable variance to the real and perceived purposes of the corporation. Government is an uneasy partner, since it is likely to view NGOs as useful and desirable partners where there is public credit to be enjoyed by association with them. The conclusion has to be that there is a model to be drawn, on which corporations can plot association or alienation from the drivers of CSR – the NGOs – depending on where those NGOs' tactical intent lies on specific CSR issues.

One such model is The Rich Window^{TM} (see illustration). The vertical axis represents the degree to which the NGOs' call to action is directed at individuals (down the axis) or government (up the axis). The horizontal axis represents NGOs' influencing tactics, ranging from direct action (left axis) to research and policy documentation (right axis). The top-left quartile consequently represents degrees of direct action aimed at influencing government policy; the top-right quartile represents degrees of research and independent policy also directed at influencing government. Meanwhile, the lower quartiles represent actions aimed at influencing individuals (employees, consumers) on the left and research and policies aimed and influencing individual behaviour on the right.

In managing a specific issue, a corporation directs its communications strategy by plotting where an NGO's tactics and target audience place it on the window. Actions are prescribed by whichever quartile an NGO occupies, as follows:

- Top-right quartile – Engage: Only in the top-right quartile can a company engage with an NGO, in debate over the quality of research and proposed policies aimed at government and the

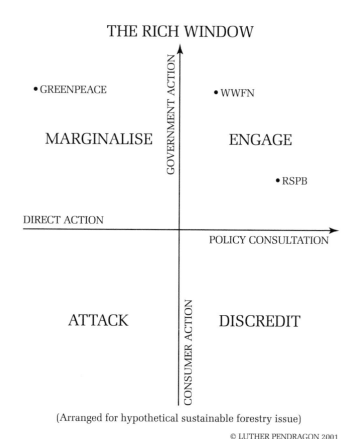

THE RICH WINDOW

(Arranged for hypothetical sustainable forestry issue)

© LUTHER PENDRAGON 2001

potential consequences that arise from them. These are likely to be NGOs driven less by ideology than by a desire to achieve special-interest objectives. There is value in joining their tables to identify mutually satisfactory aims for government policy.

- Top-left quartile – Marginalise: This is at the direct-action end of attempts at government influence. These are stunts aimed at attracting maximum attention or generating embarrassing publicity at government level. Any engagement is likely to fuel publicity and play into the NGO's purposes. The corporation seeks, so far as is possible, not to be involved and, if it responds at all, does so in plain-vanilla through a trade association or other official channels.

- Bottom-right quartile – Discredit: This is likely to be sensational research or scare stories aimed at individual consumer behaviour. Rapid rebuttal is called for, with the low quality of research or factual error exposed for what it is. Engagement is with the audience, not with the NGO, for which the value of the exercise is not in the quality or otherwise of the research – whose accuracy is of little concern to it – but rather in the effect on the audience.

- Bottom-left quartile – Attack: These are activists that are aiming to intimidate or scare individuals – employees or customers – into action that supports their cause. There is no point in any dialectical engagement, so the aim must be to attack and undermine their position, without any direct association with their actions. This is likely to involve very active media exposure of the activists' tactics, backed by force of law, with the response focused exclusively on the actions rather than the aims of the activists.

There is growing evidence that NGOs are consolidating to cover the axes of available tactics, which further complicates the issues. It is possible, for example, that a research-based NGO will have an informal alliance with activists of the Crusty variety at bottom-left. So some overlap of communications strategy may be required – a certain amount of hard-ball in the upper quartiles, for instance.

To take a real CSR issue by way of illustration, sustainable forestry – concerns for deforestation and bio-diversity – might see the World Wildlife Fund for Nature (WWFN) and the Royal Society for the Protection of Birds (RSPB) in the top-right quartile. These groups share many interests in common with manufacturers using wood, relating to security of supply, stability in supplier economies and meeting the environmental concerns of consumers. Greenpeace might be harrying cargo ships with the aim of encouraging bans on certain forms of wood-pulp – that would place it top-left. Women's groups could be making claims that paper products are treated with bleach in ways that could generate risks for consumers – claims that place them squarely bottom-right. Meanwhile, environmental extremists are picketing wood-pulp users and writing threatening letters to employees – bottom-left.

This is robust and self-interested communications strategy and is a country-mile away from the relentless auditors of the triple bottom-line and the Fluffies of CSR. What it recognises is that, while western capitalism has global responsibilities to fulfil, the most efficient methodology for their fulfillment is to continue to make more money in the developing regions in which it operates, increasing local prosperity. In this way, CSR and capitalism have common objectives. Much of European business is in denial of these central truths – like the emerging hegemony of bonds over equities, many corporations are adopting the attitude that if they don't look and pretend it's not there then the frightening new future will go away. But there's really nothing of which to be afraid. The development of global responsibilities alongside capitalism is advantageous to both causes if they respect one another (just as bonds markets can develop at the expense of equities without ruining the entire state of capitalist enterprise). But CSR matters are more advanced in Europe than they are in the States. In general, Europe is relatively empirical and mild in the way it addresses the issues compared with what goes on in the States. Things are different there.

THE AMERICAN WAY

*March 1999 – We're sitting in a windowless meeting room at
our Washington DC partners, Nichols Dezenhall, just around the
corner from Capitol Hill, where we're spending the day preparing
a presentation for an American multi-national – it's our job to
bring some European solutions to the table. Nick Nichols, the
chairman and CEO, has looked in and sits down at the table,
chewing gum and drumming his fingers. I've already worked out
that this is not the kind of communications outfit that we're likely
to find in Britain, let alone continental Europe. There's a small
alligator in a tropical tank in one of the executive's offices.
Nichols and I exchange wisecracks across the table – both of us
have sensible and clever colleagues who are doing the work –
and I elicit a dry chuckle from him occasionally. I've already
worked out that Nichols is the Sundance Kid to his Butch Cassidy
partner, the urbane and slick Republican Eric Dezenhall out of
Ronald Reagan's White House Office of Communications. We fly
up to Chicago to join the client, Nichols with his slim portfolio,
chewing for his country and becoming more animated as we
approach the action. I sense that he is happier taking out the
opposition than talking about it. Like Sundance, he's better when
he moves.*

Like L.P. Hartley's past, America is a foreign country: they do
things differently there. More accurately, in so many areas of
politics and trade America is our future – and, as they do things
differently there, we'd do well to pay attention. Some of it is bound
to be coming here – but only some of it. Tony Blair's
Prime Ministerial style has been labelled presidential by British
commentators so consistently and his support for American

imperialism so widely recorded, especially when Iraq became the issue, that there was a widespread assumption that we were being annexed as the 53rd state. The view is reinforced by Europhiliac writers, most trenchantly by Will Hutton's sequel to his New Labour curtain-raiser, *The World We're In*, and by Little-Englander Americaphobes of both Left and Right. But there remain essential differences, legacies of the two countries divided by a common language. For the purposes of a comparison of the nature of communication, the most important differences are to be found in the constitution, unwritten in Britain and enshrined in the US in the Articles of Confederation and its amendments and the Bill of Rights. As a consequence, American accessibility and its citizens' rights to information are of a different dimension to those of British subjects. New Labour has had a stab at a Freedom of Information Act, but as yet there is little indication of either greater freedom or more information. By contrast, America is culturally used to challenging its rulers and receiving answers. I recall as a young reporter in the Eighties, sitting on the edge of a New York hotel bed, jet-lagged and hungover, with a mundane telephone inquiry for the mayor's office. It's alarming and slightly shaming for the British journalist, familiar with obstructive and obfuscating press offices and other assistants, to be put through directly to the mayor himself – though at 8 am it concentrates the mind perfectly.

Some progress in Britain is being made towards open government, although on the communications side Alastair Campbell's Number 10 machine is always likely to receive scant credit from media that like to think that they are exclusively in charge of the communications process. The naming of the Prime Minister's spokespeople as they go on the record, some broadcasting of briefings and the breaking of the parliamentary lobby's communications cartel, as well as the PM's American-style press conferences that started in 2002, are all evidence of attempts to bring some limpidness to a process that is trammelled by the lack of legislative instruments of communication. It's as though we're trying to behave like we have the best that America has to offer, while protecting our right to keep the establishment secret, under its monarchical mystique.

The polar opposite is best described in Howard Kurtz's book, *Spin Cycle*, which aspired to go 'inside the Clinton propaganda machine'. Kurtz describes Clinton's press secretary, Mike McCurry, in his daily broadcast before the nation's media.

> *'He would mislead reporters on occasion ... He would yell at offending correspondents, denounce their stories as inaccurate, denigrate them to their colleagues and their bosses. He would work the clock to keep damaging stories off the evening news, with its huge national audience. Yet with his considerable charm and quick wit, McCurry somehow managed to maintain friendly relations with most of the reporters who worked the White House beat. He would go to dinner with reporters, share a beer, give them a wink and a nod as he faithfully delivered the administration's line. He was walking the tightrope, struggling to maintain credibility with both the Press and the President, to serve as an honest broker between the antagonists ... Each day, it seemed, McCurry faced a moral dilemma. He stood squarely at the intersection of news and propaganda, in the white-hot glare of the media spotlight, the buffer between self-serving administration officials and a cynical pack of reporters. The three principles of his job, he believed, were telling the truth, giving people a window on the White House and protecting the President, but the last imperative often made the first two difficult.'*

Sound familiar? To anyone on the political media circuit during Blair's first term between 1997 and 2001, McCurry is not quite a dead ringer for the Number 10 Press Secretary – beers and dinner with journalists would hardly suit the famously teetotal Campbell – but there are strong resonances. Campbell should receive some credit for aping the open, if aggressive, informality of McCurry. Yet McCurry was widely admired, while Campbell was just as widely slated. The roots of this contrast in response may lie in the American admiration for success and position and the British equivalence of dissent, envy and cynicism. But that won't quite do in a global culturism in which western attitudes are much more homogenised than once they were. More apparent is that American media and the people they serve know that they have a right to information enshrined in the constitution. This makes the President's spokesman's role clear, if difficult. His is a constitutional and accountable role between the government and the governed and, as such, is likely to elicit respect for its purpose and sympathy for its challenges. No such constitutional clarity of function or style exists for the Prime Minister's official spokespeople, who are consequently kicked about without either respect or sympathy (though, as previously noted, the lack of constitutional definition does provide the PM's spokesman with a far greater freedom of power in international, diplomatic communications than his American opposite number).

But the differences between the communications universes of America and Britain are markedly different for operational, as well as for cultural and constitutional, reasons. The faith and trust that Americans invest in commercial institutions, at the expense of non-commercial organisations, sets up an entirely separate set of social responses to messages and consequently prescribes a variety of communications styles that are, metaphorically as well as literally, foreign to European audiences. In its second annual Study of NGO and Institutional Credibility in 2002, Edelman PR Worldwide and researchers StrategyOne examined relative trust in brands in the US and Europe. In America, the top five most trusted are, in descending order, Microsoft, Coca-Cola, McDonald's, Bayer and Ford Motor Company, with trust ratings ranging from 47 per cent to 56 per cent. In Europe, the top three are Amnesty International, World Wildlife Fund for Nature (WWFN) and Greenpeace, with massive ratings between 62 per cent and 76 per cent. It's only at fourth and fifth place that you find Microsoft and Ford, with relatively measly ratings of 46 per cent and 36 per cent respectively. In America, WWFN ranks seventh, between Nike and Dow Chemical, with 43 per cent. Amnesty and Greenpeace are 10th and 11th, with 40 per cent and 38 per cent.

It may be that NGOs have strengthened their brands and are approaching parity, in credibility terms, with business and government in the US, while simply maintaining an earlier established dominance in Europe, as Richard Edelman argued was the bottom line when he presented the research in New York. I'm not so sure. It is at least possible that Americans have an ingrained trust and respect for business and government, combined with a low regard for environmentalists, that isn't matched in Europe. This would offer a partial explanation of the apparent contempt displayed by George W.

Bush's government for the Kyoto environmental accord and his personal boycott of the Earth Summit in Johannesburg. It's said that Bush's response to charges that the US is responsible for 25 per cent of the world's atmospheric pollution is to sniff the air and remark 'It smells okay to me'.

This support for the interests of industry and commerce over the concerns of environmentalists dictates an approach to the communications process that is at wild variance to the European model. The style of communications approach to NGOs from the business community in the States is one of attack and oppression. Environmentalists and, to a lesser degree, social reformers are the enemy. These are not Crusties and tree-hugging hippies, the argument goes, but highly organised, efficiently funded and politically motivated operators. The challenge is not one of accommodation and engagement, but of challenge and repression.

My friends Butch and Sundance have both written books on the subject, the titles of which provide an early indication of their theses: Nichols' is called *Rules for Corporate Warriors*; Dezenhall's is called simply *Nail 'em!* Nichols' prologue, entitled War and Appeasement and taking Neville Chamberlain and Sir Winston Churchill as part of his text, sets the scene:

> '*All too many business leaders, middle managers, public relations and politicians have somehow concluded that the wisest course of action is to appease the predators' hungry demands, address even their most illegitimate grievances, present them with tasty victuals course by course, and ensure "peace with honour" and "peace for our time" ... Will you corporate chieftains learn from history? Or will you allow yourselves, your companies, your employees, your investors, our citizenry, our consumers and our world civilisation to be dragged into a new ideological abyss?*'

According to Dezenhall:

> '*The Culture of Attack is the result of discontentment ... and declining standards of decorum in which once-repugnant forms of behaviour are now accepted. Attackers are angry because they mistake opportunities with guarantees and confuse disappointment with betrayal. They are guerrilla soldiers engaged in a*

battle for the American Dream, which many see as a perk they're owed just for being alive. When they don't get it, they attack ... Americans are the richest people on earth, yet prosperity hasn't neutralised all forms of misery. A few act out their misery by exchanging the pursuit of happiness for the destruction of the celebrity and the faceless big-business.'

Nichols Dezenhall is at the crisis-management end of the communications market. It would be wrong to suggest that their approach is characteristic of the American communications industry – indeed it would be to erode ND's competitive edge. There are legions of PR 'flacks' in the US who would attract Nichols' scorn for appeasing predators and many more who are involved in long-term profile-raising exercises, or handling investor relations on Wall Street, and who are professionally committed to engagement, rather than aggression. The worldwide PR empires that grew in the second half of the last century, such as Burson-Marsteller and Hill & Knowlton, were of this ambassadorial nature, communicating globally and consistently in the American way. And those British groups that have founded offices in New York or Washington have largely sought to emulate the American model by fitting in and securing briefs to return earnings to the London headquarters. This is not about entrenchment, so much as enjoinment. But it remains the case that America is peculiarly constituted for 'us and them' communications struggles, whether between Republicans and Democrats (still distinguishable in a way that parties battling for the middle-ground of politics in Europe are not), between corporations and their attackers or, more recently, between America itself and most of the rest of the world.

The terrorist atrocities in New York of 11th September 2001 will increasingly be perceived by history as strategic failures. If the attack was to cause new generations of indigenous Muslims to rise in jihad against the corrupt and corrupting West, then the attempt was a disappointment for its perpetrators. Western Muslim youth either looked on in horror and fear of reprisal or shrugged its shoulders and went back to its Sony Gameboy – just like the youth of any ethnicity. But, post-9/11, the characteristics of American 'us and them' attitudes have understandably hardened, domestically and on the world stage. Eco-warriors or any other kind of alternative activist are not likely only to be 'nailed' in the historically robust environment of American commercial or political debate, but to be seen as anti-American. The same applies abroad – perhaps even more so.

The challenge for Europeans – as for the populations of other continents – is to accommodate American attitudes and the communications techniques that purvey them. It's not mandatory to do so. But not to do so is to alienate land-masses and their populations from the largest and most powerful economy on earth. Whether it is desirable to do so is largely irrelevant – America is a fact, not an option. It follows that those with a professional responsibility for international communications in Europe are charged with taking America gently by the arm and leading it into different and challenging environments.

Bismarck jotted on a letter from the Russian Chancellor 'Whoever speaks of Europe is wrong, it is a geographical concept'. Similarly, the proverbial American view asked 'Who gives me Europe?' The cultural and national fragmentation of Europe, even with the growing centralisation and federalism of the European Commission and the euro-zone, offers an entirely alien legislative, regulatory, political and commercial environment into which American corporations are to operate. Wherever one stands on the concept of Europe – whether with Bismarck as a geographer (and probably as a Eurosceptic) or whether with the Europhiles and federalists – the opportunity for the management of transatlantic and transnational communications is a considerable one. For those who are any good at it, it should also be a highly lucrative one.

THE EUROPEAN WAY

September 1999 – My new colleague, Amy Kroviak, doesn't do fear. She's from Chicago and somehow that seems relevant to the ability to turn fear into irritation. Or maybe it's a talent she developed as a producer at LWT for Brian Walden. So she's irritated by the small plane that has taken us to a small airstrip in the west of England to consult a client, bucketing about in bad weather. She chain-smokes outside the reception building and talks about food safety and, though having adopted a European liberal conscience herself, about how Americans in America are astounded by support for animal rights in western Europe. 'My dad says it's based on guilt because they had to eat their pets during the war,' she says as I shield her lighter from the wind. This is Marlboro country. It's at this point that I have a small epiphany – I have travelled the States as a journalist and as an advocate and worked for Americans across Europe and of course I knew they were different from us. But I'd never really recognised how sorry they could feel for us, how foreign and inferior our savage ways could be to them. Nearly three years later, the software of the laptop I am writing this on automatically changes my spelling to American. Boy, are we in trouble if we don't handle this relationship properly.

I have previously covered how American brand values favour corporations over NGOs and environmentalists and how that position is very much the reverse in Europe. As a consequence, many American multi-nationals, whether headquartered in Dixie-land or the more cerebral mid-west, refuse or are unable to take Brussels seriously. These corporations are irritated – not afraid – by the Green influence on proposed legislation and regulation in

Brussels and either assure themselves that 'it'll never happen' or that they can get around it by being omnipotent and, well, American. Since becoming the one great, global Superpower since the collapse of the Soviet Union and having embarked on a worldwide subjugation of its attackers in the wake of 9/11, they may prove to be right in the latter assumption, though possibly for the wrong reasons.

There is no tone of irony in American voices that attack Microsoft for being too powerful in the States, while concurrently demanding competitive freedom in Europe. The US anti-trust authorities supported European Union competition commissioner Mario Monti when he examined the implications of Microsoft bundling software applications into its Windows XP operating system. When the same European Commissioner blocked General Electric's near £30bn merger with systems group Honeywell, the US Justice Department shouted that the EC 'punishes efficiency' and 'punishes success'. I wonder how punished for his efficiency and success Microsoft's Bill Gates feels. British Airways, which was running a television commercial at the time featuring the importance of flying to the US to do business transactions in person, in January 2002 withdrew with its US partner American Airlines from negotiations in Washington aimed at agreeing a new bi-lateral air treaty. BA blamed the unreasonable and one-sided conditions set by US competition regulators for approving the BA/American Airlines alliance. BA described the US proposals, by which some 220 landing slots at Heathrow would have to be surrendered, as a 'protectionist grab'. For every Cuban Camp X-Ray circumstance – the detention and interrogation camp established after 9/11 to hold al-Qa'ida prisoners – when Americans seem bemused that their European allies should object to them doing exactly as they like in their own interest, there are dozens of lower-profile examples in the business world.

The attitude behind the hegemony of the American Way may be rooted in snobbery, as the assumption of European dietary habits, more in common with the Koreans, on the part of Kroviak Snr demonstrates. Americans believe that it is a sign of weakness that European governments can be so easily intimidated and influenced by NGOs and special-interest groups in shaping the legislative

agenda. Huntingdon Life Sciences, a publicly-listed British company involved in animal experimentation, was all but closed down
in the UK by intimidation of its employees and financial
institutions until the Government stepped in to provide its banking
facilities through the Bank of England in 2001. The idea that an
American company would be driven into direct banking with the
Federal Reserve in the States by intimidation from activists is
laughable. Geography also plays its part – not simply America's
global isolationism pre-9/11, but also its internal geography. The
country is simply so large that it is almost impossible to attract
national support for activist campaigns. A friend of mine grew up
hating Gillette and Proctor & Gamble for animal testing, but never
knew any co-ordination at a national level. The result was a social
assumption that activism was a right of passage and, for all but the
most wildly committed, it was then time to grow up.

By contrast, the collection of nation states that constitute Europe
offers a consolidated and influential network of activists. The
oldest, largest and most successful Green party is German and
all mainstream west European political parties have adopted the
environmental agenda to some degree. As a consequence, the
management of issues such as waste recycling, renewable energy
and organic farming are led in Europe. Meanwhile, America could
afford, for the time being at least, to be high-handed at Kyoto. But
the crunch comes, inevitably, for American multi-nationals aspiring
to trade in the EU. Financial institutions, such as Goldman Sachs
and Morgan Stanley, have found that they had to live like the locals
in financial markets. So do the producers of goods and services.
The communications challenges are more than significant ones –
message-delivery and other products of a spin-culture aren't
adequate to serve the interests in these markets of multi-nationals
that aren't prepared to engage in the management of complex
environmental, health and social issues. Like the cases described
previously in the UK domestic market, communications effort
needs to be directed at identifying and working towards common
solutions to challenging issues – share-of-voice, persuasion,
advocacy, rebuttal, ingratiation and all the rest of the weaponry
of an established spin-culture will be next to useless, unless the
solution to those issues is addressed honestly and directly.

Among the most urgent issues to be addressed by companies trading across Europe are food safety, chemicals regulation, forestry derivatives and corporate social responsibility, which, for right or wrong, has become a central defining quality for many companies. I invite the reader to buckle down for a couple of tough paragraphs – we need to touch on what some of this will involve, but it won't last long. The issue of food safety itself contains some of the most contentious factors on the management agenda, including the establishment of a European Food Safety Authority (EFSA); the massive and emotive issue of genetically-modified organisms (GMOs); food additives, ingredients and flavourings; product labelling and animal feeds and medicines. The EU's Chemicals Review Process subjects thousands of substances for thorough review, such as PVC, vinyl acetates and PCBs. This Process further complicates the food-safety issue with the Scientific Committee on Food (SCF), which has conducted a protracted review of the sweetener Aspartame, used in diet soda and confectionery. That's before you get to endocrine disruptors, the chemicals that threaten the human-hormone system and may contribute to infertility, testicular cancer and other conditions.

Following crises of BSE (Mad Cow Disease), foot-and-mouth and e. coli and salmonella poisonings, food safety was a priority for Romano Prodi as President of the EU. As a consequence, EFSA will be a powerful body – Italy and Finland have been fighting for the perceived advantages of hosting it. It will employ some 250 people with a budget of some €40 million after three years. A Food Safety Directive is drafting into European law requirements that place full responsibility on food producers for the safety of foods – the four principles are called: scientific validity; traceability; Precautionary Principle and the establishment of EFSA. Some of EFSA's main tasks will be the identification and early warning of emerging risks; support for the Commission in crises and communication to the public on all matters within its mandate. That mandate is very broad so that, according to the Commission itself, 'it can take a comprehensive view of the food chain and provide a basis for policy and legislation'.

The Precautionary Principle (PP) is significant. It enjoys various definitions among Commission officials, but in a worst-case scenario it can (and has been) deployed to reach decisions on a 'guilty until proven innocent' basis. In the hands of those seeking a ban on additives such as Aspartame, it could be a commercially threatening device. As such, the remit of the EFSA will pose enormous challenges to companies that, directly or indirectly, face scrutiny by it. This sounds enormously burdensome, but it is not necessarily the threat to capitalist civilisation that some Americans might believe it to be, nor the sovereignty-robbing, faceless bureaucracy that those on the right-wing of British politics – in parties invariably with Freedom or Independence in their titles – would have us believe that it is. The whole BSE crisis may have been very different had all this regulatory machinery been in place, as would something as serious and protracted, but rather less high-profile, as the old debate on organophosphate sheep dips.

Nevertheless, it has to be true that, on a continent where NGOs already hold an efficient and effective sway, such regulatory mechanisms offer a means for having food ingredients and chemicals more heavily regulated, banned or subjected to the delays of moratoria more readily in Europe than is anything like the case in America or other trading markets. It follows that European regulation and legislation offers a particular threat to the commercial viability of multi-nationals. Furthermore, it would be naïve to the point of negligence to suppose that regulatory criteria will be decided by science alone – it's enough to say that today's NGOs, though treated contemptuously Stateside, are smarter, more professional and more mobile than at any time previously. Consequently, they are shaping the regulatory agenda well ahead of any multi-national that treats them with such contempt.

So what is a corporation trading in Europe to do? Clearly the adoption of American belligerence is going to be counter-productive in an environment that has fostered and revered the principles of regulation. Furthermore, the communications requirements will go way further than message delivery via media and in the lobbying sense – you might as well drop sandbags on Chernobyl. Nor does the integrated application of communications disciplines, as I have described being applied in the UK market, help much. At a base level, multi-nationals must learn to take Brussels – a tiny city punching hugely above its weight – seriously. They must adopt decent systems of intelligence monitoring so that there is early warning of regulatory attention applied to any chemical, additive, colouring, flavour, packaging material, or animal feed that is relevant to its interests or that of its supply chain. Risks must be assessed to agreed benchmarks as they arise (including the risks of doing nothing). Identify third-party industrial and political allies, engage relevant opinion-leaders and run a twin-track campaign of regulatory advocacy – the legitimate offspring of lobbying – which will likely involve reaching representatives of each relevant member state. All of which, needless to say, is supported by media communications to support your position, plus any further internal and external communications that may be appropriate for reputation protection in trading and marketing. (It is worth noting that much of this kind of activity can be consolidated into communications activity on behalf of entire industries – highly lucrative for those who can achieve it.)

There are sophisticated communications demands over and above that baseload activity. Take the issue of genetic modification. This is an issue that is far too important to the future of the planet – particularly developing economies, if arguments for the economic efficacy of GMOs can be sustained – to be left to debate between the science-friendly Tony Blair and the God-fearing Prince of Wales (big business, as we know, has got to the former; a surfeit of 'nature' may have got to the latter). Even the baseload level of communication demands that the issue is managed actively by corporates responsible for the development of the industry, rather than by corporates for competitive advantage. With US corn genetically modified and unexportable to Europe and with the US and Canada threatening complaints to the World Trade Organisation over European traceability proposals, the communicational atmosphere is – or should be – way past anything popularly associated with spin.

The demands of Europe take the role of corporate communications into a new dimension. The challenge is not so much one of integrating separate communications disciplines into an issues management approach, as one of becoming the issue oneself and thereby defining the nature of the issue to be managed. Issues of genetic modification, the environment, animal experimentation and the role of chemicals in food safety are not subject to the established and mechanical regulation of financial markets. These are frontier issues as yet uncharted by pioneering arbiters of ethics and morals. Those industries affected are shaping the issues, rather than managing them. This represents a fantastic opportunity for the European community, as well as an awesome responsibility for the European Community. As for corporations, the communicational opportunity is not one simply in which to set objectives for competitive advantage and commercial-reputation enhancement (though it is primarily that), but also one of establishing by what principles the oldest democratic continent in the world wishes to live and how it is to be constituted.

It is said that capitalist globalisation disenfranchises the democrat, with the multi-nationals calling the world's governmental tunes, rather than politicians. That may be so – and it may not necessarily be the dark prospect that anarchist organisations, NGOs, protesters and Crusties from Seattle to Genoa would have us believe. Corporations, run properly, are at least as accountable as governments, possibly more so – it is certainly quicker and invariably easier to remove the management of a publicly-quoted company than the leadership of a country. And, if it is true that the future of Europe and its constituent memberships will be decided by business rather than politics, then it is as well to pay corporations – and the way they communicate their will and manage their business – some close attention.

THE GLOBAL WAY

Late May 2000 – I'm sitting in the back room of the Blackfriars branch of El Vino with an internet entrepreneur. He is very drunk, but he can handle it. A business journalist joins us and asks breezily 'How's it going?' The internet entrepreneur averts his gaze from the claret bottle, stubs out a cigarette and says: 'I've just had the arse shot off my share price, my largest investor is demanding an exit at a cash-positive price and I'm being defamed by my rivals on notice-boards over which there's no legal jurisdiction – how are you?' The journalist fills his glass and sails on: 'Never mind. There will always be an internet.' My friend manages a chuckle. 'That's like telling someone after the 1929 crash that there'll always be a stock market. You can't uninvent the telephone. You might as well say there'll always be an England. Statement of existence is not an economic model. If I had a pound for every time someone told me there will always be an internet ... I'd have eleven pounds.' He trails off. But a point of sorts is made. The existence of the internet is a separate issue from its prosperity.

When the dot-com bubble burst, social and financial attention focused on the human drama and the sums of money that had been lost. We could have been forgiven for believing that the revolution had failed. The truth was that a number of companies had failed and they offered good media stories, partly because of the inanity of some of the individual responses to financial ruin and partly because of the delight among the middle-classes that the nerds of the revolution were no longer gazumping them for old rectories and raising the prices of exotic holidays. Intelligent dot-com executives knew that they were never 'worth' the sums of money that credulous reporters and investment mountebanks told them they were worth – at the very least, they knew they would never realise such capital sums. But they also knew that the bubble was to do with a chimera in the financial markets, not in the developing markets of communication. Intensely annoying as it was to be told so, the internet was not going to go away. The internet as a new economic paradigm – the 'new economy' – may have turned out to be over-optimistic and naïve but the new paradigm in communications was real and established. Strictly, this was the revolution of digitisation, rather than of the internet. Some of the more extravagant prophecies of Nicholas Negroponte, founder of the iconic *Wired* magazine, may have proved over-excitable – that we would want to hold conversations with our fridges – but we shouldn't doubt that the digital age was changing our society, even if it was not radically changing our economy.

The change was not confined to the internet. Advances in mobile-phone technology were changing social behaviour in ways far more profound than fogeys becoming irate on trains about people speaking no more loudly into phones than they would if the person to whom they were speaking were there. The disastrous post-war advertising campaign for a cigarette brand held that 'You're never alone with a Strand' – it failed because of the associations with loneliness. The leading mobile manufacturer has never run an ad strap claiming 'You're never alone with a Nokia phone', but if it had, the associations for the consumer might be more positive than for the lonesome contractor of lung cancer. A social effect of the digital age is that most of us in remunerative employment now have consciously to choose to be alone, or at least out of contact from colleagues, friends and family. The effect on the mobile generation, now just beyond adolescence, will be interesting to track, not least perhaps for shifting levels of extramarital infidelities. A shrewd guess might be that the trend over time in this regard is downwards – deceit and parallel-living require inaccessibility.

Whether that means that the mobile and the modem-enabled laptop are agents of greater freedom or restriction of action is a debatable point. But that the nature of our personal means of communication has changed is beyond doubt. This is generally held to be an efficacious development of democracy. The slogan for the on-line financial services firm (adopting the by now universal lower case for on-line proper nouns) interactive investor international observed that 'financial power is changing hands'. The principal offer of the internet was empowerment. Communications clout, for the first time since the divine-right monarchs, was vested in individuals. We shall come to the future implications for granular, as distinct from consolidated, communications in due course, but the effect of the internet, simply by virtue of its arrival, on the traditional balance of power in corporate communications should not go unrecorded simply because so many of those riding the wave were to drown in the flood of over-capitalisation.

This empowerment has shifted the balance of communications power from its traditional source – corporations and institutions – to consumers and individuals. There will still remain the top-down cascade of information and propaganda from multi-nationals and organs of government but that cascade is now not into the absorbent soil of society, but into a wide and deep pool, with changing currents and tides, capable of changing its own shape and direction in relation to the shifting sands around it. This represents a quiet revolution against the established communications hegemonies of corporations and politics.

Like all good revolutions, the internet has not changed human nature, only human behaviour. The internet most emphatically has not changed human motivations. As Roy Lipski, who quit the relative comforts of Goldman Sachs to found Britain's first qualitative internet research and communications consultancy, Infonic, puts it: 'What is radically new about the internet is that it facilitates patterns of behaviour that previously were difficult, or impossible, to put into action.' Nothing new actually happens on the internet. But what it does is massively extend the scope and range of human communication by reducing the constraints of geography, audience-reach, time and resources. It is simply rationalising. Pre-internet, communications methodology (particularly advertising) was concerned with reaching socio-demographic target groups in a fixed geographical environment. This was achieved through ownership or rent of the means of publishing or broadcasting, or a physical presence, such retail outlets.

There has arisen a rather silly debate in this regard over whether the nature of the future retail industry will be on-line or in-mall, as if the internet and the shop are mutually exclusive. The tiredest middle-class conversational gambit is that you can't try on a jacket or enjoy a hazelnut-syrup latte with a friend on-line. Hurrah, then, for the High Street. The fragility of this truism isn't so much exposed by a generation who explores what they want on the internet and then goes out and buys it, nor by the same generation 'shopping' for clothes (trying them on) and then buying them more cheaply on-line, but by the difference between retail communication and communal activity. The former is revolutionised by the internet; the latter untouched by it. The internet is a massive educational resource for our children, but they still go to school. No one seriously considers that they are rival alternatives (as yet).

So people haven't changed, but the means of reaching them have and those media are not owned by the multi-nationals and retail chains. We are reminded of the point made by Benjamin Wegg-Prosser of *The Guardian Unlimited* that 38 per cent of his site-visitors don't read the *Guardian*. Through newsgroups, websites, bulletin boards, chat rooms, instant messaging and email, anyone with internet access can have a world-wide presence – and potentially reach a world-wide target audience – for the cost of a local phone call. The deadening anti-climax and direct consequence of any democratic revolution isn't increased sophistication, but frivolity and debasement. Liberation means the freedom to be unsophisticated – it's why reactionaries and fogies chant 'more means worse'. So the early and most visible manifestation of the internet democracy has been lurid personal websites indulging their owners' crepuscular poetry or stag-night photos – and of course pornography. There is a different matrix of exploitations in the latter, but they are generally the result of individuals exercising their democratic right to be exploited, like it or not, rather than the classic, top-down capitalist model. The internet, if you like, is communication unspun.

Outside the hardcore action and blank-verse sites, the mass now communicates among itself, rather than being engaged by communications through mass media. The internet rubric was that it took 'the wireless' (followed by the radio) some 38 years and television

13 years to reach an audience of 50 million. AOL took two and a half years. This is the kind of market penetration that attracts the undivided attention of rather more than pornographers. Corporations have historically endeavoured to influence public perception through the engagement of substantial corporate communications resources. These resources are fuelled by the kind of budget that what were called agit-prop organisations in the Seventies and are today more prosaically known as NGOs could not hope to deploy. As in litigation, the communications prizes have invariably gone to those with the deepest pockets.

The internet has rendered that an unreliable assumption. The rationalisations of geography, access, time and budget that the internet offers have significantly undermined the corporates' advantage by enabling stakeholders of the widest variety to communicate independently of the approved corporate conduits of information and as effectively as if they had used official channels. In the discrete environments of the internet, a corporation and its detractors are in a fairer fight, or the corporation is more vulnerable and exposed to pejorative communications, depending on which side of the argument you stand.

There are three principal components to the levelling effect of the internet. First comes the economic advantage offered to its exploiters. Anyone of limited budget can command sufficient web space to establish disproportionate presence – with a working knowledge of HTML and some creativity, a pair of bedsit anarchists can, and do, take on the multi-nationals, often with sites that simulate their targets' own corporate sites with unnerving accuracy. If the content is strong enough, the well-organised activist's site may even be able to use the network and resources of the internet – on a fast-breeder basis – to reach a larger global audience than the corporations themselves, whose targets in any event may be narrower. And this is achieved on a low budget and below the radar screen of regulators, who would in any case be pressed to identify a jurisdiction in which to take prohibitive action.

Secondly, the internet has spawned a parallel universe of alternative authorities. Surfers searching for corporate information or advice are no longer confined to the manageable locations of the corporates' own sites and those of government agencies and NGOs.

The internet enables them to turn to organisations they may never have reached off-line. Not a few of these organisations will be of the loony-tunes variety, but the internet has grown up in, thrived upon and fed on an atmosphere of anti-corporatism. There now exists a credibility gap between the corporate message and public perception that the internet can effectively leverage. Finally, there are the NGOs themselves, which have proved skilled and diligent at exploiting on-line opportunities, which have been seized by activists with sufficient speed to leave corporations, relatively cumbersome in response terms, struggling to keep up. With the company struggling to win its share-of-voice in the debate, alternative sources of opinion tend to prevail.

But what is truly frightening is not the degree of success of the anti-corporates through the internet, it is the scale of opposition and detraction that it reveals. The internet did not create this dissent. It is simply a cost-effective global tool under no proprietorship. What it reveals is the scale of antipathy towards business that is out there and gaining confidence now that it has found its medium for solidarity. Against this increasingly potent and self-assured global forum for dissent is set the traditional edifice of the corporate communications function, which may not simply be less equipped to take on its on-line assailants, but is structured in a wholly inappropriate way to respond effectively. The internet is a perfect resistance movement – discrete, mobile and with no formal management structure. The corporation, by contrast, has been created on the command-and-control model. This is not only slow, but quite incompatible with the loose and informal structures of the web. It's not a question of corporate communications structures being unwilling or simply untutored in the ways of the internet – they are simply not structured in a way that could possibly engage with the web. Command-and-control does not lend itself to spontaneity. Companies not only have to learn to let go, to allow factions and individuals to engage in debate on the net – they have to learn to join in.

Examples of effective corporate engagement on-line remain fairly limited. This is partly because engagement of any kind with stakeholders is only a relatively recent phenomenon. In a command-and-control structure, the corporation felt historically obliged to be as limited as possible in its direct communications to audiences – far safer to have such communications filtered through the formal strictures of the AGM, in the confined financial-valuation circles of the City or the anodyne medium of the annual report and controllable propaganda of sterile corporate advertising. Companies did not much want to communicate with real people – customers or critics – other than through the condescending means of the newsletter. To some degree, that was altered by the neo-hippy and post-Seventies glasnost of relationship marketing, but engagements with the outside world were still in the narrowly controlled environment of corporate communications – the company decided where and when engagement was to occur and communication was tightly controlled, if not entirely one-way. It was the cascade principle adapted for external audiences. We were in the world of the stage-managed, privatised-utility AGM where ginger groups were carefully undermined, or the financial-services Q&A road-show, or the consumer-products focus group. Corporations had only really begun to grow accustomed to this limited degree of communicational transparency when the development of the internet announced that stakeholder communications were no longer within the exclusive gift of the companies' representatives. The corporation was to be discussed and examined publicly by stakeholders on an entirely independent basis. Beyond their control or management, corporations were being obliged to join in faceless engagements. They had only just grown used to face-to-face engagements with relatively small numbers of participants, usually of its own invitation who were also geographically accessible. On-line, it was fast becoming more simple to engage 5000 people as 50, in Buenos Aires as easily as in Barnstaple.

Some companies, to be fair, responded more swiftly to the explosion of communications challenges that the internet proffered in the Nineties. Volkswagen memorably responded to a complai-nants' site by adopting it, encouraging the climate of dissent and complaint and endeavouring to respond to it – looking both broad-shouldered and responsive in the process. More recently, Halifax, the building-society-turned-bank and now Halifax Bank of Scotland (HBOS), has partly abandoned the patronising world of financial-services communications – complex jargon or soothing voices on broadcast radio programmes – for direct engagement with third-party on-line discussion forums. HBOS tended initially to focus on users' confusions about product issues, but also became involved in dealing with individual customers' problems. Conventional wisdom had held that consumers don't want companies interrupting what they deem to be semi-private on-line conversations. This was probably an excuse for inertia – experience has shown that those on-line are well aware that they are posting to a public forum and are reassured that the companies involved are sufficiently concerned and responsive to be monitoring their grievances. HBOS actually created a culture of expectancy, with customers calling on HBOS to respond when an issue emerges of a concern which starts to build popular support.

Most famously, Shell, in 1999, developed this technique and its commitment to dialogue with its Tell Shell forums, a set of on-line, uncensored discussion forums inviting participation and feedback on issues as diverse and contentious as human rights in Sudan to bio-diversity and rainforest depletion. There is more to commend these on-line communications processes than to censure, since it is an enlightened form of engagement with the new granular on-line audiences that the internet offers, but the danger is that such sites do not move an issue on, unless the company responsible for such an issue does so. Open, uncensored discussion forums will not in themselves guarantee lively and constructive debate, unless commensurate action is taken. If it is not, such sites become like a CD on repeat-mode – they go round in circles (some might say spin freely) while repeating the same tunes.

With target-companies behind the curve in on-line developments, those with a greater professional interest in undermining them than mere service-complainants are likely to take advantage. We have seen how NGOs have emerged as a major lobbying force and central communications challenge on both sides of the Atlantic, with differing responses in Europe to those in the States. For the NGOs, the internet is the most powerful of communicational weapons – for many it defines them. While to some degree or other the major corporates understood the potency of the internet by the late Nineties – at least as far as recognising the need to establish a corporate website and to publish on it material regarding

the social, environmental and ethical charges levelled at them by
NGOs. But they achieved this response and engagement only after
several years of the NGOs enjoying the on-line environment almost
entirely to themselves. It is hardly surprising that a well-organised
NGO is likely to be more flexible and fleet of foot in its on-line
communications than the multi-national that it traduces. Approval
of communications, their content and deployment within large
corporations is, by comparison, painfully slow – a treatable
consequence of pyramidical command-and-control structures,
burdened with communications journey-people, the communications corridors paved with nice but ineffectual executives with
good intentions on cumbersome committees. Little wonder that
corporations continue to be outgunned on the internet.

The relative on-line sophistication of the NGOs is apparent on
sites such as RTMark's, a consolidated site bringing together
activists and investors looking to support anti-capitalist and
alternative projects. Similarly, the old parody sites – on which
activists emulated and mocked specific corporate sites (with some
wit – Nike's 'Just do it' becoming the pastiche 'Just stop it') – have
morphed into the likes of Save or Delete, a Greenpeace-operated
site that is sophisticated and consumer-friendly, considerably more
sophisticated than a simple campaign site. Its design commanded
coverage in right-on magazines such as *The Face* and *i-D*. The
purists among the anti-establishment might accuse Greenpeace of
selling out, but the site takes the environmentalists' message to
audiences not renowned for their activism credentials. These are
not always voters – some downloadable graffiti-stencils have been
enthusiastically deployed within Holloway prison. The relatively
low cost of on-line publishing has been an encouragement to
activist sites that have been narrow and single-issue in their appeal
for attention, but others have begun to establish themselves as
opinion leaders within the activist communities and have emerged
as hubs of on-line social movements. They have built credibility
and authority, developing powerful and well-respected brands in
an environment in which it is difficult to ascertain what is reliable
information and what is scurrilous rumour (though there is not
much difference in this respect between the internet and much of
the Press). Most significantly, these vanguard organisations were

among the first to recognise the importance of building networks and links between common interests and websites to combine the forces of otherwise disparate activists. Examples are IBFAN, a global network of public interest groups campaigning to reduce infant-mortality rates, and the Framework Convention Alliance, a group of NGOs and activists promoting the World Health Organisation's Framework Convention on Tobacco Control and endeavouring to prove the tobacco industry's obstruction of its progress. This represents on-line evidence of the consolidation of effort of organisations that could otherwise separately be tracked strategically for communications purposes in *The Rich Window*.[10]

The consequence of this consolidation has been that, since the millennium, the number of authoritative activist on-line voices has been in decline, but have built a consistently large audience for their sites, have ensured that their sites are well-placed in search-engine rankings and have developed partnerships that ensure that they are well-represented in debates in their areas of interest. They are groups with diverse causes, such as Greenpeace, Human Rights Watch, Sierra Club, McSpotlight and CorpWatch. It is possible to draw a parallel here between the on-line-activist media and the commercial media industry. Just as an increasingly limited number of media owners dominate the Press and broadcast media, so a relatively few NGOs and activist groups now account for a large proportion of on-line campaigning. They are growing in influence and public profile. But the consolidation of this alternative industry also means that its constituent parts are more visible and easier to track by those whom they seek to undermine, if only the butts of their attacks were better organised in their response.

Meanwhile, the fact that a relatively small number of NGOs and activists are establishing themselves as the critical mass of the on-line media, local or single-issue groups can align themselves to the global network through the resources, technical support and campaign reach of the international NGOs. One anecdote illustrates this: A group called Concerned Citizens of Norco, a deprived, largely black community some 50 miles from New Orleans and location of a chemical refinery owned by Shell, called on the

---

[10] *The Rich Window* was developed by Ben Rich and is © Luther Pendragon 2001.

support of organisations such as Greenpeace, CorpWatch and the Movement for the Survival of the Ogoni People (MOSOP), a Canada-based Nigerian activist group. In so doing, it succeeded in persuading Shell to improve its relocation and environmental improvement package. Multi-nationals often boast of global power delivering local service, but it looks like their opponents can play that game too.

The strengthening position of the NGOs in the on-line campaigning world raises compelling questions about their accountability and responsibilities. But they would claim to raise just as compelling questions to address to the multi-nationals on the same criteria. The corporations in this scenario have much to do to keep up with their opponents – putting the corporate social report online won't do. Nor do we need just ePR – the issues themselves have to be managed on-line. But the most important implication for this, the most important development in global communications, is that the internet is forcing world business – long before such a pressure exists in world politics – to concentrate on dialectical engagement rather than assertion, image-presentation and obfuscation. Since the process of political communication tends, as we have seen, to follow business communications, engagement of issues on the world-wide web may yet prove the *coup de grâce* for our global spin-culture.

CONCLUSION

THE EXCITEMENT OF HONESTY

March 2002 – Conversations with the Rt Revd Richard Chartres, Bishop of London, can take on a dream quality, in which one is a contestant on a TV game show that's a highly-charged combination of University Challenge, Call My Bluff *and* Countdown, *with an irrational fear that an answer may be demanded in Greek. I have just had such a test in one of his rooms in Old Deanery Court, just across the road from St Paul's – and feel that I've scored few points. I'm on an end of a small sofa facing the fireplace, the bishop to my left facing the sash window, while the gloaming darkens the room. Suddenly he explodes: 'How did we become like this? How did we get so boring?' Happily, it turns out that he's not referring specifically to the two of us in the room, but to the wider Church beyond the window and Ludgate Hill. We've been talking about denominational labels – conservative evangelical, liberal catholic and the like – and the self-obsessed bickering between those who believe that they represent God's One True Church. Bishop Richard is a man of many missions – one of them would appear to be to make the Church of England more interesting. He is described to me by a former aide to the Archbishop of Canterbury as 'the personification of an English bishop – Trollopian with liberalism and erudition'. When the next conservative evangelical asks me what I am, I resolve to reply that I'm a liberal-erudite Trollopian, like my bishop.*

A little over a week after this interview with the Bishop of London, *The Sunday Times* runs an interview with the Archbishop of Wales, Rowan Williams, whom the newspapers have been crawling over as that short-odds bet in the Canterbury Stakes. The Welsh valleys echo to London, as Williams tells his

interviewers: 'We are a deeply, dangerously bored society ... we should be asking "what's happening to us? Why are we so bored?"'
True, there is a difference between 'boring' and 'bored', but not much. The bored are invariably boring and the boring are often bored. It's possible that the bishops had shared their thoughts, bishops often do – it's what a synod is for. But if Wales and London had not in March explored the nature of society's boredom, then there must be something soporifically tangible in the air, something so apparent to the episcopal senses that it transcends coincidence and reveals its secular self clearly to such churchmen. It must be the case, because the Holy Spirit is not a bore.

There was further coincidence, but no sense of irony – this was not a boredom special report – that *The Sunday Times* ran on the same page a piece, by Oxford's Regius professor of divinity, Keith Ward, about how an absurdly literal understanding of God comes between modern humans and an inspiring faith. It contained the line: 'It is not that God's existence has been disproved – no, God has simply become boring and irrelevant.' This was a view that neither of the bishops had expressed – for them, it was Church and society that had grown bored and boring, rather than God. But it's clear that the capacity to bore is building as a characteristic of the decade, despite a global war on terror, the prospect of cloned human beings and the advances in telecommunications and digital technology that make personal entertainment available anywhere and at anytime. After the Consuming Eighties and the Democratising Nineties come the Boring Noughties. Why, after a protracted period of unbridled prosperity and with a global village in which to play with the most enabling technology ever developed, are we so bored? Among the Bishop of Wales' rhetorical questions exploring the nature of modern boredom were: 'Why do we want to escape from the glories and difficulties of everyday life? Why do we want to escape into gambling or drugs or any other kind of fantasy? Why have we created a culture that seems more in love with fantasy than reality? Whether that's gambling or drugs or, for that matter, the National Lottery, we should be asking ... why are we so bored?'

Why indeed? The drugs are a symptom, not the malaise itself, as Labour's ineffectual 'Drugs Czar' Keith Halliwell was to demonstrate. The fact that they are universal, rather than confined to sink estates or areas of high unemployment or even highly urbanised areas, would seem to support this. Ask the most accurate of social observers, the taxi drivers. I took a cab from Crediton station in Devon to a cottage we were renting in 1999. Crediton is a pretty rural market town: 'There was a needle-death last Saturday – always needles lying around the public lavs,' said the driver. 'Crediton is the drugs capital ...' I waited. Of the South? Of the West Country? ' ... Of East Devon,' he confirmed. You can be that specific. You can *want* to be that specific. Another cab driver in Folkestone and writes me regular bulletins from the front-line of illegal immigration and the drugs trade. Here's a typical extract:

'I first knew Darren and Royston when they were sullen truant teenagers moving quietly about the council estates, members of a small pack of watchful scavengers; like jackals looking for carrion they viewed everything in their domain as a potential theft for gain, and everybody that passed through as a potential muggee. Ten years ago Darren and Royston lived with their mother and stepfather. Their mother died recently of an overdose and the stepfather shambles about in the terminal stages of a drink- and drug-fuelled hell that will end soon in a pool of piss in a bus shelter. The days are gone when mother and stepfather would take a taxi to collect their dole Giro before going on to the GPO and then to the Warren, behind St Peter's church, where they would disappear down a pathway to meet their supplier and restock, to service their own needs and those of the stunned creatures who made it to their door. Royston and Darren are fully fledged junkies now with girlfriends they put on the game as necessary and a life driven by the need to steal daily to finance their long suicides.'

Daily and nightly he has such youngsters and older no-hopers in the back of his cab, twitching and sweating, sometimes turning nasty, at which point he can protect himself from the knife by throwing the central locking, but not from the block of concrete that might come through the windscreen. This is not Glasgow or Liverpool or Brixton or Bristol – or Miami or Rio or Mexico City or Jakarta or Hong Kong or Moscow. Or any of the other concentrations of the cosmopolitan urban under-classes. This is Crediton and Folkestone.

To claim boredom is at the source of this mess, as does the Archbishop of Wales, is a bold claim. Or perhaps he claims boredom as another symptom – he does, after all, ask why we are so bored as to want to escape reality. The cabbie reckons it's because the last traditional working-class occupations were destroyed in the Eighties, leaving an uneducated and unskilled under-class with no purpose. Old Labour statesman Tony Benn believes that the corrosive effect of 'routine lying' in public life is a contributory factor. With boredom goes cynicism and the crises of boredom are closely related to the crises of trust in public institutions. This is not a country colonel's point about respect for authority and sense of public duty. It's about not trusting public institutions to deliver. Ultimately, it's about having nothing to believe in.

For the educated and affluent classes, for whom a sense of purpose is not so dissipated as to demand a heroin habit, the difference is one of degree, but not of principle. There may be no working class in the historical sense anymore, as a recent test case in the British courts suggested. Property developers Dano Ltd wanted to build luxury apartments on land that was set aside in a 1929 covenant on the eighth Earl of Cadogan's Chelsea estate for the working classes. Dano argued that 'the words "working class" are not now capable of any meaningful definition', holding out the delightful prospect of a reformed House of Lords ultimately ruling whether there is a working class to be governed. Thatcherism may have largely abolished the working class. But there are under-classes – and the middle-classes may suffer a similar root-boredom to theirs. Their relative comfort simply dulls the desire to escape it. Post-agrarian economies that produce surpluses have developed secular western societies in which spirituality is operative only at the margins, if at all – and then driven by the obsession with self, so that the New Age religions are easily compatible with materialistic urges. More frustration and boredom. Politics, too, offer little by way of ideology, now that the only territory under dispute is the middle-ground and the relative competence of stewardship of a free-market economy, in which private enterprise is the only proven model. Such enterprise, after the most prolonged period of bull markets that western capitalism has ever known, followed by a disillusioning collapse of confidence, is itself dull. It has provided comfort without challenge, the only striving factor being the degree of self-motivation that can be conjured to claim one's share of the spoils.

Public service, in this environment, becomes an option, but not the necessity that it is in societies where and when collective, rather than individual, effort is required to survive and to prosper. It's hardly surprising that, in such an individualistic social environment, the family – as a model on which to build social development – should look tired and anachronistic. A society that increasingly dispatches its elderly people to nursing homes, so that their heirs can get their hands on inherited property assets, is demonstrating that its components have regressed to more bestial modes of behaviour than their forebears, for whom quality of life had measurements other than the length of the drive, be it in front of the house or on the golf course. The attitude infects every limb of our lives. The arts are reduced to commentaries on the latest outrages of Tracey Emin, her unmade-beds-as-art and the excesses of the Turner Prize. Articulate, middle-class, artistic soundbites are to be absorbed over the last of the claret late on a Friday night in front of the *Newsnight Review*. Listen to this from the Queen of the Zeitgeist, Germaine Greer, on *Newsnight' Review* – the subject is Sam Taylor-Wood's 'controversial' exhibition at London's Hayward Gallery: 'Ultimately I have to say that I think she is a good artist and an important artist. I think that the real message is that style is the new content.' In a spin-culture, it has ceased to be an option to appreciate or to experience art, so much as to win a Greer's stamp of approval that you are 'good' and 'important', because that's the ultimate triumph of style over artistic content. Poet and critic Tom Paulin chimes in: 'It's the absence of politics. This is the end of history. It's narcissistic, weightless, fantasy, decadent art that's somehow survived into the next century, but still saying there is nothing here and there is soon going to be even worse than nothing.' He could be talking not so much about Taylor-Wood's art as of art criticism in general and the *Newsnight Review* in particular.

The common accusation is that our media are dumbing-down. But it is the media that are reflecting the dumbing-down of our approach to politics, to business, to the arts and all areas of human endeavour in our institutions, which become not so much leaders of opinion as 'lifestyle choices'. We see that in our Church, when the predicted appointment in the summer of 2002 of the new

Archbishop of Canterbury, Rowan Williams – an appointment that was naturally leaked well in advance to *The Times* and *The Guardian* in order to test media and public reactions – is greeted with the splashed news that he is poised to publish a book that attacks Disney's influence on children. In fact, the book, *Lost Icons*, was published two years previously and examines the nature of a multitude of modern iconic influences. The triumph of style over content. We see it when, earlier in the same year, the head of the Armed Forces in Britain, Admiral Sir Michael Boyce, realises that he has been drawn into Number 10's spin-culture and has ramped expectations of a Royal Marines operation to hunt al-Qa'ida terrorists in Afghanistan – false expectations that, widely covered in the media out of Blairite enthusiasm for war-on-terror success, threatened the job of the Marines' commander, Roger Lane. Less of a triumph in the war on terror, then, than of style over content.

The good news is that people aren't so stupid as to continue to take this. They are bored by the spin-culture and want out of it. The Government recognised this around the 2001 election and belatedly made efforts to distance itself from that culture. But there is little ultimately that government can do about a culture that it didn't create, but of which it became a part. It is for the mass of people to alter the culture in which they live, in all walks of life. There may be paths out of this decadent ennui, in which the dispossessed see no greater purpose than to escape life while it is lived, until the escape is permanent, and the privileged protect themselves from life's non-professional challenges and from the militant dispossessed with possessions and an adulation of style, ignoring life's content. The choice of such paths could be forced upon us – by a prolonged reversion of the economic growth cycle, for instance, or by a global/cultural conflagration between the rational *logos*-obsessed western nations and the spiritual *mythos*-inspired tribes of the east. Or we could shake ourselves from our torpor and re-discover senses of purpose that make us less boring and less bored. We would need to find something to occupy us, rather than being occupied. We need to find something to do.

Thursday, late morning, 20th June 2002 – The office has televisions hanging from the ceiling that have mostly been showing the World Cup in anticipation of England's quarter-final with Brazil. They only get switched to Bloomberg or Sky News if clients are in. But we switch to Sky for the Prime Minister's first US-style press conference from Number 10. Blair is appealing to us over the heads of the press corps and we know what he is doing. He's still good at it though – I'm watching with a collection of some of the most cynical, metropolitan and politically-aware people around and, if they're impressed, he'll be doing more than all right for middle-England's news-bites in the early evening news. Somebody wonders how he manages to keep swigging from a cup of tea below the podium – it's only a small cup and he never seems to finish it. Maybe there's a vending machine built into the podium. Maybe he has a special hot-beverages adviser replenishing it. It's obviously resonant of the mug of tea clutched on the end of naked forearm that has made previous manly appearances, but if this is the most critical his audience gets then it's a triumph. The current Private Eye *runs with a cover of Blair saying 'From now on it's no more spin' and Campbell in the background adding 'I think that'll play really well'. Charles Moore of the* Telegraph *says 'nothing of any interest' emerges from the press conference. But that's not fair. Blair emerges from the press conference and he's interesting. For some weeks, Number 10 has been under siege and we've begun to believe that Blair is raging in his bunker that his hapless generals have failed to win the media war by not giving him enough old ladies to glad-hand at a royal funeral. This performance knocks that image down. Blair is, after all, a pretty straight kinda guy.*

At one stage in the planning process for this book, the publisher suggests that 'honesty is the new spin'. I rejected this out of hand, not just because it's wildly over-optimistic, but because it's a motherhood-and-apple-pie view. When you appeal for honesty and trust, you might as well say 'all you need is love' – it's true, in its way, but it doesn't help much. It's the sort of thing you hear on *Thought For The Day*. It is, in any event, in the nature of politics to lie and dissemble – no politician can be expected to concede that his party has no chance of winning the next election, however far behind they are in the polls. Honesty simply has no place in politics. But now I'm not so sure. It's Blair's aspiration, if only to appear more honest and less spinful, and if we need a broad cultural change, we need politics to set an example. He was saying before the 2001 election that his Government had to concentrate less on its messaging service, but that was, as *Private Eye*'s irony would have it, because it would play well. Now he has to believe it – and, more importantly, to live it. The spin-culture served Blair's purpose well in the early days of government, precisely because the issues were easy – making the Bank of England responsible independently for setting interest rates was, for instance, inspired but simple. It ceased to be so easy after his 2001 return, as the Government came to face real content, over which style alone could have no dominion – health-service provision, public transport, pensions, housing. And, of course, Iraq. He had to move from being a Prime Minister of presentation to one of rational debate and not be afraid of doing so – the Presidential press conference was a significant step in that direction, just as his subsequent appearance before an interrogating parliamentary select committee was not, because select committees are vapid, under-briefed and obsequious. It is also important that he does so because the boredom and frustration that European electors have felt during the battles for control of the centre-ground, which again are no more than battles of style over content, have manifested themselves in the partially successful re-emergence of odious extreme right-wingers at the polls. This isn't just a communications game.

So Blairism moves on. Simple assertions won't do. There need be no more happily double-counted NHS funding figures paraded as increased investment; no more claims that the Government will reduce street crime in months, when it will in reality be advances in mobile-phone technology that make the latest component in mugging less attractive for muggers. Focus groups show that the electorate want explanations and Blair is the party's greatest communicational asset when it comes to explanation. The difference is a thin one. The less easily conned, or rampant right-wing detractors (depending on your political sympathies), will have it that such press conferences as Blair's inaugural effort are about presentation rather than substance (cf. Charles Moore), but, in terms of access, an agenda that isn't dictated by New Labour and the opportunity for at least a degree of spontaneous debate, it is hard for those not on Moore's mission to argue that Blair isn't taking at least one tentative step away from the command-and-control control-freakery that was associated with the spin-culture fostered by New Labour for its first term.

A concentration on issues and the management of them, with communications being an integral part of the process, in any event has implications of honesty that emanate from the discipline of the new process. The analogy with commercial communications might be the manner in which the British record industry managed CD pricing (cf. page 163) or the video industry addressed censorship (cf. page 168). I have not a shadow of doubt in my mind that corporations will meet – will *have* to meet – the challenges of NGOs and special-interest groups where they are, rather than where they would wish them to be, just as the Church has to meet people where they are with the Gospel or remain a diminishing sect. That will require a degree of engagement and dialogue which, while sharing many of the objectives and attitudes entrenched in a more combative and confrontational past for all parties concerned, will require honesty too. Blair's June 2002 Press Conference was part of a cultural shift too, rather than simply a political re-positioning. New New Labour (as Mandelson calls it) needs to reflect the new honesty to which electors are growing accustomed in other walks of life. Look at Prince Charles calling the Queen 'Mummy' in public; look at a new Archbishop of Canterbury, appointed by the PM, who called the Government's support for a war in Afghanistan 'morally tainted'; look, for that matter, at Cherie Blair referring to the 'hopelessness' of Palestinian suicide bombers. Addressing the issue and saying something honest, whether it's immediately helpful or not, comes not far behind.

Labour is learning this and its efforts to dissociate itself from the spin-culture to which it contributed is evidence. In June 2002, the minister for Europe, Peter Hain, acknowledged that there was a 'trust problem' for the Government that would need to be addressed before a referendum on the euro. This served as a recognition that trust is central to the success of Labour's European policy. There is time to win that trust back. You cannot trust someone who is not honest with you. Honesty doesn't have a moral genesis in this context – it is a practical demand, if the Government is to fulfil its European mission. In the same way that a company will need to be honest if it is to prosper in an environment increasingly controlled by the NGOs, government can adopt honesty as a vote winner. There is plenty of time for that, during a pro-euro campaign that will tell electors that the issue is not about bent bureaucrats or straight bananas but about the cost of living – more specifically, the higher cost of living outside the euro.

The Tories have only partially learned this lesson. The more enlightened, such as Francis Maude, have spearheaded think-tanks such as Cchange (get it?) that seek to make the Tories electable by presenting an eclectic candidacy that isn't as straight, white and male as the party that has lately occupied a parallel universe – well, not that parallel, more of a separate dimension – to modern Britain. It has to be true that Conservatives will adopt more electable policies if they widen their prospective parliamentary candidates lists more inclusively. The 'one more heave' tendency, embodied by Ann Widdecombe, who would have it that political sympathies are cyclical and so the electorate will return to traditional Conservative values and policies if the party is just patient and resolute, consigns the Tories to a gradual deterioration and irresistible demise in an old folks' home.

But it's difficult to see how a wider variety of candidates can be attracted to the Conservative Party without some serious shifts in policy. Asylum policy could hardly have endeared Tories to the immigrant community. 'Traditional family units' are hardly likely to have ambitious young women beating down Central Office's door for application forms. So one is left with the feeling that the exercise of re-invention for the Tories is about image. Indeed, Maude is on record:[11] as saying that the Conservative Party has to change its image as Labour changed its own in the Nineties. But Labour didn't just adopt a new, user-friendly image – it annexed centre-left and some centre-right policies that had been the province of Conservatives. It broke with the politics of its past in its re-invention.

Former Conservative Party chairman Sir Archie Norman has called the Tories 'an unfashionable brand – the perception of the party is pretty dated'. As a former chairman of Asda, Norman will appreciate that brand values are about more than image. Asda

---

[11] *Today* programme, BBC, 24th June 2002.

didn't sell groceries because its executives were friendly (or were from a wide social and ethnic mix), but because it sold products that people wanted at a competitive price. Labour had to confront its demon in Clause 4. Conservatives will have to confront theirs in Europe. An affirmative vote in a referendum on the euro – surely within the grasp of an honest campaign – will marginalise and render irrelevant the barking tendency of the Tory Party, as the abolition of Clause 4 marginalised the old Labour left. Europe is the Conservative Clause 4.

In honesty, there was probably more that was dishonest about Labour's transformation than would be tolerated by the electorate today. Tax-and-spend was a policy that New Labour had allegedly abandoned, but turned up anyway in raised indirect taxation and came properly out of the closet in the 2002 Budget. The grinning image of Blair's New Labour owed much to the power of image over substance – the greatest image boost being not being a Tory. It's difficult to see the same trick being pulled off by an opposition party in the foreseeable future – the post-spin-culture demands this honesty factor. The electorate demands an honest dialogue with government – and expects it to be delivered. There is no way back to command and control. It's not such a catchy lyric, but things can only get more consensual. That means more access and debate. And what electors want in the post-spin-culture is honesty. It's the new brand value.

A problem is that, in the mouths of politicians, expressions of honesty turn to dust. Like humility, as soon as you claim you have it you've lost it. It can only be about how you behave, rather than what you claim. More accurately, it's about how politicians allow those who represent them to behave, because – as any student of *Newsnight* will confirm – the politician's job is to defend the policy corner. In that sense, it doesn't matter much whether they are believed or not, so long as their opinions appear to be honestly held and soundly argued. The voter may make a decision based on those latter qualities of honesty and soundness, rather than political belief. It follows that the task of political communication does not principally lie with the politician. Nor can it lie with special advisers – the 'spads' – the burgeoning number of whom, however unjustly, have been marked as irredeemable components of the old spin-culture.

No, political communication must be driven by the Whitehall civil-service machine of GICS – by no means without the assistance and collusion of the spads – if the necessary public trust and confidence in government communication is to be re-established. In a private presentation to the Institute of Public Relations on 22nd April 2002, GICS' Head of Profession, Mike Granatt, spelt out the means by which this trust and confidence would be rebuilt and maintained. These means could be categorised as consistency, clarity, transparency and accountability.

Consistency requires long-term investment in not only the dry human-resource areas of staff and training but also in communicational relationships – and not just with the freshly diluted Lobby system. The concentration on the traditional Lobby, combined with an economic squeeze on newspapers that ran down specialist correspondents, contributed significantly to the corrosive juices of spin, counter-spin and a culture of ringside reporting that has marginalised reasoned and rational debate and analysis. Clarity demands clear roles and demarcation lines for permanent specialist civil servants working alongside spads. Without doubt and despite the high-profile horror stories, of which Jo Moore's is the most cautionary, spads bring challenge, creativity and a wider range of recent experience to Whitehall. Likewise, GICS is the essential in-house component, the incubator and reservoir of government experience (including previous governments) and track-record, ability to apply creativity without rule-breaking and the source of an essential critical mass of senior managers. Without this buffer and reservoir, no amount of importation, from whatever private-sector source, could develop and maintain a credible government communications service.

The GICS-plus-spads model is a combination worth considerably more than the sum of its parts. For its part, GICS makes an offer to internal and external stakeholders. For ministers and the rest of Whitehall, GICS should provide confidence that it's the communications will be responsive and deliver sophisticated and cost-effective advice and action within the rules; those outside the Government must have confidence that GICS will deliver the facts in an honest, timely and cost-effective manner within the rules.

Spads are nothing new. There are just more of them – around 70, or twice as many as the Tories ever had, with nearly 30 in Number

10. Ministers need devil's advocates, conscience-keepers and back-watchers (though fewer back-stabbers, a role too often adopted voluntarily). Furthermore, civil servants appreciate informal party-political sounding-boards on policy matters and a proper communications conduit to hand for the referral of party-political activity. It might be added that the media too need authoritative sources for party-political emphasis and nuances. To work most effectively, spads need induction, guidance and training in Whitehall – standards have suffered through lack of formal integration. They need leadership and mentoring independent of their ministers. What they do not need is executive powers.

The demarcation of the roles is for GICS to provide the factual explanation and description of policy, information distribution and management of budgets and resources. This leaves the spads clear for ideological justification and party-political manoeuvres, the cut and thrust of politics – and some explanation and description when required. Both GICS and spads must liaise and co-operate within their fields of activity and both should have direct advisory access to ministers. But the difference in their professional roles requires regular and clear exemplification – the relative political freedoms of spads have too often been the subject of fudge; similarly the restrictions on civil servants have similarly been dangerously blurred. These are different creatures, though they may work together constructively. The differences need to be clearly identified and celebrated.

To be effective, that requires transparency. Codes of conduct, unlike the private sector, which lacks the public-interest imperative and is, in any event, not subject to effective application of regulation, need to be published and assessments reported to Parliament. This will need to be completed and enforced by the heirs of Sir Nigel Wicks, whose eponymous committee succeeded the Nolan Committee as the arbiter of standards in public life. Accountability is spawned by the clarity of the various roles. But it is important to stress that GICS is a civil-service function that rightly reports directly to the permanent secretary, as the senior civil servant in particular departments. Spads must report directly to their ministers. As temporary civil servants, they have technically reported to permanent secretaries. This has been a ghastly recipe for compromise and conflict of interest, with a permanent secretary feeling obliged to protect a spad when he or she should rightly go, or a minister feeling able to dump responsibility for a spad on his permanent secretary. The machinations between Stephen Byers as transport secretary, his permanent secretary Sir Richard Mottram, spad Jo Moore and civil servant Martin Sixsmith was only the most visible of an intolerable system of working.

The model is transferable to the business world. Globalisation and the anti-capitalist movements it has spawned; the international NGOs and their well co-ordinated social-health and environmental agendas; societal co-ventures with governments to establish a world order that accommodate advances in frontier sciences such as genetics – all wrapped in one-world information technologies – mean that corporate communications must develop into something more sophisticated than bright young men and women on the phone to the capital markets. In the US, Washington is commercially as important as Wall Street; in Europe, Brussels is as vital to corporate prosperity as London or Frankfurt. Corporations – the engines of economies – need to engage in open and honest dialogue with a vastly wider variety of stakeholders than those who hold their shares, if they are to prosper. Similarly, well-developed in-house corporate communications resources need to be supplemented with the challenging and properly deployed talent of their own breed of 'spads'.

Businesses can usefully replicate the Government's holy alliance between GICS and spads. Corporations will require their own slick internal 'civil services', while drawing in those communicational specialists and generalists who understand the outside world and can play it to corporate advantage. That advantage, however, will only narrowly be served by the old networks that can provide press and on-line share-tipsters. There is too much to play for in developing Worlds – First, Second and Third – in which global corporations are paying the pipers and calling the political tunes, with governmental co-operations and consents.

The stakes are high. The influencing professions and trades – politics, law, journalism, advertising, PR and communications – face a crisis of confidence among those they serve at a time when their self-confidence is high, because spin-culture has undermined the credibility of communications professionals. The truth is that they are not believed. It's a dangerous position to be in, when there is so much to play for in politics and commerce. Just as a vacuity has occupied the centre-ground of political life, offering opportunistic right-wing extremists to make ground across Europe, so a lack of voice in the business world provides an empty platform, with a sound system turned up loud, for those with extreme anti-capitalist agendas. Those influencers have only themselves to blame. Our children thirst for media-studies courses, because the business of image and attitude and their transmission is attractive to them. It's why pop and rock jump the generations, but we have made the content of major, life-affecting issues boring. We have covered politics and business with the tarmac of a spin-culture and then wonder why the grass isn't growing.

Government and business can share the role of rebuilding trust and confidence in institutions, even when those institutions are widely challenged. Such institutions – whether they are a Government, a Church, a corporation or a newspaper – need only to be believed as a first step, rather than necessarily believed in. The way to that trust and confidence is through the sort of vibrant, honest and rational debate that has been stifled by a spin-culture that has inured people to what they believe. But people are intuitively progressive, drawn invariably to improving their lot over sinking into ennui and atrophy. We have reached that stage in the way we communicate, in politics and industry, through media and to one another, in the establishments and institutions we accept or reject and in our relationships with those with whom we agree and disagree. There is more to life than what we think about it. We have to *do* too. That means being brave enough to use communications as a means of action, not positioning; of joining the debate, not evading it.

Again the stakes are high. It may be that the Queen Mother's lying-in-state debacle will not be the iconic event by which Blair's regime is remembered. War is becoming one of his defining characteristics, from presiding over the fall of Milosevic to marshalling a global coalition – including that of public opinion – for military action in Iraq. A prerequisite of war is belief in a cause. We do belief badly in Britain. Richard Addis, a former editor of the *Express*, returned in the summer of 2002 from editing the *Globe & Mail* in Toronto to a job at the *Financial Times* in London. He remarks that there is now a marked difference between the cultures of debate in the UK and North America. In Britain, he suggests, it is usually sufficient to state a clever-clever position gleaned from the media. Across the Atlantic, like never before, this is likely to be listened to politely before you are asked: 'Yes, but what do *you* believe'.

War concentrates our minds on belief. In the long run, broadening and deepening a culture of deliberation about what we believe can only be a good thing to emerge from the darkness of conflict. This does not have to make politics more ponderous or more deferential, but it does rely on collective commitment to the public sphere. In the end, making structural adjustments to the way institutions communicate formally – or, for that matter, the way that culturally diverse nation-states formally communicate – will only take us so far. While government has a responsibility to lead, there is little it can do while acting alone about a culture that it didn't create and of which it became a part. It is for the mass of people to alter the culture in which they live, in all walks of life. In particular, this raises a nagging question about the power and responsibilities of the media which, while struggling with the same pressures and demands faced by all other communicators, have nonetheless managed to avoid a widespread debate about the effects of their own behaviour.

When the US has finished sorting out the world, we can look forward to concentrating on the development of post-spin communications, whose ability to flourish will depend on a much wider debate, which is only just beginning. Ultimately, the priorities I have outlined should not only return politics, our business and our institutions to the didacticism in which they should be engaged, but will also make them more fun. That fun has largely departed in recent years, with journalists and spin-doctors complaining about each other in increasingly tedious ways. They and we should be having arguments and enjoying them.

Bibliography

Armstrong, Karen, *The Battle for God* (2000)

Bentley, Tom and Stedman Jones, Daniel (eds), *The Moral Universe* (2001)

Dezenhall, Eric, *Nail 'em!* (1999)

Friedman, Thomas, *The Lexus and the Olive Tree* (1999)

Giddens, Anthony, *Runaway World* (1999)

Hartley, L.P., *The Go-Between* (1953)

Henderson, David, *Misguided Virtue* (2001)

Hollingsworth, Mark, *The Ultimate Spin Doctor* (1997)

Hutchinson, George, *The Last Edwardian at No. 10* (1980)

Hutton, Will, *The State We're In* (1995), *The World We're In* (2002)

Jenkins, Simon, *Newspapers, The Power and the Money* (1979)

Kurtz, Howard, *Spin Cycle, Inside the Clinton Propaganda Machine* (1998)

Leapman, Michael, *Treacherous Estate, The Press After Fleet Street* (1992)

Mandelson, Peter, *The Blair Revolution Revisited* (1996, 2002)

Nichols, Nick, *Rules For Corporate Warriors* (2001)

Nuttall, Jeff, *Bomb Culture* (1968)

Oxford English Reference Dictionary (1995)

Patten, Chris, *The Tory Case* (1983)

INDEX